Beyond the Spirit of Empire

RECLAIMING LIBERATION THEOLOGY

Beyond the Spirit of Empire

Theology and Politics in a New Key

Néstor Míguez
Joerg Rieger
Jung Mo Sung

scm press

© Néstor Míguez, Joerg Rieger and Jung Mo Sung 2009

Published in 2009 by SCM Press
Editorial office
13–17 Long Lane,
London, EC1A 9PN, UK

SCM Press is an imprint of Hymns Ancient and Modern Ltd
(a registered charity)
St Mary's Works, St Mary's Plain,
Norwich, NR3 3BH, UK
www.scm-canterburypress.co.uk

British Library Cataloguing in Publication data

A catalogue record for this book is available
from the British Library

978 0 334 04322 5

Typeset by Regent Typesetting, London
Printed and bound by
CPI Antony Rowe, Chippenham, SN14 6LH

Contents

Acknowledgements

We would like to acknowledge the support of various people and organizations in the writing of this book. Our academic communities have provided space and support for us to do our work as scholars and activists: The Methodist University of São Paulo, in São Bernardo do Campo, Brazil; the Instituto Universitario ISEDET in Buenos Aires, Argentina; and Perkins School of Theology at Southern Methodist University, Dallas, USA. William B. Lawrence, the Dean of Perkins School of Theology, Southern Methodist University also funded the first of our meetings in Dallas and further research assistance. Additional funding was provided by the Office of Research and Graduate Studies at Southern Methodist University and by a Collaborative Research Grant of the American Academy of Religion. Support for the translation was provided in part by the funds of the Wendland-Cook Professorship at Perkins School of Theology.

We are grateful to PhD student Peter Jones for translating Sung's chapters from the Portuguese and Míguez's chapters from the Spanish, Philip Wingeier-Rayo also helped with the translation of Míguez. Thanks to PhD student Kevin Minister for compiling the index.

Introduction

A German Methodist professor of theology in the United States, a native Korean Roman Catholic in Brazil, teaching and writing in the areas of education, theology, and economics, and an Argentinian biblical scholar of Spanish and Italian ancestry who works part time with aboriginal people converted to Pentecostalism . . . what is it that brings them together?

This book, with its three authors, was forged in different places: in meetings of the three in Dallas and Buenos Aires, but also in partial meetings: Joerg and Néstor exchanged ideas in Oxford, England; Jung and Joerg conversed in San Diego, in the United States; Néstor and Jung met at a university in São Paulo. The book, dealing with the global Empire, emerges as a symptom of globalization. It is a critical reflection on how we live; it is nourished by the very ambiguity that it questions.

Thus, we see Empire from distinct angles, from different experiences, and with formations that are dissimilar in focus and scope, although they converge in certain core orientations. Through dialogue we have discovered that this diversity congregates around a shared need: to consider human life 'from below', from the locations of the dispossessed, the victims of plunder and prejudice, the excluded, whether for reasons of economics, gender, ethnicity, politics, or ideology. Nevertheless, the reader should be warned that we will not emphasize any of these in particular; rather, our purpose is to investigate the system of domination that we know as 'Empire', its characteristics and claims, and the search for better alternatives.

The three of us can be characterized, in some manner, as engaged in liberation Christianity: a theological tradition that emphasizes critical reflection. Nevertheless, in different ways, each of us has expressed the necessity of certain revisions of the tendencies and directions that have been increasingly identified with this perspective. For this reason it makes sense to continue producing theological reflection, maintaining the necessity of actualizing it through new dialogues and in conversation with other approaches, beginning with new experiences, proper or assumed, in conversations with other authors, double-checking the theories, epistemological suppositions, and undisclosed assumptions of this theological perspective. It takes more than repeating the affirmations, many of them valid and illuminating, that inspired us at a certain moment in time. That has already been said elsewhere, and this is where we begin.

Today we must analyse new components of our realities, take into account the changes suggested in the last 30 years, assume the new discussions and contributions of the social sciences, and project ourselves towards the future in different ways, keeping in mind that past efforts do not pass without leaving traces, without becoming some kind of memory, and moulding in this way reflections on religion and faith. We listen to and appropriate certain critiques because we are reclaiming a heritage and because we are interested in supporting and nourishing it. But that in itself leads us to rethink certain things because this is the way to maintain the life of that initial calling, of that inevitable commitment that faith imposes on us.

Let us return to our theme: to think about Empire is to think about our reality, to see through the games that it plays, to see its new – and perverse – ambitions and tools of domination. It is to discover the mechanisms with which it imposes itself on people's consciences, with which it claims its unique right to the universal dominion to which it aspires, and with which it organizes its hegemonic discourse. The plurality of perspectives, our own and those of others, is important because it helps us to point out the weaknesses of Empire. This plurality of perspectives challenges Empire's demand for unified perspectives and foundations, suggesting limits and complementarities. Although Empire itself embraces superficial plurality and fragmentation, these impulses remain on the surface and therefore allow Empire to maintain its unified force.

The same diversity that brings us together and distinguishes us can be seen in the development of the chapters. Although the topics were exhaustively discussed between us, each has assumed the responsibility of writing some of them. This explains the diversity of style, language, and approach. Nevertheless, this book is not simply a collection of articles and chapters. If we assume authorship together it is because, beyond respecting the peculiarities and emphases that each one has expressed in his writing, every chapter was discussed and critiqued by all of us; and each chapter was rewritten based on suggestions and reflections of the group. This is how we construct our complementarity, without denying our diversity. Free expression of each author

distribution of chapters Next

includes the openness to be modified by the contributions of others. This is why all self-references of the authors are plural in form.

In the distribution of tasks, Néstor wrote the opening and closing chapters of this book, as well as this introduction. Joerg took on the topic of subjectivity, which is explored in chapters two and five. The two central chapters, in which we consider the theme of transcendence, we owe to the work of Jung. This results in a 'chiastic' structure: the development of the second part of the book is a mirror image of the development of the first. In this way, the book opens by raising the problems of Empire from its ideological-political side (chapter one), then shows how it affects the construction of subjectivity (chapter two), and finally emphasizes the religious dimension that Empire assumes, having claimed a sense of transcendence and omnipotence (chapter three). In the second part of the book we backtrack along that path, but we backtrack in a forward direction, showing where a new reading of the transcendent must lead us (chapter four), how to re-evaluate ways of constructing subjectivity (chapter five), and, finally, thinking about how to discern, in the midst of the imperial darkness, an improvement through the recovery of the *res publica*, of the popular, and of the messianic dimension in human history (chapter six). We want this final reflection, as a conclusion, to stay within the theological environment that inspires us, but we also seek in turn to establish its relevance to the political, social, economic, and cultural realms in which the theological exists and develops.

When we began to discuss the themes of this book, we found ourselves in the most aggressive period of the politics of the administration of US President George W. Bush. The international political and economic scene was dominated by that administration's invasions of Afghanistan and Iraq, by its threats of extending the conflict to Iran, and by its refusal to acknowledge the Palestinian government, by its politics of internal control through the so-called 'Patriot Act', by its expansion of financial politics, and by its threats to countries that resisted its financial models and demands for the adjustment of the state. We saw many people being reborn into the idea of what might be called a 'North American Imperialism', including some North American ideologues, who developed great enthusiasm for this idea and who made arrangements to ensure its dominant place in the world. Nevertheless, we refrain from discussing this alternative here, although the idea remains.

When we met for the last time, to complete the book, however, conditions had changed: the financial markets had collapsed and were in deep crisis, a new President of African-American origin was governing the country where the principal world power resides, announcing that he would try to dismantle the military conflicts of the previous administration and promising respect for the rights of everyone. One step towards this goal was the gradual closure of the US prison in Guantánamo Bay, Cuba. In this context, distributive conflicts were re-emerging as the primary issues of concern, with protests and strikes in the most developed countries, in the face of massive unemployment and other problems. As a result, the state was forced to take a decisive role in the economy, although distinct governments understood this in different ways and offered different proposals. Another mark of this new situation is that the consequences of aggression towards the planet's ecosystem turn out to be more visible, and the illusion of unlimited growth starts showing its weaknesses.

While acknowledging these developments, we prefer to base our reflections on a less provisional analysis. Since we consider the whole world of financial capitalism as a confluence of the imperial vocation, we wonder why there is a particular 'incarnation' of the wandering spirit of Empire in this context. We are interested in 'the spirit of Empire': that is, in seeing what moves this conglomerate of forces that generates this particular form with its propensity for total domination, what spurs the underlying motivations of imperial companies, and what creates this intangible and secret ruse of forms of power that seek to circumvent all controls, which constantly increase in excessiveness.

Reflecting on the weakness of Empire must not allow us to forget that the thrust of Empire can reappear in new guises, and this insight obliges us to think closely about the opportunity to overcome this understanding of power with a political ethics that enables other ways of organizing politics and the political. In this sense our work aims to look for an 'imperial way of life' that transcends the partial expressions of different historical circumstances, rather than for mere historical coincidences that might show what imperial groups have in common, what circumstances have allowed their rise or decline, and so forth. As theologians, we are interested in analysing this imperial spirit at another level: investigating what shapes character, what makes an empire what it is, what makes human beings seek, admit, or resist the imperial way, what allows us to see, though still in the midst of imperial demands, that there is another human way of being.

The tendencies of expansion and the desire for unlimited control, of immeasurable accumulation and the pretension to be able to mould subjectivities and to be imbued with a sense of transcendence, are some examples of what some human beings want to be when they want to be divine. To this end, certain forces are mobilized, certain dynamics created, and a way of managing life on the planet delineated, and this is what we call 'imperial'. Nevertheless, it is our conviction that to arrive at the imperial domain is the end (in the sense of the destruction) of all politics, although not necessarily the end (in the sense of the objective) of all politics. The Empire that keeps expanding in search of its own safety and control is the ultimate threat to human freedom. Meanwhile, the lives that desire to be human must look for a better political vision than the imperial one, and continue searching for that which reaches beyond Empire. That is why resistance to this encroachment of empire is mobilized. Moreover, in proposing and advancing the possibility of living beyond Empire, resistance recovers the public that Empire threatens to destroy, reinstalls the sense of freedom and hope, and stirs up the forces of the messianic. In this sense, the proposal of a theology that criticizes and overcomes the imperial vision and establishes a new vision, which we will call 'laocratic' rather than 'democratic' (as the Greek term *laos* refers to a broader group of people than does *demos*), is also political.

Not every authoritarian political system or dictatorship is imperial, unless it has the necessary strength to pull things off. This is necessary to keep in mind so as not to confuse the particular mode that we call imperial with other forms of political or economic domination, or with cultural impositions or ideological constructions. Human relations, as we know and experience them historically, are marked by a certain level of inequity, which exists at the core of the family, embodied in the primitive clan, or in the group of hunters who mark their territory. Inequities and injustices, underlying or explicit, as well as conflicts exist even in these early beginnings of society and are projected in practical and symbolic forms of violence, which are complex and take different political forms. Nevertheless, it would be a simplification if we were to lump all these forms together in a common theological diagnosis that holds that the human being is a sinner and that everything is resolved in this affirmation.

On the contrary, the ability to identify the proper marks of each of the forms of injustice and oppression is what allows us to confront them. Although we will never eliminate 'human sin', it is possible to look for ways to limit its consequences, to relieve suffering. This signifies the recognition of our limits, of the need for mutual control and complementarity, and of the existence of a plurality of ways of seeing and living human life and understanding its place on the planet, which is what Empire destroys when it seeks to unify all under one rule and under its control. To recognize the destructive capacities of the human being, directed against itself, against the environment that sustains it, and against other human beings, is to accept that it is necessary to set limits and regulations. Such limits and regulations allow for the display of the creative potentialities of every human being, for possibilities for solidarity and love, as well as for the expression of human dignity.

This is why our proposal involves a reflection on the effect of this imperial spirit on human spirits, especially of those who remain more strongly exposed to the inequities and injustices that the imperial system generates. We do not impose our hope of 'redemption' on them, which would load on their already weary backs the political responsibility of modifying reality and transforming the system. But we perceive in them the most visible effect of the consequences of the pride of Empire. Furthermore, we also acknowledge their capacity to express the reality of the struggle, in reactions of resistance and anticipation, a struggle that is not only their own but also belongs to all those who bind themselves together as people. In this sense our proposal is a 'demo-cratic' or 'lao-cratic' search, which seeks to be aware of all the dimensions and also of the limits of any and every proposal of power, which recognizes the presence of the most affected in every social system, and which shows its continuing need for transformation.

It is in this sense that our theology wants to recover the place of the transcendent, of something that is always beyond what Empire contains and what it wants to enclose. Only when we are in this space of the transcendent, which Empire cannot contain, can we fashion a radical critique, which can never be carried out if we begin with the postulates that Empire consecrates in its immanence. However, this transcendence is not known through some form of omnipotence or through the justification of immanent power; it is only known through a presence in the crucified one who has risen, in the mourner who raises his voice, in the poor person who does not give up, in the victims of ethnic, racial or sexist prejudice who claim their condition as whole human beings, in the excluded who still make their mark on the people. It is in this sense that we believe in the possibility of overcoming Empire, of anticipating in ourselves the hope of another possible world, a world where all worlds have a place, and a messianic kingdom, which we may never achieve in our history but which constitutes the vision that encourages us, sustains us and to which we pledge our lives.

I

Empire, Religion, and the Political

The themes of Empire and imperialism have re-emerged in what is now a global debate about the concentration of power. Discussions about the meaning and understanding of these concepts have arisen in numerous books and controversies throughout the twentieth century. In Marxist circles they have been studied and debated as the highest stage of capitalist domination. Even though Marxist theories have now entered into a crisis and are being revised, the concept of Empire and the controversy about imperialism as the expression of late capitalism today occupy an important place in political science and philosophy, as well as in the definition of the problems confronted by global systems today. And not only among critics linked to sectors of 'the left' or those who consider themselves of Marxist heritage, beyond how one would qualify these characterizations, but also among others who claim some forms of Empire as necessities within social and economic postmodernity, as we will see in this book.

This discussion will focus particularly, then, on the latter part of the twentieth century and the beginning of the twenty-first. Whether through direct reference, as in the text that in some ways started this discussion (*Empire* by Antonio Negri and Michael Hardt),[1] or indirectly, when we refer to 'postcolonial theories', it is not our intention to add one more revision of these concepts or to enter fully into the controversy, although we cannot avoid it completely. Rather, we will look at what we call 'the spirit of Empire'. With this expression, which we will leave open for the time being and recall later in search of greater precision, we refer not so much to the political and economic mechanisms that shape what we characterize as Empire, although that cannot be excluded, but rather to an *ethos*, a way of thinking and doing, a *Weltanschauung*, and even a certain theology that demonstrates the imperial spirit, which is innate to the form of social organization that we visualize as Empire. That is to say, we refer to those conditions of subjectivity and of cultural self-conception that Empire generates in itself and in others, but that are simultaneously a result and a condition

I

of its mode of establishing its politics and of exercising its economic dominance. Empire is a particular formation of government and power and, given its pretence to be global, generates a 'collective spirit', an anthropological construction, that allows and approves of certain behaviours, reactions, feelings, and attitudes of the social and political actors, that shapes a certain logic and way of conceiving life, and that imposes and translates itself into values and a hegemonic *Weltanschauung*. Of course there is no single univocal homogeneity, and this produces, in turn, certain antagonisms: along with a 'spirit of Empire' there emerges a counter-imperial vision, which should not be ignored. Our intention is precisely to clarify what constitutes this opposition, and to discern what this spirit of empire is and what can arise as an alternative and an expectation, a different way of conceiving power and human life.

This chapter introduces and states the problem and sets out the pattern for the other conditions that we highlight as the 'spirit of Empire'. For this we are giving an overview of the political and economic dimension of what we mean by Empire, and then introducing the two dimensions of our proposal: the construction of subjectivity and the relationship between Empire and transcendence, the religion of Empire, its trinity of economic power, military power, and 'spirit'. In our capacities as theologians, this last area will perhaps be the space where we will make our greatest contribution. Of course, we are aware that not everything can be resolved at the spiritual level, and that problems of political and economic nature help to establish and communicate the 'spirit'. But we also understand that Empire has a configuration of subjectivity and a force of communication, a 'spirit', a self-conception that helps it to sustain and impose itself. And without a capacity for independent thinking, without a 'freedom of spirit' that is capable of decolonizing oneself and creating a cultural alternative, to live up to a subjectivity of anticipation, the task of overcoming the imperial configuration is not resolved. The question is not just about the current situation, but rather whether we are capable of overcoming the present situation; thus we must ask: with what are we left after Empire? If Empire leaves behind an imperialized human being, in whom the spirit of the Empire remains, then there will not be an 'after', because we will still have a humanity predisposed to the acceptance of domination, even if the current powers and imperial configuration in the political, military, and economic planes are in decline.

Empire as a political-economic formation

What do we call Empire? What is its origin? Apart from the debates about whether it is possible to understand current Empire in line with earlier political and military imperial formations in history, and apart from the slippery semantics that form the trajectory of such a broad and varied concept, one should recognize that if one continues appealing to the term 'Empire' it is because it somehow represents in our collective imagination a continuity that allows us to apply it to certain historical situations (despite their differences) and not to others. It is interesting to rescue this diachronic element in order to see the common 'spirit' that would appear to establish itself as appropriate to imperial configurations.

The concept of Empire was born and consolidated in Rome. Of course there were expansive powers in the history of the East[2] and West before the advent of Imperial Rome, but there is certainly a 'quantitative and qualitative leap' that differentiates the reality of the Roman Empire from earlier forms of power. This difference lies in the convergence of two factors: on one hand, the explicit quest for totalitarian power, to include the inhabited world under one unified political entity, and on the other hand, to achieve a conglomeration of the different components of this power in a single project.[3] Perhaps the closest antecedent in the West is the brief but significant era of Alexander the Great, which prepared the political, military and cultural conditions for the Roman Empire. We can say that the Roman Empire itself emerged with the victory of Octavian Caesar (who was later declared Augustus) in Actium in 31 BC. From this moment, with the concentration of power around the victor and the necessary adherence of the distinct sectors of the capital city of Italy and of the different provinces (nations, kingdoms, and conquered peoples), as well as adherence to his government from the different strata of Roman society (patricians, the *populus* and *plebs*), a political conglomerate was created that met no significant opposition. Rome conserved its republican organization with the formal controls represented by the tribunals, plebiscites, and Senate, but adapted to a situation in which the confluence of economic, military, and political powers and the ideological construction of *Pax Romana*, with its corresponding theology of *Pax deorum*, created the Empire.

Empire should be understood (then and now) not as an institutional form of polity but as a way of exercising power through different legalities (and illegalities). Its formation is built on its capacity to bring together the interests of certain elites, beyond different institutional organizational possibilities and without decisive influence

3

from national or ethnic limitations, and on its capacity to mobilize the strengths of a different order for those interests and to avoid the controls and balances that regulate the exercise of power. For the sake of clarity we separate the concept of Empire from imperialism and the so-called 'expansive monarchies'. The Roman Empire, as an antecedent and model of imperial power, was designed as a concentration of power that affected all of the people who lived under its domain (including the *plebs* who lived in the city-state from which it emerged). Imperialism is a moment in the construction of the Empire understood as such, and it is more precisely the eagerness to conquer that moves a nation to impose its power over others with the desire to exploit.[4] In turn it is necessary to differentiate Empire from the expansive monarchies of Antiquity that launched territorial conquests to expand their domination, displace other peoples, or subject them as vassals. Nevertheless, in these expansive monarchies it was always clear that domination came through a victorious military power, based on strength, and that it provoked the resistance of local monarchies (even when they were formally faithful to the dominant monarchs), who waited for any occasion to break the status quo and recover their autonomy. Perhaps Darius and Cyrus, during the Persian domination of the Middle East, were able to show a different face during their rule, appearing as 'benefactors of humanity'.[5] But it is with Rome and its concept of *Pax Romana* that the idea of expansion was joined to the concept of unity, of unifying the whole world in its totality, of making Empire and humanity coincide. Although imperial dominion was not hidden, the colonized elites found that it was convenient for their own existence and power to conform to this power as a means of survival, clearly aligning themselves in the exploitation of their own people.

It is not our intention to create a 'history of empires' or to show the degrees to which various configurations that have been so labelled actually realized this type of political form. We are interested, rather, in investigating the conceptions and political 'spirit' that emerge when these historical situations occur, the ways in which the imaginary and symbolic structures of power, which ideologically sustain the hegemony in imperial times, are constructed. From our position as Christian theologians, it is not a minor detail to point out that the beginning of the Christian experience took place in the context of the first global Empire. Nevertheless, in our subsequent analysis we will focus our attention particularly on the current imperial configuration.

What do we mean by Empire?

Many have attempted to establish the characteristics of Empire. Hardt and Negri's book *Empire*, which is at the centre of a larger controversy about the topic, offers us an idea of Empire as a network, a formation of power that constitutes a way of exercising power that extends globally without a unified centre. It is not our interest here to discuss this concept. We will consider its truths and insufficiencies later in the following chapters in order to see what really is involved in the imperial spirit and ideology. In this sense, the idea of an empire that limits and does not respect any sovereignty except its capacity to impose, to regulate all life on the planet, helps us to see what makes up an 'imperial mentality'.

In another analysis, the World Alliance of Reformed Churches (WARC) has in an ecclesial document proposed the idea that

> Empire . . . [is] the convergence of economic, political, cultural and military interests that constitute a system of domination in which benefits flow primarily to the powerful. Centred in the last remaining superpower, yet spread all over the world, empire crosses all boundaries, reconstructs identities, subverts cultures, overcomes nation states and challenges religious communities.[6]

What stands out in this definition is the idea that Empire is a particular configuration of power, which is characterized by the conjunction of economic power and certain political, military, and civil organizations, as well as government structures. Those powers that were destined to control one another, to sustain themselves in tension, and to limit their reach through oppositions and confrontations, are now co-opted by the same project or understanding of power. They are jointly aligned and organized according to a single shared objective. They are fed by a common *ethos* and annul the validity of other powers and the emergence of different options. This occurs through the convergence of certain elites who produce practical alliances or establish power relations that allow them to relativize other concurrent powers. Although they may have some conflicts and minor disagreements, they are unified by their decision to control and dominate, and are in agreement on the way to do it. The public sphere is submitted to the coercion of this united force, which is ready to control everything, impose its order, and impede the access of others to decision-making spaces. In a nutshell, they convert the public sphere into a game on a restricted playing field that they already dominate.

5

Empire emerges precisely out of the weakness of political mechanisms to withstand situations of tension, to provide avenues for the expression of conflicts in a way that does not hide or destroy them but rather makes conflicting interests transparent. That is to say, imperial power is born from imbalance, the child of the lack of moderation, the lack of control. However, within a nation or people there must exist internal mechanisms that lead to the accumulation of power, and then the possibility that this accumulation of strength be expressed in the capacity to involve other nations and peoples under their dominion. In other words, imperial situations are the result of the fragile balance of power faced with the onslaught of accumulated interests. Again, we can see a good example of this in the Roman Empire. There were internal tensions generated in the time of the Republic, and the lack of political definition led to the establishment of the triumvirates, brief moments of power-sharing that impeded the parties involved from resolving the political fortunes of the conquered. When, after the triumph in Actium, those balances and tensions were broken and power was consolidated in the hands of Augustus and the hegemony of the elite landowners of the city of Rome, the Empire was born and *Pax Augusta* was imposed. With concepts borrowed from Antonio Gramsci, we could say that hegemonic situations are the outcome of times of organic crisis. To the extent that relations among nations, and even the concept of the nation-state, have entered into a crisis in our globalized world – which manifests itself with increasing strength since the dissolution of the Soviet Union – we find ourselves in a situation ripe for the emergence of this type of empire with global pretensions.

It is precisely from this global pretension, of bringing everything under its dominion, that imperial politics claims that there is no space for dissension, alterity, and antagonism. To explain the use of the concept of hegemony, Ernesto Laclau and Chantal Mouffe state that 'its very condition is that a *particular* social force assumes the representation of a *totality* that is radically incommensurable with it'.[7] In the case of the current Empire, like that of the Roman Empire, this 'totality that is radically incommensurable with it', is, more or less, that of all humanity. The discourses of the Empire, through its designated spokespersons, precisely claim to define what it is that the totality of humanity wants, or needs, what is good for all, and, finally, what cannot be avoided (this will be explained in the chapter on the 'transcendence' of Empire). In the third chapter we will examine some of these claims that humanity can approach its fullness and self-realization only within the parameters that imperial power establishes.

Of course, no human power is capable of achieving this totally – at least this is our hope. But historical situations can arise in which some regions for a time experience a broad consolidation of power capable of conditioning all human behaviour under its influence, even life itself. Such power is introduced into the means of production and the reproduction of life itself in such a way that it is transformed into what some authors call 'bio-power', generating a 'bio-politics' that, as we will see, threatens to destroy politics itself as a human activity.

As we said earlier, on an analytic plane it is useful to distinguish between 'Empire' and 'imperialism', reserving this second term for the expansive (mostly territorial and economic) tendency that manifests as confrontations with other nations. One can conceive, and this has occurred historically, of a nation that is internally structured as republican and democratic, its formal constitution at least calling for 'participatory' institutions of government, yet is imperialist in its foreign policy. As a matter of fact, the Roman Empire, as we pointed out, was formally a republic throughout its existence. Nevertheless, although its republican form was maintained, an analysis of Roman foreign policy after the rise of Augustus (although the process had already started in the previous century with the expansion of Roman power in the Mediterranean basin) shows how the *res publica* – in other words, true participation and citizenship guarantees in public affairs – declined, as dominant interests removed from the sphere of collective decision-making the options that might harm them. 'Citizenship guarantees' became increasingly insignificant, and the distinctions of power that enabled the formation and maintenance of the imperial elite within the state itself acquired normative power. In the Roman Empire, in its second century, citizenship was extended, becoming almost universal to all free men. This was possible because citizen rights had been stripped, except for formalities, of all their political content. A legal distinction was created between *honestiores* and *humiliores*, with political rights being reserved only for the former, who were the members of plutocratic elites, and with the latter excluded from decision-making power and direct access to law. In this way, the older citizens of the Roman *populus* saw how the Empire signified the emptying of their republican rights, even though these rights still existed formally.

This same dynamic is manifest in other situations: the exploitation of the resources of conquered nations, which fundamentally benefits the governing elites of the imperialist power, leads to increasing internal accumulation that, in turn, ends up upsetting the configuration of power within the metropolis. In this way, even if republican structures are still in place, in practice there is a disparity in power and resources that causes the institutional controls to fail. The 'patriotic laws' dictated by the 'republican' government of the United States in recent years demonstrate the advance of the central power over that of citizens' rights, annulling, in many cases, the balance that would suppose the intervention of the judicial and legislative branches. Modern and post-modern empires cannot simply impose a legal distinction that does not recognize equality before the law; instead, they declare 'exceptional circumstances'.[8] In addition, as we will show later, this incidence of inequality in the power structure takes the form of unequal participation in the market, or simple exclusion from access to goods, and the recognition of entire portions of the population as being under conditions of what Giorgio Agamben, borrowing from Walter Benjamin, calls 'bare life'.[9] If democracy is resolved in the market, then those who cannot participate in the market cannot participate in democracy, and those who control the market control democracy. That is to say, politics has been eliminated and replaced by the economy, and not just by any economy but by that which sustains the financial capitalism of the total free market.[10] Whoever cannot participate in the market becomes a non-subject, a non-person. Applicable to this situation is what Reyes Mate states about the understanding of the oppressed: 'To them is applied this mode of politics called biopolitics, because in it is seen all that this collective human activity [politics] can have of will and rationality, to remain at the mercy of biology.'[11]

The change from Republic to Empire does not always modify the institutional forms of government, but it does force modifications of the power structure. In this way, the institutions of the Republic worked formally in Rome, but they all responded to the same economic interest. They aligned themselves with the government's sole objective and were subordinate to the rule of the Caesarean elite. The wealth of the patrician landowners who sat in the Senate, the tribunals that represented the *plebs*, the military power, the official artists who were protected by their patrons, the varying stoic philosophers who dominated the intellectual scene and the spectacle offered to the masses, even the architecture and statues in the cities and the circulation of Roman coins contributed to a concentration of power with the intention of leaving no space for any alternative. The local elites also participated in this, whether those established through the Roman practice of founding colonies under war veterans licensed from the army, or those native elites that had made agreements with the imperial power. Religion was not an exception: the Roman pantheon integrated all gods, all were tolerated and had their festivals, but all were subordinate to the only god that truly mattered, that had its statues throughout the Empire, and whose veneration was incorporated into local worship styles: the *Divus Caesar*.[12]

This strength of the dominant power modifies the conditions for citizenship. The Roman Empire was able to universalize citizenship precisely because it stripped it of its meaning. Modern and postmodern imperial power follows the same path. The citizen has been abstracted in representation, in such a way that there is no response to the citizen but to its ghost, emptied of real human content. On the one hand, there is the juridical fiction of legal rights; on the other hand, there is 'bare life' deprived of rights. These rights have been absorbed by the 'market', which ignores the citizen in the consumer.[13] In this democracy the people are an 'idol', who are 'represented' in order that they be dominated and emptied. There are some self-appointed 'priests' who claim to speak in their name as their representatives. But nobody represents nor can anyone ever represent the voiceless, precisely because they are inaudible; their silence (forced, believed, etc.) questions everything said on their behalf. Democratic discourse is emptied and replaced by the powerful voice of the market. The 'representatives of the people' remain captive to business 'lobbies', when the businessmen or women do not themselves directly run as 'representatives'. The representatives do not respond to those whom they represent, as the people are not present, but to the demands of a power that has wrapped up into one project of domination the various aspects of human life and activity. This is the 'democracy of the Empire'.

This emptying of democracy, which is, in the end, the annihilation of politics, creates precisely the space where the imperial possibility is inserted. The democracy is left without its foundation, which comes to be a significant void, and without a foothold in reality. Postmodern deconstruction reveals the precariousness of any reference to reality, and especially to any transcendent reality. This lack of any fixed reference for democracy opens up a crack that allows Empire to occupy the concepts of democracy, liberty, and citizenship, and to absorb them into its own discourse, newly construed as expressions of its vocation for domination. The analyses of Claude Lefort tend to show that, in its rejection of a transcendent foundation, democracy remains exposed to being emptied of meaning: 'Democracy inaugurates the experience of a society which cannot be apprehended or controlled, in which the people will be proclaimed sovereign, but in which its identity will never be definitively given, but which will remain latent.'[14] The Empire fills this vacuum and offers itself as the transcendence that ends up anchoring and subordinating political life, securing its totalitarian rule.

The pretension of a global Empire

Today we are witnessing a moment of imperial consolidation, with the difference that this Empire is provided with a development of technological communication that allows it to aspire to a greater potential totality than that enjoyed by the empires of the past (in reality, every empire claims this, but the historical and technological conditions did not make it possible in earlier times). The entire world should conform itself to a single mode of operating in the economy, of conceiving politics, of managing power, and to a supreme military power. Just as the diversity of gods that come from a variety of cultures and religions were accepted in the Roman pantheon, they are all accepted only after recognizing the guidelines imposed by the Empire. Perhaps a metaphor is helpful to illustrate our point. In the food court of the shopping mall there are a variety of shops representing different cultures. One can find Thai food, Italian pizza, Chinese rice, German sauerkraut, Mexican tacos, Argentinian beef, or Japanese sushi. Even the distrusted Arabs can offer their kebabs right next to an American hamburger stand. The only condition is that all the food stands must serve fast food, which is imposed by the globalized model of consumption. The dominant aroma will be that which the air conditioner imposes. And the profits will sustain the whole system or, better still, fatten the owners of the system.

But everything must fit inside the 'shopping mall': that is to say, everything must adapt its existence according to the capitalist business framework and the consumer society. Because this global Empire is the empire of late financial capitalism, the economic core pulls everything together with its virtual power as well as its various political, military, and cultural powers. All the diversity of the world is reduced to one licit path – towards the Empire – of managing the economy. The true network that contains the Empire is the international financial network: to which the people and their expectations, cultures, and nations must submit. As a matter of fact, as postmodern, post-Marxist, and multiculturalist currents have often insisted, not all antagonisms have their roots and resolution at the level of the economic sphere or the class struggle. But it is also true that the globalization in which these antagonisms are developed and expressed bears the stamp of late capitalism, and all the struggles are traversed by its 'laws', by the interests that it unleashes and puts into play, by the threat that it imposes on them, which claims to represent and organize the 'totality'. In this sense, and also in others, the Empire is 'totalitarian'.

In the background, in this imperial conception, democratic formalities must serve to secure one aspect of the economy: the global market. In reality, as the situation in Palestine since the triumph of Hamas demonstrates (to take a paradigmatic case), the conception of democracy that the Empire intends has nothing to do with the government of local majorities, but rather with the submission to the will of the powerful (not even to the law, since it breaks its own laws). Through the simple method of applying the label 'terrorist' to any political movement, nation, or population, that grouping is transformed into an exile from the political arena, left with no rights. And more clearly, if the 'free market' is not guaranteed to rule over the totality of human life, then there is no 'democracy'. The object of a democratic government in an imperial style is not the government itself, the possibility of politics, but exactly the opposite: the total annihilation of politics, its total disappearance in light of another mechanism – the market. This is to say, as we mentioned before, that the public domain becomes an object of transaction for private interests. The state and politics, the public domain, beyond its forms and formalities becomes captive to this game of interests of the global elite. *Demos*, from which the word democracy is derived, as a theoretic source of power – and even more the *laos*,[15] which cannot exercise the rights of the citizen nor of the consumer – is replaced by the financial power of the market; democracy conforms to *jrematocracia*.[16]

So much is this the case that in the economic jargon imposed by the businesses of hegemonic communication 'the markets', or even in the singular 'the market', does not refer any more to places for the exchange of goods, where producers and artisans sell and exchange their products. It does not even refer to the most abstract derivations of the celebration of the buying and selling transaction. Rather the market now refers to financial games. The notion that the 'market formulates prices' within industrial capitalism has now given way to finances. The great fortunes of today are not established by the possession of material goods but rather from bank accounts, financial wealth and other forms of 'virtual goods' such as trademarks, patents, images, use of business 'logos' in the form of merchandizing, and so on. Things virtual, fantasy or fetish, to use Marxist language, have replaced, scammed, and annulled what is real. It is just like the story of the witty tailors who scammed the emperor by selling him a robe of non-existent cloth and telling the gullible crowd that only the wise can see it. So everyone refrained from telling the emperor that he did not have any clothes on, for then they would be considered stupid. Today we all believe that things exist that others say exist, even though personally we do not see them. But in this case we have all been forced to wear these invisible robes and we all fear to discover that we are naked. The only one who is dressed is the emperor.

Yet, just like human life, the virtual system needs access to the material world and its resources. The system needs to have available all the economic, technological and energetic resources of the world, and it places them under the care of the financial market. So, in a nutshell, those who do not have money do not have a right to the resources that make life possible; in other words, they do not have the right to exist. But the rights that theoretically exist on the political plane – human rights – are emptied of their potentiality, having become rights without resources. On the other hand, when these resources do exist they must be placed at the disposal not of the imperial state (distinguishing it from classic imperialism) but of the private interests that constitute the economic marrow of the Empire. In today's situation this extends beyond any particular nation-state, even if the United States constitutes its political and military centre. It is not that the imperial state has ceased to exist or that its role is diminished; rather, it is redefined as a function of ensuring that the economic interests of the global elite have at their disposal the resources necessary for business, development, and domination. For example, Bolivian natural gas is important, the Bolivian people are not. Therefore it is necessary to privatize Bolivia's energy resources, and if the current Bolivian government reverses this process and ignores the voice of the market, then it will continue to be regarded as part of the 'axis of evil' and as an object of imperial aggression. This is precisely what has occurred.[17] Iraq's oil is crucial, even if it has to be extracted from under the corpses of the Iraqis who refuse to give it away. In summary, the restricted sector of the 'global class' (the elite among the financial groups, who also control, either directly or indirectly, production companies) have assumed the exclusive right to become owners of the world. Everything becomes precarious in the face of imperial power. But the empire itself becomes precarious, in turn, in its relationship to human law and to the possibilities of the survival of what we can still call nature. If democracy continues to rest on unstable foundations, through its renunciation of its transcendent aspects, then the Empire continues to endanger life on the planet because of its totalizing appetite for global dominion and possession.

Another one of the many consequences brought about by the financial nucleus of the global Empire is the transfer of human rights from persons to things or financial and juridical fictions. For example, capital can flow freely around a borderless world and financial transactions can take place 24 hours a day through the internet in any market and from any place where there is a computer terminal. The demand arises that products must be commercialized, with no strings attached (especially those that favour the wealthiest sectors), and free trade agreements are imposed without eliminating the subsidies with which the most concentrated sectors of the economy privilege their immediate environment. But the mobility of everyday people, real human beings, especially if they are poor or from the 'Third World', is increasingly restricted. The Berlin Wall falls and capitalist interests penetrate Eastern Europe, but a fence is built to exclude poor Mexicans from having access to the developed world.[18] Businesses and manufacturing plants move in order to exploit cheap labour in poor countries, but immigration and human mobility must be restricted because they threaten the imperial environment and 'identity', just as the elites are protected by the high walls and private security of the gated communities in which they live. The ideological war is transformed into a war against the poor. The natural human person's right to health is set aside (in the United States more than ten per cent of US Citizens – and many more of its residents – do not have health insurance). Real human beings, of flesh and blood, who suffer from HIV/AIDS do not have their right to health care guaranteed because they are dependent on the patent rights of the pharmaceutical companies, on the registered trademarks that do not even recognize the scientists who invented the product. The pharmaceutical company reserves the rights to charge for the trademark; meanwhile the researchers, the real and natural people who work to produce the medicine, are but 'employees', only 'sub-persons' of the legal entity that manages them, that contracts them or fires them at will. In other words, the 'juridical person', the virtual world, takes the place of the real existing human being and their rights.

> From the point of view of transnational corporations, human rights as the rights of bodily human beings are nothing more than distortions of the market. They operate and calculate on a world scale and for them the entire world is just a space where distortions of the market appear.[19]

By placing the laws of the market, which are driven by the love of money (the pursuit and maximization of profit), at the centre of its valorizing system, the financial empire reverses and inverts the significance and meaning of human life as understood outside the empire. Corruption is the norm (the Nobel laureate in Economics Joseph Stiglitz documents in recent works how corruption has been the basis of the 'structural adjustments' imposed by neoliberalism).[20] Everything is based on the law of profit: Mammon is God.

Imperialized democracy

Neoliberalism has been the central tenet of the dominant political current of recent years. This is so well known that it is not worthwhile to dwell on it in an ideological discussion, but we would like to bring attention to how it influences the spirit of Empire. Neoliberalism, its most well-known spokesman being Friedrich A. von Hayek, begins with the hypothesis that the human vocation is realized only in extreme individualism. In his conception, instincts towards goodwill and solidarity are only the bad aftertastes of a past that must be left behind in order to assume the true final realization (proposed in almost evolutionary terms) of the human species: its profoundly individualistic rationality. This expresses, curiously and paradoxically, its 'natural' condition: Hayek unites, to use an alternative way of speaking, 'being in itself' with 'being for oneself', but in this case, playing with the words, we can understand 'for oneself' to have nothing to do with consciousness but with inexhaustible egoism – the insatiable desire to consume. This is, in itself, a 'gift' of Empire. Only free competition in all the spheres of life can produce true liberty, and any interference will only reduce the possibilities for human expression. This principle should be protected from any element that impedes one's freedom to consume, and even the state (and, as a result, politics and democracy) should be reduced to its minimum expression. The government should do only what is necessary to allow the market to operate freely. Therefore, concepts such as 'solidarity' or 'social justice' are explicitly despised in Hayek's writings as expression of past oppressions that must be overcome.[21]

The concept of total competition between human beings, which is derived from Hobbes, paradoxically transforms egoism from the greatest sin (at least in some Christian traditions) into the means of salvation. In the Gospel according to Hayek, Milton Friedman, and other neoliberal theologians, egoism is a salvific virtue and love is a mortal sin. This is where this way of conceiving human life participates in the 'spirit of Empire'. The connection to the other is denied: the other is always a competitor, never a neighbour. The other is a threat to my freedom, never an opportunity for working together. My only concern should be to do what I desire (although in reality, as we will see, my desire is actually the desire of the other – see Chapter 2). This tension that conflicting interests signify can only be resolved through the triumph of one and the annihilation of the other. But what is not explained is that, when this competition is for vital goods, losing means frustration, desperation, and death. Just as with the gladiators of the Roman circus, to lose is to die. 'You're a loser' is the expression of scorn for another human being, the final expression of the arrogance of the spirit of Empire. Here there is only room for the winners, those who dominate and control, the powerful who will never concede, nor resign their will for communal benefit; they must be willing to despise the lives of the weak, considering them 'collateral damage' in their quest for accumulation. The rich functionary described in the Gospel who distances himself from Jesus is their hero, and the 'Good Samaritan' a primitive idiot.

This extreme individualism, despite the sermon on freedom (although freedom is defined in negative terms: the absence of restrictions to the will), is still totalitarian. Only now the political sovereign is not the Leviathan capable of containing mutual aggression, restricting freedom, but the invisible and wise god that makes it possible: the market. The market does not absorb the volitions of its subjects, it realizes them. But the right of citizenship is given only to those who possess the only document valid in the market economy: money.

This is the new ground of the dispersed unity of individualized humanity. This extreme individualism is essentially anti-democratic because it destroys the concept of *demos*. There is no longer a 'people', a space for constructive discussion, or the possibility of collective action. The totality of the market and its 'invisible hand' replaces civil society and politics as the entity that co-ordinates and directs the existence and actions of individuals. The state is reduced to its policing function, to playing the role of the guardian of private property (of owners, obviously, without reviewing the historical process of appropriation). In this way, everything is decreed to private initiative, *beati possidentis*, and public life practically disappears. The state must not own, manage, or distribute anything. Neoliberalism is incompatible with the notion of *res publica*.

In addition to the attack on politics by extremist neoliberals, which results in the emptying of democracy, there is also an attack from the consensualists that is no less dangerous. Postmodern culture, in spite of disguising itself as open and tolerant, is complicit and a necessary participant in a system that does not tolerate alternatives and demands submission to the only universal law. If everything must be included in a globalized world, then, from this point of view, dissent from the parameters of globalization becomes a problem. In this new reading, democracy is the way to address and resolve dissent and arrive at a consensus. But for the empire, this consensus is predetermined, and it can be nothing other than the freedom of the market, a consensus around the unimpeded functioning of global capitalism. Any other possible consensus is, in this vision, profoundly 'undemocratic'.

In this way, by raising the problems in abstraction, as if late capitalism was not already a firmly established framework, as if there were no power asymmetries that determine all social participation, those who conceive of democracy as a 'search for consensus' end up becoming allies, whether they like it or not, of the Empire. Under the existence of the Empire the only attainable consensus is the validity of the Empire. Any other consensus would not be allowed by the forces that today sustain the Empire, and it is difficult to conceive of the Empire conceding economic, military, or cultural power, as well as its preconceptions, to achieve a non-imperial accord. Forcing a 'consensus' is part of the task of creating hegemony.

Chantal Mouffe, in her book *On the Political*, has developed this thesis with clarity.[22] On the one hand, she challenges the visions of authors such as Ulrich Beck and Anthony Giddens and the label they apply to the present age of 'reflexive modernity'.[23] The consensus of these authors, as well as of some other postmodernists and multiculturalists, some implicitly and others explicitly, is that there is no alternative to capitalism. What we are left with, then, and the solution Beck proposes, is what he calls 'sub-politics', or 'politics from below', where resistance can be expressed.[24] He argues that the fundamental conflicts in the world today are no longer of a distributive nature, and that the conflicts of identity must be negotiated beginning with the postmodern principle of ambivalence, which enables the dissolving of the conflicts through relativization. The political bodies of modernity do not make sense anymore and forums of experts, politicians, business people, and citizens that can achieve a consensus that allows for mutual co-operation should take their place. Similarly, Giddens speaks of a 'dialogic democracy' where 'experts' play a fundamental role.[25] When one analyses these texts '*in nuce*' it seems that what they are proposing is the illusion of a mix between direct democracy in small non-political circles and the emergence of a new aristocracy of knowledge, the experts. This is the suggestion of Giddens' 'third way', which could lead to a cosmopolitan social order.[26] The intervention of Tony Blair's government, to whom Giddens was an advisor, in several international conflicts can indicate to us how this 'third way' is applied in practice: the recourse of dialogic democracy, should its outcomes not match the expectations of the Empire, is to military violence. One may ask oneself, together with the legitimate criticisms of Mouffe, which we will not repeat here, if we combine this with the dominion of global capitalism, what else do we have besides a totalitarian empire, where consensuses are sought in order to resolve questions of identity, but

only and beginning within the rigid guidelines established by the existing, unmodifed global system? On the other hand, when one looks at
the distribution figures for the world's resources and the tendencies
toward the accumulation of capital, one can ask what it means to say
that 'conflicts are no longer of a distributional nature', as Beck holds.[27]
This intentional myopia concerning the conditions of global capitalism
is necessary for the purpose of creating 'post-politics'. 'Post-politics'
are necessary because politics are dangerous. The Empire is resolved
thusly, in a 'post-democracy'.

Jürgen Habermas and his communicative ethics take us in the
same direction, although from a different place. In this case we follow Mouffe's critique as well, in the sense that all these conformists
presuppose the necessity of Western-style liberal democracy, rational
behaviour, and the rule of global capitalism as the logical economic
expression of this rationality.[28] But to conceal this subjection of the
political to the economic, for which they criticize Marxist orthodoxy,
it is necessary to set aside the relation between politics and economics.
They defend the autonomy of the political and then destroy the political without destroying the economic. Thus, in this isolation of politics (which turns out to be seemingly contradictory in relation to their
'holistic' conceptions), they end up proposing to reduce politics to
issues of the moment, or to render it inoperative. With which once
again the exercise of the truly political is left solely in the hands of the
global elite, whose experts will convince all the rest of the consensuses
necessary for its survival. In any consensus some situation of domination subsists. Consensus and unity generates the idea of a possible
'totality', and ends up producing worship of the imperial hegemony.

Empire, communication and subjectivity

As we have already seen, forces today hegemonic on a global scale are
resolved in their attempt to shape the subjectivity of imperial subjects
or, it is almost necessary to say, to enthrone them as the only 'truly
(in)human' subjects, and in the destruction of the *demos* as subject,
its replacement being an object of the colonization of mentalities. It
is no minor detail that capitalism and liberal 'rationality' are seen as
'the superior state of humanity', the destiny of humanity. The imperial
subject is, necessarily, a proud subject, which must justify its imperial
enterprise as a humanizing enterprise (see the arguments of Robert
Cooper in Chapter 3). It reflects what humanity must be, which,
thanks to its existence, humanity has become. Whoever is not like

them is half-human or, better still, an infant who must be guided by the imperial parents to adulthood, sometimes by force through punishments and beatings, especially if one is rebellious. In order to avoid these extremes the Empire offers to 'educate' citizens (subjects) in the imperial way of doing things.

The means of communication is one important area to highlight here. Global communications businesses (misnamed the 'media', given that they convey their own ends), which answer to the same interests, create the sensation that the desires established by the market are the only valid ones, the only possible ones, the only path that leads us to that fullness enjoyed by imperial subjects. To that end, the realities of all real subjects, the environments in which they emerge and live, are made virtual. Whether in the news or soap operas, reality is made virtual and dissolves into nonsense. Private lives are exhibited in public like spectacles while public resources are privatized. Desire is induced and oriented toward commercial interests. The law communicated by the consumerist market is 'just do it'. Instantaneous is the norm, the primitive impulse is converted into the only motive, in such a way that one adopts the symbolic proposal of the Empire, eliminating mediations that might emerge from creating the symbolic itself. Appearance is everything, even though there is much behind it, as we will discuss in the next chapter.

What is new? Where can we get it? How much is it? These are the most frequent questions asked by our colonized youth. Individual satisfaction dissolves the sense of solidarity. In this way, a series of factors contribute to generating an imperialized subjectivity as the spaces of freedom disappear. The only freedom that survives is the freedom of the market, where the human being either remains subject to the dominant interests or is expelled. There is only room for desire generated in hegemonic domination.

It is important to clarify the concept of hegemony here. Today it is a worn-out concept that is debated in some currents of 'post-Marxist' political philosophy.[29] This is not the place to revisit this debate. In our conception, hegemony is a dimension of social construction where the factors that provoke domination come into play, and that operates in the field of the political culture, and in that intermediate space in which the relation is generated between politics and subjectivity (as much in the individual as in collective subjects) of those who become social and political actors. This is not equivalent to domination or imposition. It is the internalization of the imperial consensus, the participation of the dominated in the ideological space of the dominant, which is assumed as one's own ideological construction: 'the dominant ideology is the ideology of the dominated'. The dominant symbolic structure is integrated into the expressions of those rendered subaltern within it, and they end up incorporating this symbolic into their self-images. It is not a simple resigned acceptance of domination but rather an active incorporation, which introduces the worldview, the 'spirit' of domination, as a dominant *ethos*. The social conjunction operates according to the symbolic structure that hegemonic forces generate, in such a way that even what appears diverse is expressed within the same symbolic structure; it is, therefore, totalitarian. Hegemony supposes an absolute immanence of the system (which, therefore, is considered transcendent) in the circularity of its way of conceiving and expressing reality (the symbolic). Reality remains subject to the configuration that imposes the dominant subjectivity, although this subjectivity has been formulated in a fantasy that ends up fantasizing the world according to its particular interests and without recognizing the real of reality as external to its discourse.

This is precisely that to which hegemony aspires: the possibility of eliminating the control of those who might claim it, their claims having already been incorporated as subaltern in the symbolic structures of those who have assumed the power of the totalizing demand. The hegemonic consensus exists so long as those other claims cannot be identified within the symbolic structure that the powerful propose. This formulation of other demands can change relations of power. When relations of power begin to change, it is because they acquire the capacity to manage autonomously the demands of certain sectors, or find or appear to find a possibility for the social insertion of other interests and forces that begin to seek other ways of managing political space and expressing their antagonistic interests. A new symbolic emerges from the cracks that are produced in this game of immanence, breaking down the totalizing fantasy, and names the real from another mediation, from another formulation of the human experience, from another way of being alive.

Democracy as 'anti-imperial' requires this breaking of the hegemony or, in the struggle for hegemony, the presence of anti-hegemonic forces. Democracy demands a certain incapacity to resolve differences, a certain degree of ambiguity of recognizing tension as inevitable. But this ambiguity, to differentiate it from the ambivalence Beck proposes, is not an excuse to avoid conflict but rather a recognition of its necessity, of a certain state of indefinition, of a struggle for meanings, of a distributive dispute that renders democracy dynamic, the occlusion of which brings the end of politics and, therefore, of freedom. It is the place where conflicts are aired and regulated: they are not dissolved, reduced to a consensus, or submitted to the dynamics of the market. They are recognized and expressed in political terms to generate political action.

The fictitious representative character of the imperial Republic empties reality and presents us with its fantasy as if it were reality. The task of politics is not to present a virtual substitute (utopian politics) but rather to install symbols that link it with the reality of the people and, therefore, once again place in the centre of the public sphere antagonisms and controls that are appropriate to a diversified exercise of power. In other words, that which the Empire has emptied from humanity through its construction of a virtual reality, this hall of mirrors that the Empire exhibits as its infinite power, must be returned to the human and to the dimension of ambiguity, of unpredictability, of participation that, paradoxically, can only be proclaimed as a break, an irruption. That is to say, as in the well-known story, but now reversed, it becomes necessary to admit that 'the emperor is dressed and has left us naked'. The spell, or in this case, the submissiveness, cannot resist the voice of the weakest, of the child who tells it like it is, of the sick one who describes suffering, of the undocumented person who nevertheless exists.

The Empire and the times

'Normal' times are those where there are hegemonic struggles, where the dominant powers legitimate themselves through the act of exercising their own power, where the power of violence – physical or symbolic – effectively secures the possibility of a 'stable' government. In this sense, the 'normality' of the empire is its capacity to suspend the law, in Schmittian terms, to declare itself sovereign, or to suspend politics, to resign democracy, to dissolve the *res publica* even under republican formalities.[30]

Formal democracy thrives on 'normal' times. This is why it is acceptable not to seek justification in anything transcendent. Democracy itself cannot aspire to any kind of absolute because doing so would definitely install the hegemony. Democracy must constantly feel threatened by the irruption of the absolute, conscious of the precariousness of every condition of power, of the instability of the asymmetries that establish it today, in order to avoid absolutizing itself as an Empire. It must recognize the 'laocratic' claim as a time of gratuity, of the paradox that the absolute is claimed from the materiality of life.[31] Indeed, the Empire 'de-eschatologizes' politics because it ignores the absolute that comes to it from outside itself in order that it be able to realize it in itself. But the human being never can represent the absolute and can never achieve it. When we attempt to achieve it we become authoritarian, totalitarian, and eventually monstrous, as the Book of Revelation depicts it.

But facing these 'normal' times there always appear, threatening, those times where ambiguity can be expressed; where the immanent fantasy of the system is touched by the transcendence of reality; where another claim appears, the 'laocratic' claim, which struggles against the retention walls built by the empire, against the exclusion that its excessive pride constructs. Since the real is in time, the only way that the Empire can be eternal is to dissolve the real into its pretension of eternity, into its virtual potency. For this it is necessary to ignore the real life of real human beings, and to replace it with the virtual life of virtual human beings, with their juridical fictions and 'invisible hand'. When that is not enough, weapons appear.

The imperial ideology, as much in the past as now, is necessarily 'de-eschatologizing': just as there can be nothing 'outside' the Empire, something that is free of market forces, so there is no future, no next. The next can only reproduce the now. There is no coming system, no other time possible, because the Empire is defined as eternal, the end of history. It presumes that it does not have to explain its actions to anybody because its power validates its existence. It proposes to eternalize this lack of control and lack of accountability. Time passes without having an impact on the condition of things or on the limits of its power: these are the 'normal' times of imperial domination.

The threat to the empire and its normalcy is a break in this passing of time without the 'passing' of time. From there, all the 'anti-imperial' movements need to generate a distinct temporality, and they must introduce an eschatological horizon, a temporal rupture that calls normal times into question. The introduction of an eschatological expectation is the adventure of hoping for (and provoking) the rupture of normal times, in which there emerges a crack in the linear rationality of the powerful. This is what the Empire and its agents fear. They fear the time in which a prophetic voice will sound out. They fear it because it will bring into view the 'laocratic' cry, the reality of the fundamental dissatisfaction of the majorities.[32] They will fear it even more if this multitude becomes a *demos*, if they call for the re-establishment of democracy, again bringing validity to the *res publica* not just as a formality but with substance. In this we differentiate our idea from that of Hardt and Negri, who state that the multitude itself questions the Empire. In contrast, we argue that this occurs only when its state of *demos* recovers, when we reclaim participation in the public arena, and when we reinstall channels that allow us to act upon the closed totality of the Empire, to break it down and transcend it.

This is an unavoidable part of the political aporia: opposite this claim to eternal immanence is the space of the transcendent, from where it is necessary to raise the critique of Empire. In the ambiguity of the religious there resides a transcendence that has been erected as a guarantor of empires (when transcendence is made immanent in the sovereign who represents it); but at the same time there has always existed a transcendent voice, the dimension of the prophetic vision, that has emerged as the last space of critical revelation. To the degree that human relations have been imperialized, criticism of the empire can only come from an *extra novis*, from an outside that manifests its limit (this idea will be developed more extensively in Chapter 3). It is here that 'laocratic' power, the cry of the excluded, of the non-persons of the empire, becomes a dynamic factor in political time, announcing messianic times, eschatological times, if you can forgive the theological language that today has become a reference in political writing.

Eschatological times are the times when the Absolute irrupts and the Empire cannot extinguish it, times of the real (against Hegel, where the Absolute is ideal, and does not irrupt, but rather constructs itself in its manifestation). This presence of the exteriority that irrupts in the immanence of the system is the prophetic contribution to political philosophy, and from there we come back to read the biblical text in a political key.

We do not say, as some argue, that the power that will destroy the Empire is in the most humble, poor, meek, excluded, and marginalized. This would place tremendous responsibility on their shoulders, another burden. We are saying that, in its unwelcome presence, in its impossible disguise, in the deaths and crosses painted on the wall of shame, the spirit of Empire is revealed, and in the face of this spirit of death, from the reserve of anti-hegemonic feelings of the people, the spirit of life is expressed.

Notes

1 Antonio Negri and Michael Hardt, *Empire*, Cambridge, MA: Harvard University Press, 2001.

2 We avoid entering, for lack of knowledge, into the histories of the great ancient Eastern kingdoms (China and Japan) and their characteristics. A comparative study could shed additional data and light on our topic.

3 This is the vision that is presented by Polybius in his view of the Roman

Empire, which is conceived as 'the exemplary model' of total power. See the comments of Hardt and Negri on this (*Empire*, pp. 314–16). See also Domenico Musti, *Polibio e l'imperialismo romano*, Naples: Liguori Editore, 1972, pp. 15–17 and passim.

4 See Musti, *Polibio*, p. 17: 'Potessimo definire ad esempio l'imperialismo come tendenza al dominio con sfrutamento.' The following pages will justify the development of this concept.

5 Examples can be found in José Severino Croatto, *Las Culturas del Antiguo Próximo Oriente*, Buenos Aires: ISEDET/EDUCAB, 1994.

6 See a report from the 24th General Council of the WARC, held in Accra, Ghana in 2004, entitled 'Globalization and "Empire": A Challenge to Christian Mission', available online at http://warc.jalb.de/warcajsp/side.jsp?news_id=125&navi=1.

7 Ernesto Laclau and Chantal Mouffe, *Hegemony and Socialist Strategy: Towards a Radical Democratic Politics*, 2nd edition, London: Verso, 2001, p. x, italics original.

8 The considerations about 'exceptional circumstances' come from the interventions of Carl Schmitt and Walter Benjamin. They later became fundamental material for the considerations of Giorgio Agamben in his *Homo Sacer* and later works.

9 See Giorgio Agamben, *Homo Sacer: Sovereign Power and Bare Life*, trans. Daniel Heller-Roazen, Stanford: Stanford University Press, 1998, p. 65.

10 This returns to the old discussion of Marxism at the beginning of the twentieth century about the relationship between economics and politics, and the latter's relative dependence or autonomy. This cannot be discussed here, but it is discussed in, among others, Laclau and Mouffe, *Hegemony*, Chapter 1. See also J. Elias Palti, *Verdades y Saberes del Marxismo*, Buenos Aires: Fondo de Cultura Economica, 2005.

11 Reyes Mate, *Contra lo políticamente correcto: Política, memoria y justicia*, Buenos Aires: Editorial Altamira, 2006, p. 17.

12 Néstor O. Miguez, *El tiempo del principado Romano*, Mimeo: ISEDET, 1998.

13 See Zygmunt Bauman, *Liquid Modernity*, Cambridge: Polity Press, 2000. For a somewhat different perspective see Nestor Garcia Canclini, *Consumers and Citizens: Globalization and Multicultural Conflicts*, Minneapolis: University of Minnesota Press, 2001.

14 Claude Lefort, *L'Invention democratique: Les Limites de la domination totalitaire*, Paris: Fayard, 1981, p. 173; cited according to the translation in Laclau and Mouffe, *Hegemony*, p. 187.

15 If the Greek words *demos* and *laos* refer to free men, the first is used more frequently in Greek texts, while the second is much less frequent – with the exception of the Greek translation of the Hebrew Bible (LXX), which uses it about 2000 times. *Laos* is used in Homer to refer to the troops, the common soldiers, as distinct from the chiefs and aristocrats who commanded them, or to the common men, as distinct from those that exercised government. *Demos* also has some disparaging uses, but in Athens it acquired a new meaning by referring to free men with property. It implies certain rights of citizens: for example, participation in the assemblies and a certain level of influence within

the government. With time it came to indicate a people, a determined group of persons with common characteristics. In addition, in some Greek cities and then in those cities throughout the Roman Empire that spoke Greek, the word *demos* was used to refer to the town assembly. *Laos*, on the other hand, maintained the meaning of the undifferentiated masses, of simple common dwellers or inhabitants of a region (some linguists derive the German word *Leute* from this root). In this book, we will use this difference to indicate those who have greater participation in governmental decisions or access to some forms, although reduced, of social participation (*demos*), in contrast to those who have been excluded from all power to decide and are 'leftovers' of the imperial system (*laos*).

16 We construct this neologism from the Greek *jrema* (goods or money, also a matter or business): that is to say, the power or government of money, or government where wealth constitutes the bases of the exercise and legitimization of power.

17 On the nationalization of Bolivian energy resources, see the BBC report 'Bolivia Gas under State Control', 2 May 2006, http://news.bbc.co.uk/2/hi/americas/4963348.stm. On the then US Defense Secretary Donald Rumsfeld's 'Latin American Axis of Evil', see Eric Fish, 'Axis of Evo: Bolivia's Model of Leftism', *Academy and Polity* 28.2 (2006), available online through the Harvard International Review at http://www.harvardir.org/articles/1541/.

18 Upon considering the impact of these 'walls' it is appropriate to remember that approximately 300 people died trying to cross the Berlin Wall during its existence (the figure is over 900 if you include the deaths of all those trying to cross the border between the two Germanies between 1945 and 1989). Meanwhile, the death toll for people attempting to cross into the United States from Mexico during the last eight years is estimated at ten times this amount, well above 3000 (figures and documentation can be found online at http://en.wikipedia.org/wiki/Immigrant_deaths_along_the_U.S.-Mexico_border).

19 Franz Hinkelammert, 'La economía en el proceso actual de globalización y los derechos humanos', *Revista de Interpretación Bíblica Latino Americana*, 30 (1998), pp. 8–16.

20 See his 'Corrupting the Fight Against Corruption', available at http:/www. project-syndicate.org/commentary/stiglitz75.

21 On these points in Hayek's thought, see especially Chapter 1, 'Between Instinct and Reason', in *The Fatal Conceit: The Errors of Socialism*, Chicago: University of Chicago Press, 1988.

22 Chantal Mouffe, *On the Political*, New York: Routledge, 2005.

23 Mouffe, *On the Political*, pp. 35–63.

24 See Mouffe, *On the Political*, pp. 38–9.

25 See Mouffe, *On the Political*, pp. 45–6.

26 See Mouffe, *On the Political*, pp. 59 ff.

27 Mouffe, *On the Political*, p. 37.

28 Mouffe, *On the Political*, pp. 83–9.

29 A reference point in this debate is Laclau and Mouffe's *Hegemony*, as well as the debates that have occurred around authors such as Slavoj Žižek and Judith Butler.

30 See Carl Schmitt, *Political Theology: Four Chapters on the Concept of Sovereignty* [1922, 1934], trans. George D. Schwab, Chicago: University of Chicago Press, 2006; and Giorgio Agamben's reflection in his *State of Exception*, trans. Kevin Attell, Chicago: University of Chicago Press, 2005.

31 On the *laos*, see n. 15 above.

32 For the North American public (and also for some Europeans), the claim is usually that it is the minorities who voice the dissatisfaction of the poor, of the victims. Yet, when considered at global level, the minorities are the privileged and the majorities those who have been exploited or excluded.

2

Empire, Religion, and Subjectivity

It is often overlooked that empires shape not only political and economic structures but also cultural, intellectual, religious, and personal
realities. In the current situation of Empire, people's subjectivity is
shaped in new ways, often unconsciously.[1] Unlike in many empires
of the past, subjectivity is not necessarily subdued by force and out-
right cultural repression (such as past missionary efforts to 'civilize the
savages' or expectations of conformity in the 'melting pot') but through
more subtle mechanisms, which include new media and the advertising industry (as is often noticed), and through cultural and religious
dynamics that are less visible. Moreover, while subjectivity and desire
have always been shaped by relations of production – work in the fields
shapes peasants, factory labour shapes factory workers, and the office
shapes office workers – we now need to take a closer look at how consumerism shapes people. The immense desire to consume that we witness today is not natural but has to be produced, as advertisers know,
in order to keep the system afloat. The global shift from 'Fordism' to
'Toyotism', for instance, creates new relationships between consumerism and production; where in the old days subjectivity had to be made
to conform with rigid forms of industrial production (Ford's Model T,
for instance), now subjectivity can have some impact on industrial production (cars can be produced and equipped according to the wishes
of consumers). While production is still key and the invisible fetters
of salary that have replaced the visible iron fetters of slavery must be
taken into account, we also need to take another look at consumerism
and the even more subtle fetters of desire that it produces. Already in
1955 the connection between production and consumption was seen
clearly by US economist Victor Lebow:

> Our enormously productive economy . . . demands that we make
> consumption our way of life, that we convert the buying and use of
> goods into rituals, that we seek our spiritual satisfaction, our ego

satisfaction, in consumption . . . We need things consumed, burned up, replaced and discarded at an ever-accelerating rate.[2]

What is at stake in this ritualization is not just what is commonly criticized as 'materialism' or consumerism; the material and the spiritual cannot be separated that easily. At stake is how subjectivity is shaped in these processes.[3] The analysis of these mechanisms will allow us, in a second step, to identify alternative possibilities for the formation of subjectivity and desire, pointing beyond the structures of Empire.

Nevertheless, despite these softer patterns shaping subjectivity and the self, we cannot afford to neglect the role that force and repression play. Under the current conditions of Empire, soft power is complemented by hard power, which includes military action and acts of torture; the increased use of hard power in recent years has reshaped relationships on all levels in a short amount of time. With the presidency of George W. Bush, violent interventions (often religiously sanctified) have become more common in international relations – two preemptive wars in Afghanistan and Iraq speak for themselves – but they have also become more common in relations at the national level, all the way down to the level of personal relationships. There is an often-neglected history of violence that paradoxically goes hand in hand with the introduction of a certain laissez-faire capitalism that has shaped things on a global level for the past three decades. Examples include the violent overthrows of governments, from Chile in 1973 to an attempted overthrow in Venezuela in 2002, with the US lending some levels of support in both cases; reported clashes with protesters and the unreported and increasingly violent methods of the police that are often used against peaceful protests; and dramatically rising levels of domestic violence in certain regions.[4]

Nevertheless, as Michael Hardt and Antonio Negri remind us, as long ago as the sixteenth century Machiavelli understood that the use of violence and force must be short-term and limited.[5] Military force is the weakest form of power, hard but brittle. The limits of hard power are precisely what the US has experienced in its military interventions in Afghanistan and Iraq, with the added twist that hard military power seems to be less and less able to change the world. The Vietnam War provides another example of this phenomenon, as does the Soviet invasion of Afghanistan. These failures have produced some new perspectives and greater appreciation for soft power. In December 2007, an AFP News report stated that 'after six hard years of war, the United States is awakening to the idea that "soft power" is a better way to regain influence and clout in a world bubbling with instability'. What is most interesting is that, as the report says, 'nowhere is the change in thinking more advanced than in the US military, which is pushing for greater diplomacy, economic aid, civic action and civilian capabilities to prevent new wars and win the peace in Iraq and Afghanistan'. The US Defense Secretary Robert Gates, the successor of the hawkish Donald Rumsfeld, now calls 'for a dramatic increase in spending on civilian instruments of power'. As an expert at the US Institute of Peace, Robert Perito states: 'In conflict prevention, of course, there is very little military component to that. It's mostly all political and economic. That's the other thing that is going on.'[6]

With the increasing awareness of the brittle nature of military action, the current situation of Empire can perhaps be described in terms of a passive–aggressive climate. As far as the United States are concerned, what happened in New Orleans is just as telling as what is going in Iraq. In the aftermath of Hurricane Katrina and the flooding of the city in 2005, the world was stunned by the passivity of the US government, which seemed unable to intervene on behalf of the victims at any meaningful level. Years later, many people affected are still in limbo, unable to return. What is less known is that there were indeed actions taken, and many economic and political leaders, from Milton Friedman to the members of the Heritage Foundation, noted the golden opportunity: elite neighborhoods were rebuilt quickly and without restrictions, the school system was largely privatized by issuing school vouchers, and the way was even paved to the introduction of a flat-tax.[7] In this passive–aggressive climate, catastrophes of all kinds are exploited, through both inaction and action at all levels. While the aggressive action of the two US wars after the terrorist strikes of 11 September 2001 has proven deeply ambiguous, another action encouraged by President Bush may prove to be more decisive in the long run. One of his first injunctions after that fateful day was to encourage people to go shopping. Consumerism is an important part of the passive–aggressive package of Empire. A reflection on subjectivity, Empire, and religion demands that we pay attention to both hard and soft power and to the ways in which they are now working hand in hand.

In this chapter, examples are frequently given from the context of the United States. While Empire is bigger than the United States, that country has a special place in the formation of Empire today, as there is a 'deep alignment with global developmental processes – and the "project of modernity" – that gives the American system its durability and global reach', as G. John Ikenberry has pointed out.[8] A reminder by James Petras and Henry Veltmeyer puts things further in perspective: 'Imperialism is not a policy, a conspiracy, or a product of any single administration, but a structural reality with political determinants and an economic basis.'[9] It is this bigger structural reality that we need to investigate, yet the situation in the US is in many ways symptomatic of it.

In light of these varied phenomena, the role of theology and religious studies in analysing these developments hardly needs an apology. The spirituality of consumerism and its rituals, the work ethic that is shored up by various modes of production, and the religious imagery employed in the war efforts – one Republican congressman even stated that it was God who cleaned up New Orleans, and Vice President Cheney noted that empires cannot rise without God's help[10] – all testify to the effectiveness of theology and religion. We urgently need a critical investigation that will help us understand human limits and the limits of our grasp of the divine.

A short history of subjectivity[11]

In past empires, human subjectivity and desire have often been subdued by force and direct cultural repression. The varied approaches to religion serve as a case in point. While the Roman Empire at the time of the emergence of Christianity displayed substantial levels of cultural and religious tolerance, those who explicitly rejected the emperor cult faced persecution and execution. In the days of the Spanish Conquest of Latin America, fire and the sword played a significant role in the conversion of the natives, and even alternative attempts at conversion frequently applied direct cultural pressure.[12] Nineteenth-century colonialism, while more inclined to tolerate the diversity of others – including, to a certain degree, religious diversity – still followed a hierarchical logic according to which some subjectivities were valued more than others, resulting frequently in projects of 'civilization' or, in the case of religious institutions, in 'mission'.

Nevertheless, modern colonialism introduced an important shift. The theology of the modern colonial mainstream – liberal theology – is built on the freedom of the self and the endorsement of human subjectivity. The work of the German theologian Friedrich Schleiermacher set the stage. What is often overlooked, however, is that the self of modern liberal theology was developed in relation to a colonial fantasy: it came into its own on the back of the colonial other, often without being aware of it.[13] There are at least two subjectivities in modernity: one dominant and the other subjugated. Dominant modern subjectivity is increasingly shaped by a sense of the self's ability and power. René

Descartes built an entire philosophical system on the self's ability to represent itself; industrialization raised the level of self-confidence of the industrialists and stakeholders by amplifying the human powers of production and by envisioning larger and larger projects; and political overthrows of older feudal systems by the middle class in France and the United States contributed further to a sense of empowerment.

The depth dimension of the dominant self in modernity is important and vital: deep down, at its very core, liberal theology holds that the self points to God and thus seeks to cultivate this dimension of subjectivity. And even for those moderns who do not endorse the divine, there is an essence or identity to this self that keeps it grounded and able to 'walk upright'.[14] Nevertheless, modern Empire, the modern academy, and modern religion resemble each other because they are all built on this self in terms of another depth dimension – the relation to human others who are rarely acknowledged in their full subjectivity. These others are often far away, in the colonies, but some are also at home, for instance the Jewish population of Europe. Not surprisingly, modern efforts at hermeneutics, are closely tied to efforts at understanding the other.[15] While these relationships show certain degrees of mutuality and attempts at communication, the self of the colonizer (or of the owners of the means of production, or of the educated) remains firmly in control, making use of mechanisms as varied as romanticization and repression (see below).[16]

While modernity is built on the dominant self of the philosophers, the religionists, the industrialists, the explorers, the revolutionaries, and the politicians of that era, in a postmodern situation this self has been eroded in various ways. 'First-world' liberal theology, for instance, is no longer about the depth dimension of what Schleiermacher called the 'feeling of absolute dependence' that ties humanity to God; now theology is about any feeling that promises to make us happy and provides instant gratification. Even postmodern spirituality is taking shortcuts, as it often promotes short-lived happiness without commitment. This trend throws some light on the difference between colonial and postcolonial times: just as the heavy-handed power structure of the colony has been replaced by more subtle expressions of power, the intense relation of dependency that ties together colonized and colonizers appears to be no longer required either. Such relations thrive, like multiculturalism, on superficial relations and a few fleeting images of the other (either on TV or through the commodification of other people's culture through ethnic restaurants, music, or art). This helps us understand why televangelism works so well today: a few fleeting images of the divine Other suffice too.

There is, however, another side to this. While postcolonial imperialism is not easily visible for the privileged, whose subjectivity appears to be more and more flat and one-dimensional – not long ago imperialism itself seemed hardly necessary any more – the violence produced by this situation is deadly for many people both at home and around the globe, and it severely impacts their subjectivity. In the United States, for instance, the situation in the prisons is telling: there is little oversight or structure in many of these institutions and often people are imprisoned without due process for long periods of time. As a result, the subjectivity of the guards is virtually omnipotent (an attribute of the divine in classical theism) while the subjectivity of the inmates is systematically eroded. The fact that the US intentionally supports prisons where due process is explicitly rejected, such as the detention camps in Guantánamo Bay that defy international law, is even more alarming. Add to that the ongoing investigations of the use of torture by US military forces, and the picture of a benevolent Empire that lacks strong manifestations of dominant subjectivity shifts. The fact that this violence is allowed to continue points to a complex reality that has to do not only with a conspicuous lack of awareness but also with a self-image that is generally benevolent and that takes for granted the good intentions, high moral standards, and divine endorsement of one's own position.[17] This is why the slogan 'God bless America' is still palatable to so many US citizens.

The violent nature of Empire is not the sole responsibility of the administration of George W. Bush, however, although the 'Project for a New American Century' that informed much of his policies called for greatly expanded military spending in order to maintain the position of the US as 'the world's sole superpower and the final guarantee of security, democratic freedoms and individual political rights'.[18] The 'Bush Doctrine' of preemptive war speaks for itself. As early as the 1990s, however, after the fall of the Soviet Union, the US was involved in two dozen open military campaigns – more than all its campaigns since World War Two, even if the strategies of 'low intensity warfare' are not counted. The 'Clinton Doctrine' combined bombing campaigns with the use of proxy armies which resulted in minimal loss of life among US soldiers.[19] The fact that Clinton's strategy encountered fairly little resistance in the US has to do with these negligible losses and the fact that the loss of lives elsewhere, including substantial civilian casualties, were rarely reported.[20] Chalmers Johnson has talked of the 'Empire of the bases', mostly unknown to the majority of Americans.[21] In this context, dominant subjectivity takes on a particular shape; while we may tell our children not to bully other children, these national and international displays of violent power shape us unconsciously and thus more effectively.

Against this backdrop we can return one more time to the less dramatic and violent developments that are part of this situation. Postmodernity appears to presuppose the death of the dominant self, just as modernity presupposed the death of a dominant God. Several theological schools, from neo-orthodoxy to postliberalism and 'radical orthodoxy', join this choir – although some of them use this opportunity to return to the image of a dominant divinity. Contemporary self-understanding thrives on the critique of metaphysical ideas of the universal human self, endorsing fairly harmless images of otherness and difference ('why can't we all get along?'). The problem is, however, that the dominant self (and its dominant subjectivity) is not thereby erased, even as it may be flattened a bit. In fact, neither the self nor God is really dead – dominant subjectivity and dominant transcendence do not disappear so easily – and both keep haunting us. What is repressed from consciousness returns in the unconscious, as Freud pointed out. In this book, we claim that both subjectivity and transcendence are alive and well; it is just that they exist in dramatically distorted and often hidden and repressed forms. As we pursue these realities, it is not necessary to go back to the safety zone of conventional metaphysical images. Images of the self and God now need to be reassessed in the midst of the messiness of life in the Empire.

In light of these comments, it may not be surprising that alternative notions of subjectivity are undergoing transformation as well. The modern image of the heroic subject, able to take on and change the world, has at times been appropriated by protest movements as well. The youth rebellions of the 1960s, driven by middle-class unrest, often exemplified such attitudes. Yet when these dominant subjectivities failed to produce the desired results quickly, mostly because they overestimated their autonomy and underestimated their beholdenness to the status quo, fatigue and burnout were often the result. In this context, the dominant models of subjectivity led into an impasse that fed back into the status quo: it was not even necessary to suppress these subjectivities in totalitarian fashion, since such illusions of dominant subjectivity were bound to fail sooner rather than later, just like the theological notions of the divinity's dominant subjectivity in certain misappropriations of liberation theology by the middle class.[22]

Subjectivity and Empire today: four perspectives

The automatic subject and the religion of the free market

Contemporary Empire appears to be less interested in the active domination of other people's subjectivity and desire that characterized modern colonialism. Most foreign wars are now fought in the name of democracy and freedom rather than colonialism and conquest. In Iraq, for instance, the US does not promote the kinds of efforts at civilization that would have been typical for nineteenth-century colonialism, and missionary projects are officially discouraged to the point that religious organizations are only allowed to deliver humanitarian aid. In the nineteenth century, by contrast, the US supported the establishment of missionary schools in the Americas and elsewhere in the hope that they would help shape the subjectivities of those who were seen to be in need of formation. Today, economic networks assure the dominance of Empire more reliably than any colonialism, and the tactics of Empire have shifted.

Nevertheless, these economic networks shape up in close connection with political, cultural, and religious realities. Religion takes on an important function in this context, whether it is aware of it or not. To be sure, each of these realities shapes up somewhat differently in different contexts, and so they are characterized by a certain open-endedness; consequently, there is no clearly definable essence to the political, the cultural, or the religious. There is no universal category of religion, for instance, that would allow us to assume that all religions are identical. Furthermore, there is considerable overlap: the dynamics at work in the world of corporate business, for instance, are not just economic but also cultural, political, and religious, and sometimes it is hard to tell where one ends and the other begins. For these reasons, the approach taken here will focus on particular constellations. Religion for the purposes of this argument is tied to Christianity under the current conditions of Empire in its actual manifestations, which have cultural, economic, and political characteristics.

There are subtle mechanisms at work in the contemporary situation of Empire that continue to shape subjectivity and desire. Empire now seems to have incorporated the lessons of Freudian psychoanalysis that subjectivity and desire are best shaped unconsciously. The advertising industry (embodying a combination of cultural, religious, and economic concerns) represents the most sustained effort at shaping subjectivity and desire at the level of the unconscious. The messages of advertisement are carried not by the slogans and statements geared to address the conscious levels (who would really believe that a soft drink is the 'real thing'?), but by the associations produced in the unconscious: shaping desire, feeling good, and producing identity (what is called 'branding' in advertising lingo – religionists might call it 'initiation') is the key. Even the world of advertisement, however, does not yet reach to the bottom of the mechanisms that shape subjectivity and desire under the conditions of contemporary Empire. Advertisement itself is a symptom of broader shifts, piggybacking on cultural and religious dynamics whose effectiveness is often even less visible. Our hope is that, by identifying those dynamics, alternative options for the formation of subjectivity and desire can be identified that will provide viable alternatives to the lure of Empire.

In this context, dreams of the autonomous and autocratic self, whose subjectivity unfolds freely, have faded for good reasons. Our postmodern disillusionment is so deep that even idealists now have some sense that the self is no longer master in its own house. Rather than vanishing, however, subjectivity becomes more and more a function of the structures of Empire, economic, political, cultural, and religious. In his influential analyses of postmodernism as the 'cultural logic of late capitalism', Fredric Jameson has identified 'a new emotional ground tone'. Wide-ranging changes in culture and the economy are no longer tied to external phenomena alone; these changes transform the very core of our selves, our subjectivities. While materialist traditions of thought have long argued that shifts in economics and politics produce shifts in the ideal realm as well, we may be facing a new intensity of this phenomenon owing to the larger scale of these shifts in the global economy and to a host of more subtle mechanisms. How do these dynamics shape subjectivity?

When the question is posed in this way, the formation of subjectivity is no longer primarily a matter of individual psychology. There is a collective quality to subjectivity that can be seen in certain emotional responses to Empire. In the United States, for instance, studies of emotional responses to Hurricane Katrina found that many people were emotionally 'flat';[23] a different kind of flatness is manifest in the Iraq war: the general public loses interest while 30 per cent of Iraq war veterans return emotionally disturbed, twice as many as in the Vietnam war. Suicide rates among Iraq war veterans are significantly higher than the rates of combat deaths.[24] Add to that Jameson's observation of a new prevailing emotional mood in postmodern times that he identifies as 'depthlessness' (related to the insights of poststructuralism, according to which subjectivity is formed in the interplay of signifiers without the signified). These phenomena of 'depthlessness' and 'flatness' become clearer when we take a closer look at how capitalism works. Here another less visible colonization process is under way that seeks to assimilate subjectivity and desire; due to the inextricable connection of various levels of reality, religion and God-talk are included here as well. How does subjectivity become a function of capitalism?

It is often overlooked that capitalism is not primarily about money or capital but about relationships and power; but what shapes relationships is money. Subjectivity, too, is shaped in these ways. Karl Marx noted the automated character of subjectivity in capitalism. There is an 'automatic subject', which comes into being as a function of the accumulation of capital and the production of surplus value. The subjectivity of all classes is reshaped in the process – not only that of the working class but that of the ruling class as well. In other words, dominant subjectivity is an illusion; even the subjectivity of the owners of the means of production is automated and reduced to the functions of capital accumulation, which has become an end in itself under the conditions of capitalism.[25] Marx analyses the actual mechanism at work in the following way: as money circulates, money purchases commodities whose sale produces more money (this is the meaning of his famous formula M–C–M); money (M) and commodity (C) in this formula are thus merely different modes of value. What matters, then, is how the relationship of money and commodity produces value, and this value is what produces the automatic subject. Value 'is constantly changing from one form to the other without thereby becoming lost, and thus assumes an automatically active character'; or, translating more literally from the original German text, value 'thus is transformed into a automatic subject'.[26] Just as the commodity is stripped of its being (the value of a chair is no longer in its use or in how it was produced), those whose lives are enveloped in capitalism are also stripped of their being (the value of the entrepreneur or of the worker depends on the value produced in the circulation of money).

There is something narcissistic about this automatic subject. Curiously, Marx talks about it in terms of what might be called a 'trinitarian narcissism':

> Instead of simply representing the relations of commodities, it [value, the automatic subject] enters now, so to say, into private relations with itself. It differentiates itself as original value from itself as surplus-value; as the father differentiates himself from himself qua the son, yet both are one and of one age: for only by the surplus value of £10 does the £100 originally advanced become capital, and so soon as this takes place, so soon as the son, and by the son, the

father, is begotten, so soon does their difference vanish, and they again become one, £110.[27]

While Marx does not draw out this theological line of argument, we should seriously wonder whether not only our images of the self but also our images of the divine become a function of the automatic subject in the production of surplus value.

The classic notion of commodity fetishism – when related to Freud's notion of the fetish as surrogate object of desire – further illuminates what is at stake. As we have seen, in capitalism the value of material objects is not based on their inherent nature but on social relations. More specifically, material objects become surrogates (in which 'the social character of men's labour appears . . . as an objective character'), and the relationship of these material objects transforms and models human relationships.[28] According to Marx, 'there is a definite social relation between men, that assumes . . . the fantastic form of a relation between things'.[29] Even critics of Empire and capitalism often overlook this fundamental insight, namely that human relationships are more and more shaped by the relationships between commodities. This oversight resembles the logic of certain forms of religion, idealistic forms of Christianity no doubt among them, where 'the productions of the human brain appear as independent beings endowed with life, and entering [sic] into relation both with one another and the human race'.[30]

Commodity fetishism is, therefore, not simply the attachment of people to material things – a common critique found especially in religious circles – but the curious and much more problematic phenomenon that the relations between things unconsciously shape the relations between human beings and thus human subjectivity at its deepest levels, including religion.[31] What is also hidden here is that, as we compute values of different products, we also compute 'the different kinds of labour expended upon them',[32] and thus we compute the different value that we attribute to different human subjectivities. Just as some objects are worth much more or much less than others, some subjectivities are worth much more or much less as well. Just as the value of commodities depends on their position in the market and thus on their relationship to other commodities (independent of their use value), the value of people's subjectivity – expressed in their labour – also depends on these factors. Value, is thus 'a relation between persons expressed as a relation between things'.[33]

In other words, commodity fetishism covers up the real kinds of relationships that tie people together. Pushing beyond Marx's economic analysis, we might say that in this system human relationships are now measurable in terms of commodities and become structured like the relation of commodities. It is not so much, as Michael D. Yates says, that 'inside the workplace the freedom of the market disappears'.[34] It is more that the relationships inside the workplace between workers and others are rigidly determined in terms of the relationships between the commodities that they produce and the value of other commodities produced elsewhere. This does not bode well for the subjectivity of workers in a *maquiladora* whose products are sold cheaply; it is no accident that human rights abuses in these settings are common. Ultimately, workers everywhere are affected as their contributions are seen as less and less valuable; unemployment in this situation amounts to a complete destruction of subjectivity.[35] Moreover, relationships outside the workplace follow these models as well; the growing divorce rate, for instance, in some ways mirrors the relationships of commodities whose contribution to value needs to be constantly adjusted according to the fluctuations of the market, a phenomenon of which the trophy wives of the rich and famous represent merely the tip of the iceberg. There is also a religious component that is often overlooked. The religion of the free market that identifies the divine with success and the maximization of value undergirds these kinds of formation of relationship and subjectivity, and Godself becomes part of the market.

These reflections on how subjectivity is produced in the free-market exchange of commodities remind us of the shortcomings of our usual approach to these matters: 'Business ethics' is of little help here as it does not examine the logic and the structure on which business is built and how it forms subjectivity.

Mimetic desire and sacrificial religion

There is, however, another side to this. While subjectivity is increasingly becoming a function of the market – economic globalization makes sure of this as it reaches ever-farther regions of the globe and into the remaining white spots on the capitalist map at home – the subjectivity that is produced through the mechanisms of the market has various layers. As Friedrich Hayek, one of the original architects of the current free-market logic, has pointed out, a progressive society 'increases the desire of all in proportion as it increases its gifts to some'.[36] In other words, the subjectivity that is produced at the top levels of the free-market society takes on a special role in the formation of the subjectivity and desire of others.

A special kind of desire is at the heart of this production of subjectivity. This desire is not natural but constructed. The confusion between the concept of desire and need in capitalist societies, noted by Jung Mo Sung, is a crucial factor in this construction.[37] Liberal and neoliberal economies are based on demand, conceived as 'desire made viable by purchasing power'.[38] Demand is infinite since, unlike needs, desires are infinite as well. Thus, unlimited desire provides the basis for unlimited consumerism. As a result, limited resources must be negotiated with potentially infinite desires.

The notion of mimetic desire, developed by René Girard, helps us to analyse the central role of desire at a deeper level. Mimetic desire is not the ordinary desire of particular objects but the imitation of other people's desire.[39] This concept throws new light on consumerism (conventionally understood as desire for objects) and what drives it. Mimetic desire as imitation of desire puts the one whose desire is imitated (the model, in Girard's terminology) in a conflictual relation with the one who imitates desire (the disciple);[40] this mechanism is not limited to individuals but works with collectives as well. In the US, mimetic desire could be colloquially described as 'keeping up with the Joneses', with all the consequences for a never-ending rat race that takes over people's lives completely. While mimetic desire thus creates tensions, for the poorer nations it can have truly disastrous consequences because it demands that, in order to keep up with the wealth in the rich nations, the wealthy of the poorer nations need to appropriate more wealth and concentrate income in their own hands.

Girard assumes that this kind of desire is 'the basis of all human relationships',[41] yet it seems to us that today mimetic desire has reached a new level. One of the characteristics of the current conditions of Empire is that mimetic desire is aggressively promoted. It goes without saying that the advertising industry is built on furthering that sort of desire: we want not simply the objects that the happy people in the commercials have but we want that which makes them so happy. Beyond the advertising industry and its global reach, however, there are also what might be called 'ambassadors of the Empire' – John Perkins has called them 'economic hit men' – who spread the desires of the elites of the Empire to the elites of other countries, with the intention that 'those leaders become ensnared in a web of debt that ensures their loyalty'.[42] Mimetic desire is played out even at the highest levels of society.

Mimetic desire helps us to understand some of the deeper levels of human relationships and subjectivity under the current conditions of Empire. Subjectivity itself becomes what we might call 'mimetic subjectivity'. Competition is not simply based on the scarcity of desirable objects, as is often assumed, it is based on mimetic desire.[43] What drives economic progress, consumption, and the progress of the structures of

Empire from this point of view, is that others want what the wealthy already have. The result is the extraordinarily intense competition that has come to be accepted as the essence of free-market economies. It is not hard to see that there is little room for subjectivity and an active subject, except at the very top of society. But even there a constant battle ensues about who tops the lists, who is wealthier and more powerful, whose houses are bigger and yachts more expensive. Mimetic desire can indeed never be satisfied. The problem is compounded, of course, for those who cannot keep up. When they are drawn into this system, they can only perceive themselves as failures, as theorists from the Southern Hemisphere have pointed out.[44] What makes mimetic desire so effective in the pursuit of Empire is that it seems to have a snowball effect,[45] and it seems that we are witnessing this effect in extreme forms today. Moreover, there is a built-in reciprocity that leads to further escalation, since, in Girard's words, 'the model is likely to be mimetically affected by the desire of his imitator'.[46]

These mechanisms are immensely powerful but, like the mechanisms of the automatic subject, they often go unnoticed. This is no accident, since it is the role of culture to cover up those mechanisms and the feedback loops of mimetic desire.[47] There are some religious undertones here since desire is not tied to the object as such but to its transcendental promise. This parallels to a certain degree Marx's notion of commodity fetishism: that is, the sense that a commodity points to a deeper reality than itself.[48] Thus, subjectivity remains linked to a transcendent vision; it is shaped by mimetic desire that is itself infinite and that promises infinite happiness beyond the desired objects.

Yet mimetic desire cannot grow infinitely. Girard analyses the limits of this desire as well. As the tensions rise in which subjectivity is produced, at one point the opposing groups unite and direct their rejection toward a single person or minority group; this is when the process of sacrifice begins, in which a scapegoat is selected who is made to bear the tensions.[49] In this situation aggression 'takes a break'; the scapegoat is now the only one acting.[50] According to Girard, scapegoating and sacrifice are the typical mechanisms followed in the ancient world. There, religious sacrifice was the prime mechanism for curbing the escalation of mimetic desire and its violent effects: 'The function of sacrifice is to quell violence within the community and to prevent conflicts from erupting.'[51] This process is brought to a halt with the onset of Christianity, he notes, and the belief that Christ is the ultimate sacrifice and thus the end of it.

Nevertheless, the logic of sacrifice does not seem to have ended altogether. Girard's sense, expressed in the 1970s, that 'in our own world, sacrificial means have degenerated more and more'[52] does not quite capture what is going on now. From the perspectives of Latin America, for instance, the logic of sacrifice as that which helps to mediate social tensions seems to be alive and well. The sacrificed are those who appear less competent, who resist the laws of the market, and those who seek to regulate the market, as Jung Mo Sung has pointed out.[53] These observations from Latin America and elsewhere are crucial because they have led Girard to admit to the political use of his theories.[54] In the contemporary US, the sacrificial logic seems to return in various ways in the willingness to sacrifice others. The pressures are so high that at times no direct action by the government is necessary: if immigrants are perceived as a threat, for instance, all that is needed to get a sacrificial dynamic going is removal of government protection. The actions of self-empowered militias along the southern US borders are one example.

Another place where a sacrificial logic returns is in the context of the sacrifice of US soldiers. This attitude appears to be supported by the widespread assumption of God's own sacrificial logic manifest in the cross of Christ, a basic tenet of fundamentalism that is taken for granted by most evangelical and even the majority of mainstream Christians in the US. The phenomenal success of Mel Gibson's movie *The Passion of the Christ* (2004), in which Christ's sacrifice is depicted in all its gory details – Gibson's Christ is a superhuman sacrifice even in terms of the superhuman amount of blood that he loses – demonstrates how deep-seated this logic still is. This logic of sacrifice is even more effective when it is augmented by a logic of self-sacrifice among the soldiers themselves, many of whom are willing to risk their lives so that mimetic desire can once again flow freely, going to death for the motto that 'freedom is not free'. The truth is that freedom of mimetic desire is indeed not free. The military thus acquires a new function – enabled by the fact that most of the soldiers come from the lower classes that are more easily sacrificed. A strange phenomenon arises as a result of this logic: while war protesters have compensated for accusations that in the past they did not show respect for US soldiers, their current slogans 'support our troops – bring them home alive' have proven mostly ineffectual. Rather than earning praise as the real supporters of soldiers (as opposed to those who send them to their death or to a future of crippling disability for spurious reasons), it appears as if the protesters are those who fail to support the soldiers in their real mission – that of self-sacrifice, which keeps mimetic desire (one of the pillars of Empire) going. Unmasking this sacrificial logic becomes an important role that can perhaps best be achieved by theology.[55]

The formation of subjectivity can here be seen in a new light. It becomes part and parcel of the empire through the mechanisms of mimetic desire that are stoked in order to guarantee further expansion and success. Girard's later comments on the usefulness of mimetic analysis as an instrument of suspicion against everything that we express in our speech thus point in the right direction.[56] The return of the sacrificial logic with such a vengeance that large groups of people begin to identify with it and develop ideas of self-sacrifice should give us pause. The situation in the US is especially chilling in this regard, as soldiers are not the only ones; many working people seem to accept a similar logic of self-sacrifice when they proudly take on more and more work for less and less pay, and when they accept that their lives can take a disastrous turn any minute owing to the lack of healthcare and other life-supporting services provided not only to their European colleagues but more and more to their Latin American neighbours as well.

Shock treatment and the religion of omnipotence

Neither the automatic subject nor the subjectivity formed by mimetic desire, however, seems to be enough for Empire. The formation of subjectivity is augmented by methods that are yet more intentional than even the most aggressive promotions of mimetic desire. This sets the contemporary situation of Empire apart from the more implicit developments of capitalism in the past and leads us beyond the analyses of Empire put forth only a few years ago.[57] In what follows, we feel reminded of efforts to produce a sort of omnipotent top-down power that is reminiscent of the images of classical theism.

One of the time-honoured maxims of those who seek to build empires is to divide and conquer, a strategy sometimes employed even by the divine in order to preserve its unilateral power (this is one way to interpret the Tower of Babel story in Genesis). 'Divide et impera' was the motto of the Roman Empire, repeated through the centuries and picked up once again in modern times. In a letter to Thomas Jefferson, James Madison states: 'Divide et impera, the reprobated axiom of tyranny, is under certain qualifications, the only policy, by which a republic can be administered on just principles.'[58] The interesting question, of course, is who needs to be divided. In past empires, this phrase often referred to other nations that were to be brought under control (the Romans, for instance, divided Palestine into five parts), or to specific military strategies. Today, when Empire has adapted to democratic principles, the Empire needs to prevent people from empowering themselves by organizing around common interests. In the US, this strategy can be seen most clearly in the aggressive campaigns against labour unions and against new efforts of workers to organize themselves. The powers that be would be severely threatened if a group of people that shares powerful concerns, such as the erosion of real wages and the deterioration of schools and other social infrastructures, could not be divided.

In recent history, however, a much more radical form of divide and conquer has made headlines in connection with the treatment of prisoners in the US 'War on Terror'. While the definition of torture is being debated, the fundamentals of divide and conquer are all present in the treatment of prisoners but mostly exempt from the debate: isolating prisoners and confining them to small solitary spaces is common practice; seeking to control sensory and mental stimulation is also common, manifest in milder forms in efforts to restrict and control the flow of information and communication, and visible to the public in the pictures of hooded Iraqi prisoners. Most forms of torture are variations on those themes, such as confinement to spaces that are so small that prisoners can neither stand nor lie down; incarceration in dark spaces without sensory stimulation or food and water (hoods, earplugs, immobilization of limbs, and so forth are also used for that purpose) alternating with incarceration in spaces where blaring music and blinding lights are experienced; shock treatments through severe beatings, electrocution, simulated drowning (recently made famous in the US media as 'waterboarding'), and exposure to extremely hot or cold temperatures. Those and many other methods are not only described in US army handbooks but have recently been defended in public. 'Waterboarding', for instance, appeared to be justified because it was said to have produced information or prevented terrorist attacks in the US.[59] Note, however, that the retrieval of information is most probably not the primary concern of these methods, as torture is notoriously unreliable.

The common denominator of all those methods is nothing less than the absolute restriction of the self – the subjectivity – of the afflicted. Restricting subjectivity, if not simply trying to erase it, is seen as having several benefits. In the case of criminals, it seems to limit the possibility of criminal activity. In the case of prisoners of war, it is part of winning the war. It even has an impact on those who are not directly affected since it threatens their own sense of self. In Iraq, for instance, US-sponsored TV channels show confessions of terrorism by ordinary citizens who have been brutalized and thus robbed of their subjectivity[60] – the brutality itself does not need to be shown; the signs of it, such as swollen and bruised faces and shocked appearance, suffice.

public acceptance of violence in prison including rape

While many of these practices have not been publicly debated until recently, the common assumptions about more ordinary prison life have contributed to similar dynamics. The public acceptance of violence in prison – including rape – serves to intimidate those who can never be sure that they will not end up in similar places themselves due to simple 'mistakes'. In the US, this includes racial minorities who are subject to racial profiling, such as the senior African American professor at Southern Methodist University who would continually be stopped by the police when driving through the all-white neighbourhood. This problem is particularly severe in areas of political conflict or war since no one is safe from these mechanisms and fear is spread even among those who never experience imprisonment. In Iraq, for instance, 70 to 90 per cent of inmates in US prisons are released after a while because they were apparently held 'by mistake',[61] creating a situation in which everyone feels threatened. The problem is clearly much bigger than individual cases of abuse or random mistakes. There is something systematic in these shock treatments that affect large areas of the population around the globe. In Latin America, for instance, the populations of whole countries were held in check as hundreds of thousands of people disappeared during the time of the military dictatorships of the 1970s.[62]

Most important to our topic is that these threats have severe implications for people's subjectivity, both individually and collectively. On the side of the perpetrators and others who benefit from this situation, there is a sense of power and control that is hard to achieve anywhere else in real life and resembles the sort of omnipotent power that borders on classical theist images of the divine. On the side of all those who are not in control, whether abducted and tortured or not, there is a sense of vulnerability and danger that resides in the symbolic order just as much as in reality. Note that, in situations of torture, simply showing the instruments is often just as effective as using them.

Naomi Klein has investigated the systematic nature and the impact of such threats. This approach goes back to psychological experiments of the 1950s that were later publicly condemned by the CIA, who had funded them. Despite these condemnations, however, the experiments nevertheless found their way into the handbooks of the US military, such as the famous *Kubark Counterintelligence Interrogation Handbook*. In 2006, a report by a Defense Department interrogator was published, which recommended a careful reading of the Kubark manual.[63] The chief investigator of the psychological experiments of the 1950s, Dr Ewen Cameron, assumed that his patients needed to be 'depatterned', returned to a blank state of mind, and regressed back to infancy. This was achieved through electroshocks many times stronger and more severe than had ever been tried in medicine. In addition, he would use multiple drugs and chemicals to subdue his patients. Cameron would also use isolation chambers and long periods of drug-induced sleep. His main goal was to control and restrict both continued sensory input and memory in order to erase them.[64] As Kelly Oliver has pointed out, 'the colonization of psychic space in oppression operates in large part by denying access to the operations of meaning making'.[65]

Today, these strategies are also being applied on the macro level. Klein identifies three stages of how shock is applied or exploited.[66] Tremendous experiences of shock are generated by war, terror, political overthrows, and natural disasters. While natural disasters are not human-made, their shock value can be just as useful since those affected – especially if they are deprived of means to escape, such as transportation and funds – also experience extreme restrictions of their subjectivity. In a second step, corporations are allowed to exploit the situation and introduce economic shock therapies. This step has been endorsed officially not only for Hurricane Katrina but also for coups d'état by none other than Milton Friedman of the Chicago School of Economics, who believed that 'only a crisis – actual or perceived – produces real change'.[67] The third stage is the eventual arrival of police, soldiers, and interrogators.[68] Today, these uses of shock are no longer simply an occasional tactic or a strategy; they make up a billion-dollar economy that still lacks the sort of analysis that other prominent economic developments have received in the past.[69] In other words, these sorts of shock treatments and divide-and-conquer methods are no longer the kinds of planned acts on which conspiracy theorists dwell. They are now integrated into the economic environment that shores up Empire and its increasingly godlike (omni-)potence, and they have therefore assumed a life of their own. The consequences for subjectivity and the self of those who are actively and purposely excluded from this sort of power are devastating.

The logic of shock helps understand better the actions of the US in Iraq. While during the entire 1991 Gulf War about 300 Tomahawk cruise missiles were used, between 20 March and 2 May 2003 more than 30,000 bombs and 20,000 cruise missiles were deployed – 67 per cent of the total number ever made.[70] This was more than enough to send an entire country into the state of shock. The authors of the 'Shock and Awe' method explicitly state that the goal is to win not just by overwhelming fire power but by taking care of 'the public will of the adversary to resist', with the goal of 'rendering the adversary completely impotent'.[71] Klein also describes how sensory deprivation was part of the war effort, as communications were completely immobilized and the lights went off – many Iraqis reported that the loss of telecommunications was among the most stressful parts of the attack – and how the country felt stripped by the tremendous looting that was not controlled by the US military. Eighty per cent of the items held by the National Museum of Iraq were taken, a fact that amounts to a tremendous loss of collective memory. All these factors worked together in an effort to create a clean slate. As John Agresto, who worked under Paul Bremer as director of higher education reconstruction in Iraq, stated for his area of oversight, the stripping of universities and schools provided 'the opportunity for a clean start'.[72]

Klein discusses these approaches in terms of a religious fundamentalism that clings to its beliefs, no matter what the facts or the consequences. The beliefs are clear: they are the three assumptions of the Chicago School that the public sector needs to be privatized, corporations freed from any obligations, and social spending reduced. This fundamentalism, the growing evidence suggests, has been furthered not primarily by democratic means but by forms of coercion.[73] Milton Friedman fervently believed that the introduction of economic freedom – by whatever means necessary – would lead to political freedom, and probably to religious and cultural freedom as well. But the history of the past 30 years of pursuing this logic tells another story.

However, more is at stake than a particular economic fundamentalism. There appears to be a deeper religious assumption about the way the divine works in the world, namely from the top down and in omnipotent manifestations of power that must not be questioned. This is the spirit of the 'American theocracy' described for the US by Kevin Phillips.[74] The deeper problem, of course, is what kind of theocracy is envisioned. If it is seen that the notion of divine omnipotence is key, the problem is not just conservative Christianity and the Republican Party; mainstream and even liberal Christians are not off the hook either. Extending this logic, human subjectivity must be shaped in this image. Those who appear to be closer to the divine – those at the top in positions of power and privilege – must rule and all others must be held in check and be divided, shut down, or reprogrammed (even milder proposals for re-educating people should be scrutinized). A final paradox should be noted here that indicates where resistance might begin: the more power someone has, the greater the fear of losing this power: 'Paranoia is the disease of power.'[75]

The subject according to the realism and the religion of the status quo

A final perspective helps us to theorize and analyse some of the deeper layers of what is going on in all of these processes of the formation of subjectivity. This perspective, which draws upon the insights of psychoanalysis, subaltern studies, and postcolonial theory, makes sense only if the tensions in which subjectivity is shaped – including the ones discussed in the earlier sections – are explicitly noted and foregrounded. Without awareness of these tensions, the insights of postcolonial theory are too easily confused with postmodern concerns for more harmless forms of otherness, difference, and 'the endless flow of signification'.[76]

There is a particular sort of realism under the conditions of Empire that is expressed in the form of general assumptions that must not be questioned. 'There is no alternative', as the British Prime Minister Margaret Thatcher used to assert. Realists such as Thatcher in England and Ronald Reagan in the US, and almost all who subsequently held powerful positions in what has been called the 'free world', truly believe that their system is the only one possible. The fall of the Soviet Union seemed to provide additional evidence. To be sure, this sort of realism can be found not only in economics and politics but in matters of culture and religion as well. Whatever can be said in defence of these positions, their biggest shortcoming is that there is a complete lack of awareness that things look different from other points of view, especially from the margins and the underside. It is as if economic theory could learn nothing from taking into account the stories of those who are crushed by economic structures, or as if religion or culture could be studied in terms of the great minds alone without awareness of the consequences for the 'least of these'. Unfortunately, this is how these various fields are still mostly studied, but there are other options.

Jacques Lacan's distinction between realism and the real provides a first clue. What counts as reality, and what realism picks up, is what is commonly accepted as true by those who are part of the status quo. Statements such as 'everyone knows' or 'it is a commonly accepted fact' are based on the assumption that there is only one valid view of reality. The master narratives and constants of a given culture and what is perceived to be 'common sense' all belong to this realm of reality (which Lacan later termed the symbolic order). The various nationalisms, patriotisms, mainstream religions, and dominant subjectivities all belong here. The real, by contrast, is precisely that which escapes the realist perspective.[77] More specifically, the real is that which has

46

been pushed underground and repressed by the realist perspectives; here we need to talk about the dark underbelly of nationalism, patriotism, mainstream religion, and dominant subjectivities. As that which has been repressed, the real is not only invisible to realism – it is its alter ego, the back on which realism is built. The real is something like the collective unconscious of the dominant subjectivities. This collective unconscious is produced in analogy to the individual unconscious in moments of repression. Furthermore, since it shares in reality as a whole, this unconscious incorporates all of its aspects: economic, political, cultural, religious, and so on.[78]

In postmodern times realism has grown more sophisticated and branched out to incorporate an awareness of otherness and difference not yet evident in the realisms of Thatcher and Reagan. Postmodern pluralism and multiculturalism no longer contradict realism but have become built-in features; multinational corporations benefit from this ethos because it allows them to become more sensitive to cultural or religious idiosyncrasies in different locations. Yet there is a significant difference between the postmodern emphasis on otherness and difference that are tied to the free flow of signification, and the otherness and difference that are tied to the repressions produced in the real.[79] Unlike the postmodern version of the free flow of signification, which tends to see multiculturalism as fun and as a way to turn a profit, reflecting on repression and the real allows us to analyse severe asymmetries of power that correspond to the contemporary condition of Empire.

Lacan's interpretation of the relation of men and women, which can also be applied to other people on the margins, helps us to understand what is at stake. Women and other marginalized people are not simply part of free-floating otherness and difference; they find themselves in repressed positions, often either romanticized or demonized – the two sides of the same coin. In the repressive and highly asymmetrical world of patriarchal empire, men draw up idealistic images of women, colonizers draw up idealistic images of the colonized (the 'noble savage'), and well-to-do Christians draw up idealized images of 'the poor'. In doing so they acknowledge otherness and difference in a seemingly positive way but they also reassert control: they are the ones who determine what the other is really like. They are the realists who think they understand these others better than these others understand themselves. Colonizers tend to speak about the colonized in plural terms, as Albert Memmi has observed: 'they are this'; 'they are all the same'.[80] Joerg Rieger has noted a similar tendency in Christian theology to speak about God in such general ways.[81] Nevertheless the colonized, women, and other marginalized groups tend to defy these

On the myth of individualism

stereotypes, and we can now see why: their lives cannot be confined by realism because they also exist as part of the repressed real, excluded from, and invisible to, realism. As Lacan notes: 'There is no such thing as *The* woman, where the definite article stands for the universal.'[82] This does not mean that women and the marginalized are not real – just the opposite: they are so real that they cannot and must not be defined in terms of the realism of those in power – a realism that is really a fantasy.

The myth of individualism illustrates what is at stake. Most contemporary realists would assume that individualism is a fundamental reality. Many economists would affirm it as a good thing – individual initiative is supposed to drive the economy, as, for instance, the dominant models of the Chicago School of Economics propose. Many religionists or pastors would criticize it, noting that we should be less individualistic, while assuming its reality. From the perspective of the real, however, things look different. Individualism is the sort of master narrative that those in power who share in the dominant subjectivity tell about themselves in order to cover up and repress the real – that is, all those who have contributed to their success and those on whose backs their success is ultimately built. This repressed world of the individualist includes teachers, parents, and peers, but also housekeepers, workers who produce at low wages, and all the other service providers and subordinates in the command structure. Note that individualism is a necessary narrative for the dominant subjectivity. The seemingly self-made dominant subject must tell realism's story of individualism and repress the real; this is the only way to avoid being challenged by another kind of subjectivity that is part of the real. The Lacanian notion of the repressed real helps us see that there is no autonomous subject. Individualism is merely the myth of the powerful; even the dominant subjectivity cannot exist in isolation. Oppressors who seek to safeguard their own subjectivity by perpetuating the master narrative of individualism simply fool themselves because their identity is invariably built in relation to others and, more specifically, on the back of others. In this context, communitarianism does not fare much better because it builds on the myth of individualism, behaving as if there really were individual subjects out there whom we would have to draw together in community. In either case, the ugliness of the self, built on the back of others, will come back to haunt us.

Frantz Fanon expressed the subjectivity that emerges in the real in the strongest possible words: 'Now the *fellah*, the unemployed man, the starving native do not lay a claim to the truth; they do not *say* that they represent the truth, for they *are* the truth.'[83] The truth of this subjectivity is not tied to realism but to the real; it is that which has been repressed, pushed below the surface. Whatever has been repressed becomes the truth of the system – not in romantic or universal terms, once and for all, but in that particular situation of repression. Fanon is aware of the constructed nature of the truth of this subjectivity when he states that 'the black soul is a white man's artifact'.[84] The postcolonial theorist Homi Bhabha brings together Lacan and Fanon when he describes how identity is produced in the colonial situation of the 'in-between' – in the pressures between 'the colonialist Self and the colonized Other – for example as the white man's artifice inscribed on the black man's body'.[85] The two subjectivities, dominant and repressed, are inextricably tied together in special ways; there is even a secret desire that is bound up with that which is repressed to which we will have to return in the next part of this book. Perhaps this also helps us to understand to some degree our irrational fear of the other – there is a sense deep down that the subjectivity of the other could indeed have the power to unravel our own subjectivity. A related notion of truth can be found in Salman Rushdie's *Satanic Verses*, where a drunk reminds us of the hiddenness of truth from the perspective of those in power: 'The trouble with the Engenglish is that their hiss hiss history happened overseas, so that they dodo don't know what it means.'[86] Even though its truth is hidden, however, it is clear that dominant subjectivity is built on it and depends on it.

The dominant subjectivity of realism in some ways resembles the free-floating postmodern subject; what is often overlooked is that these free flows are closely related to the free flow of capital. Yet these free flows are illusory because they blend out the reality of the underside; in the illusion of free-floating subjectivity the poor have disappeared,[87] just as the bone-breaking reality of labour has disappeared in the illusion of free-floating capital. In either case, the phenomenon of repression does not go away, and so realism's free flow of capital is confronted by a depth dimension, where the repressed unconscious somehow grounds the conscious and points to alternative subjectivities. There are some close parallels here to liberation theology's 'preferential option for the poor'. While the theological apparatus seems to be lacking in these assessments, there is a common sense that, by connecting to the real, the poor, we put ourselves in touch with that which really matters, that which is most in touch with the heartbeat of life – the roots of a different religiosity altogether, which shares more in common with the person and work of Jesus Christ than with realism's imperial civil religions (which are now said to have taken both liberal and conservative forms).[88]

The binary of oppressor and oppressed, or of dominant and repressed subjectivity, is now considered to be too simplistic by many. This is one of the targets of postcolonial critique, which favours the notion of hybridity and rejects as Eurocentric categories the clear binaries between colonizers and colonized. It does indeed make sense to observe the messiness of real life and the fact that people have multiple allegiances and identities; the formation of subjectivity is always complex. Moreover, since official colonial relationships are for the most part a matter of the past, the relations between oppressors and oppressed have become more complex and less visible. Nevertheless, today we live once again in a situation of grave power differentials, which are in many cases just as stark as before, as the examples above have shown. As the rich get richer and the poor get poorer, with the middle class often being pulled down, the binaries will not go away. Fanon's sense that 'the colonial world is a Manichean world',[89] that is, a world marked by sharp dualisms, is making a return in our time. Even the middle will have to make up its mind sooner or later.[90] We have never been clearer about the fact that the end of formal colonialism does not imply the end of imperialism.

In this regard, the insights produced in the field of subaltern studies have been helpful. Broadening our view of the margins, especially by including those groups who do not possess a unified class consciousness, such as peasants and the poor,[91] subaltern studies have developed new concerns and new tools for investigating life at the margins. From this perspective, binaries still exist, although without the absolute character of the binaries of the status quo.[92] John Beverley connects subaltern studies to the Lacanian real: the subaltern is 'that which resists symbolization, a gap-in-knowledge that subverts or defeats the presumption to "know" it.' As a result, the real always needs to be understood in specific contexts.[93]

What are the marks of the emerging subaltern subjectivity? From the perspective of the subaltern it becomes clear that subjectivity must not be romanticized. Unlike those in power, subaltern people have a sense that they are not autonomous individuals. They experience in their own bodies on a daily basis that their subjectivity is produced by all the forces described in this chapter: the flow of capital, mimetic desire, shock treatments, and repressions; neither individualism, ethnocentrism, nor naïve communitarianism or nationalism are real options here in the long run. But neither can the subalterns afford simply to write off their subjectivity; they desperately need it in order to survive, and it may well be that these subjectivities are among the few things that can challenge Empire at a time when the dominant subjectivities have accommodated to it. It has often been pointed out that subjectivity in general is questioned precisely at a time when marginalized people have begun to gain some subjectivity. Gayatri Chakravorty Spivak's question whether the subaltern can speak needs to be seen in this light. She is certainly right if she means that there are alternative subjectivities that are not recognized by the status quo. Nevertheless, while subaltern subjectivity counts little under the conditions of Empire – just check its declining pay cheques and shrinking support structures – it does provide alternative ways of life that contain some surplus that might make a difference.[94] Perhaps the subjectivity and agency that are emerging here can be rethought in terms of Jesus' subjectivity and agency, which can do without Satan's offer to rule the world (Matt. 4.8–10). We will come back to this in the second part of this book.

Investigating the subjectivity of the colonized, Homi Bhabha makes an important observation:

> The [dominant] subject cannot be apprehended without the absence or invisibility that constitutes it – 'as even now you look/but never see me' – so that the subject speaks, and is seen, from where it is not; and the migrant woman can subvert the perverse satisfaction of the racist, masculinist gaze that disavowed her presence, by presenting it with an anxious absence, a counter-gaze that turns the discriminatory look, which denies her cultural and sexual difference, back on itself.[95]

Since subjectivity, whether dominant or subaltern, is produced under the pressure of immense power differentials, we need to think about subjectivity in the relation between the dominant and the subaltern. Without investigating dominant subjectivity and its one-dimensional realism from below, we will not be able to see the whole picture, and we will remain clueless about subaltern subjectivity. To be sure, while there is nothing romantic about subaltern subjectivity it pushes us to investigate the underside that cannot ultimately be controlled and this subaltern subjectivity may well be our best guide for understanding what is going on with the powers that be. Finally, subaltern subjectivity may provide alternative kinds of inspiration – the key function of religion – that point us in new directions towards the (narrow) 'way that leads to life' (Matt. 7.14).

Notes

1 Note that subjectivity is not merely a sideshow of empire. As Kelly Oliver, *The Colonization of Psychic Space: A Psychoanalytic Social Theory of Oppression*, Minneapolis: University of Minnesota Press, 2004, p. 26, has pointed out, following Frantz Fanon: 'The success of the colonization of a land, a nation, or a people can be measured through the success of the colonization of psychic space. Only through the colonization of psychic space can oppression be truly effective.'

2 Victor Lebow, 'Price Competition in 1955', *The Journal of Retailing* (Spring 1955), p. 7, as quoted in Michael Jacobson, Laurie Mazur, and Ron Collins, *Marketing Madness*, Boulder, CO: Westview Press, 1995, p. 191.

3 'It is necessary to be clear that in a consumer society like ours the pressure to consume more and more is not merely a problem of "materialism," in the sense that people are judged and located in society according to their patterns of consumption. Personal identity is today profoundly linked to consumption' (Jung Mo Sung, *The Subject and Complex Societies*, unpublished translation by Peter L. Jones, p. 39).

4 Between 1999 and 2004, there has been a 50 per cent increase in domestic violence in several Texas counties, for instance. See *Tyler Morning Telegraph*, 4 May 2007, available at http://www.tylerpaper.com/article/20070504/OPINION0306/705040314/-1/OPINION.

5 Michael Hardt and Antonio Negri, *Multitude: War and Democracy in the Age of Empire*, New York: The Penguin Press, 2004, p. 332.

6 Jim Mannion, 'Led by the Military, War-weary US Awakens to "Soft Power"', 13 December 2007, available at http://www.sqlspace.com/viewtopic.php?f=88&t=50831.

7 Naomi Klein, *The Shock Doctrine: The Rise of Disaster Capitalism*, New York: Metropolitan Books, 2007, pp. 4–5, 410.

8 G. John Ikenberry, 'American Power and the Empire of Capitalist Democracy', in Michael Cox, Tim Dunne and Ken Booth (eds.), *Empires, Systems and States: Great Transformations in International Politics*, Cambridge: Cambridge University Press, 2001, p. 194. While Ikenberry could still point out that part of the success of the US was that its democracy and relation to international institutions made it 'less threatening to the rest of the world' (p. 194), we have now seen the political, military, and economic power of the US at work, which Ikenberry played down somewhat in 2001.

9 James Petras and Henry Veltmeyer, with Luciano Vasapollo and Mauro Casadio, *Empire with Imperialism: The Globalizing Dynamics of Neo-Liberal Capitalism*, London: Zed Books, 2005, p. 32.

10 Richard Baker, quoted in Klein, *Shock Doctrine*, p. 4. In a 2003 Christmas card, Vice President Dick Cheney quoted Benjamin Franklin: 'And if a sparrow cannot fall to the ground without His notice, is it probable that an empire can rise without His aid?'

11 In English, the term subjectivity generally takes a more passive meaning, in the sense of 'being subjected'. Yet there is also a more active meaning, in the sense of the quality of being a subject, or 'subjecthood'. Both meanings are present in Portuguese and Spanish. Peter L. Jones, translator of Jung Mo

Sung, emphasizes this second meaning by using the word 'subjectity'. Jung Mo Sung, *Subject in Complex Societies*, p. 78, takes his cue from the work of Franz Hinkelammert. In order to make a similar point in English, we often talk about subjectivity and agency as related terms; see especially Chapter 4.

12 See, for instance, the work of Bartolomé de Las Casas, as discussed in Joerg Rieger, *Christ and Empire: From Paul to Postcolonial Times*, Minneapolis: Fortress Press, 2007, Chapter 4.

13 See Rieger, *Christ and Empire*, Chapter 5.

14 Ernst Bloch talked of *'aufrechter Gang'* (the ability to walk upright) as that which differentiates humanity from animals.

15 One example is the work of Friedrich Schleiermacher. See Rieger, *Christ and Empire*, p. 205.

16 In *Christ and Empire*, Chapter 5, Rieger shows how Schleiermacher's often benevolent relations to the other still reinforce a hierarchy of power.

17 See also Rosemary Radford Ruether, *America, Amerikkka: Elect Nation and Imperial Violence*, London: Equinox, 2007, p. 2.

18 'Rebuilding America's Defenses: Strategy, Forces and Resources for a New Century', A Report of the Project for the New American Century, 2 September 2000, p. 4, available at http://www.newamericancentury.org/ RebuildingAmericasDefenses.pdf.

19 Andrew J. Bacevich, *American Empire: The Realities and Consequences of U.S. Diplomacy*, Cambridge, MA: Harvard University Press, 2002, Chapter 6.

20 See Ruether, *America, Amerikkka*, p. 182.

21 Ruether, *America, Amerikkka*, p. 192; see also William Blum, *Rogue State: A Guide to the World's Only Superpower*, Monroe, ME: Common Courage Press, 2005.

22 In the United States, for instance, liberation theology has often been appropriated in terms of the activism of the Social Gospel movement, where well-meaning Christians sought to 'Christianize' the social order and shape it in their own image. This context, as well as its failure, is the backdrop for Joerg Rieger, *Remember the Poor: The Challenge to Theology in the Twenty-First Century*, Harrisburg, PA: Trinity Press International, 1998.

23 Flatness is one way of responding to tremendous amounts of stress and is one of the symptoms of post-traumatic stress disorder.

24 The mainstream media have reported this multiple times. See, e.g., http:// www.cbsnews.com/stories/2007/11/13/cbsnews_investigates/main3496471. shtml.

25 See Robert Kurz (ed.), *Marx lesen! Die wichtigsten Texte von Karl Marx für das 21. Jahrhundert*, Frankfurt am Main: Eichborn, 2006, p. 57. 'The circulation of money as capital, is . . . an end in itself. . . . The circulation of capital has therefore no limits' (Karl Marx, *Capital: A Critical Analysis of Capitalist Production*, vol. 1, trans. from the 3rd German edition by Samuel Moore and Edward Aveling and ed. Frederick Engels, New York: International Publishers, 1948, p. 129).

26 Marx, *Capital*, p. 131. Der Wert *'verwandelt sich so in ein automatisches Subjekt'*: original German text, in Kurz, *Marx lesen!*, p. 97; see also Kurz's introduction, p. 56. The relation of Commodity–Money–Commodity is trans-

formed into the relation Money–Commodity–Money, with the end result being Money–Money (Marx, *Capital*, p. 124); note the parallels to poststructuralist notions of language. The result is surplus value. Surplus value becomes subject: 'In truth, however, value is here the active factor [German: *Subjekt*] in a process' (Marx, *Capital*, p. 131).

27 Marx, *Capital*, p. 132.

28 Here is the full quotation: 'A commodity is therefore a mysterious thing, simply because in it the social character of men's labour appears to them as an objective character stamped upon the product of that labour, because the relation of the producers to the sum total of their own labour is presented to them as a social relation, existing not between themselves, but between the products of their labour' (Marx, *Capital*, pp. 42–3).

29 Marx, *Capital*, p. 43.

30 Marx, *Capital*, p. 43.

31 'The labor of the individual asserts itself as a part of the labor of society, only by means of the relations which the act of exchange establishes directly between the products, and indirectly, through them, between the producers' (Marx, *Capital*, p. 44).

32 Marx, *Capital*, p. 45. Money plays a role here too, for it is the 'ultimate money form of the world of commodities that actually conceals, instead of disclosing, the social character of private labor, and the social relations between the individual producers' (p. 47).

33 Marx, *Capital*, p. 45, n. 1.

34 Michael D. Yates, 'More Unequal: Aspects of Class in the United States', *Monthly Review* 59.6 (2007), p. 3.

35 The severe consequences of unemployment for the subjectivity of workers in Europe are discussed in Ulrich Duchrow, Reinhold Bianchi, René Krüger, and Vincenzo Petracca, *Solidarisch Mensch werden: Psychische und soziale Destruktion im Neoliberalismus – Wege zu ihrer Überwindung*, Hamburg: VSA Verlag, Publik Forum, 2006, pp. 105–26. The authors talk about mass unemployment as 'traumatization at the core' (*Kerntraumatisierung*).

36 Friedrich August von Hayek, *The Constitution of Liberty*, Chicago: University of Chicago Press, 1960, p. 45.

37 Jung Mo Sung, *Desire, Market and Religion*, London: SCM Press, 2007, p. 32.

38 Sung, *Desire, Market and Religion*, p. 31, n. 3.

39 René Girard, *Violence and the Sacred*, trans. Patrick Gregory, Baltimore: The Johns Hopkins Press, 1979, p. 146. Girard notes that 'desire itself is essentially mimetic, directed toward an object desired by the model'.

40 Girard, *Violence and the Sacred*, p. 147, points out that the disciple can also serve as model, 'even to his own model'. However, neither the model nor the disciple understand what is really going on, why the tensions exist.

41 Girard, *Violence and the Sacred*, p. 147; René Girard, 'Mimesis and Violence' in James G. Williams (ed.), *The Girard Reader*, New York: The Crossroad Publishing Company, 1996, p. 10, even points out that 'imitation or mimicry happens to be common to animals and men'.

42 John Perkins, *Confessions of an Economic Hit Man*, New York: Plume, 2004, p. xiv.

43 Girard, 'Mimesis and Violence', p. 10, notes that in animal life scarcity also occurs but that it is not sufficient to explain why low-ranking individuals would be inspired to challenge the dominant group.

44 See, for instance, Sung, *Desire, Market and Religion*, p. 41.

45 Girard, 'Mimesis and Violence', p. 12: 'As an object becomes the focus of mimetic rivalry between two or more antagonists, other members of the group tend to join it, mimetically attracted by the presence of mimetic desire.' See also Girard in Hugo Assmann (ed.), *Götzenbilder und Opfer: René Girard im Gespräch mit der Befreiungstheologie*, Thaur: Verlagshaus Thaur and Münster: LIT Verlag, 1996, p. 268.

46 Girard, 'Mimesis and Violence', p. 12.

47 Girard in Assmann, *Götzenbilder und Opfer*, p. 268.

48 See also Sung, *Desire, Market and Religion*, p. 47.

49 Girard, 'Mimesis and Violence', p. 13.

50 Girard in Assmann, *Götzenbilder und Opfer*, p. 269.

51 Girard, *Violence and the Sacred*, p. 14.

52 Girard, 'Mimesis and Violence', p. 17; on pp. 16–17, Girard notes that 'victimage is still present . . . but in degenerate forms that do not produce the type of mythical reconciliation and ritual practice exemplified by primitive cults'. And he adds that 'this lack of efficiency often means that there are more rather than fewer victims'.

53 See Sung, *Desire, Market and Religion*, p. 45: 'The hunger and death of millions of the poor, all over Latin America and other countries of the Third World, are sacrifices that should ensure that further sacrifices will no longer be needed.'

54 See, for instance, the conversations of Girard with Latin American liberation theologians Hugo Assmann, Franz Hinkelammert, Julio de Santa Ana, Jung Mo Sung, and others in Assmann, *Götzenbilder und Opfer*.

55 Sung, *Desire, Market and Religion*, p. 48.

56 Girard, in Assmann, *Götzenbilder und Opfer*, p. 260.

57 See, for instance, the analysis of Michael Hardt and Antonio Negri in *Empire*, Cambridge, MA: Harvard University Press, 2000.

58 Letter from James Madison to Thomas Jefferson, 24 October 1787, available at http://press-pubs.uchicago.edu/founders/documents/v1ch17s22.html.

59 See for instance, Mark Bowden, 'The Point: In Defense of Waterboarding', *The Philadelphia Inquirer*, 12 December 2007, available at http://tinyurl.com/qauyct.

60 Klein, *Shock Doctrine*, p. 371.

61 Klein, *Shock Doctrine*, p. 370.

62 This destruction was systematic. In Argentina, for instance, the children of disappeared parents were given to those in power and their friends, an action that matches the category of genocide, where children from one group are transferred to another group. The Grandmothers of Plaza de Mayo in Buenos Aires are still investigating and protesting.

63 See Klein, *Shock Doctrine*, pp. 38–46. The Kubark manual is focused on the destruction of resistance and refers to experiments at McGill University; in the 1983 edition, a stronger warning of the risk of later lawsuits can be found. Written in 1963 and declassified in 1996 (with deletions), the manual is on the

web at http://www.mindcontrolforums.com/kubark.htm.

64 See Klein, *Shock Doctrine*, pp. 25–38. For a visual report on Cameron's practices see http://www.youtube.com/watch?v=K1ZNgsNBi8c.

65 Oliver, *The Colonization of Psychic Space*, p. 128. Another mechanism is confining people to a world of meaning without the ability to participate in the production of meaning.

66 Klein, *Shock Doctrine*, pp. 25–6.

67 Quoted in Klein, *Shock Doctrine*, p. 6. When crisis strikes, Friedman explained, 'the actions that are taken depend on the ideas that are lying around'. Preparing such ideas is what he saw as the basic task for economists. Friedman saw both coups d'état and natural disasters as golden opportunities. In a letter after Hurricane Katrina struck, he suggested that this was the time for radical reform. Instead of rebuilding public schools, he proposed school vouchers – a suggestion that was realized through the founding of charter schools, leaving the school board with four public schools instead of the 123 that existed before the hurricane. It is not surprising that Friedman worked closely with Chilean dictator General Augusto Pinochet after he toppled the Allende government in 1973. See Klein, *Shock Doctrine*, pp. 4–7.

68 While this third step kicked in quickly in Iraq, in New Orleans it took longer. Just before Christmas 2007, tazers and batons were used on protestors outside New Orleans City Hall. See Naomi Klein, 'The Shock Doctrine in Action in New Orleans', *The Huffington Post*, 21 December 2007, available at http://www.huffingtonpost.com/naomi-klein/the-shock-doctrine-in-act_b_ 77886.html.

69 Klein, *Shock Doctrine*, p. 306, talks about it as 'an unprecedented convergence of unchecked police powers and unchecked capitalism, a merger of the shopping mall and the secret prison'. These developments are hidden from the public since disaster capitalists do not seek the limelight like their dot com predecessors.

70 Klein, *Shock Doctrine*, pp. 331–2.

71 Quoted in Klein, *Shock Doctrine*, p. 333.

72 Quoted in Klein, *Shock Doctrine*, p. 338, with further details on pp. 334–7.

73 Klein, *Shock Doctrine*, p. 18.

74 Kevin Phillips, *American Theocracy: The Peril and Politics of Radical Religion, Oil, and Borrowed Money in the 21st Century*, New York: Viking, 2006, pp. 101–3: 'The world's leading economic and military power is also – no one can misread the data – the world's leading Bible-reading crusader state, immersed in an Old Testament of stern prophets and bloody Middle Eastern battlefields.' Duchrow et al., *Solidarisch Mensch werden*, p. 162, talk about an inclination to 'play God' that is part of a global neoliberal mindset.

75 Elias Canetti ('Paranoia ist die Krankheit der Herrschaft.'), quoted in Duchrow et al., *Solidarisch Mensch werden*, p. 153; there is also a sense that this sort of absolute power leads to personal fragmentation and isolation in those who pursue it: p. 175.

76 For one such critique of postcolonialism see Alex Callinicos, 'Wonders Taken for Signs: Homi Bhabha's Postcolonialism', in Mas'ud Zavarzadeh, Teresa L. Ebert, and Donald Morton (eds.), *Post-Ality: Marxism and Postmodernism*,

College Park, MD: Maisonneuve Press, 1995.

77 The real, according to Lacan, is that which 'is beyond the *automaton*, the return, the coming-back, the insistence of the signs': Jacques Lacan, *The Four Fundamental Concepts of Psycho-Analysis*, ed. Jacques-Alain Miller, trans. Alan Sheridan, New York: W.W. Norton, 1978, pp. 53–4. The *automaton* here is the symbolic order, the master narratives that dominate a given context. In contrast with the postmodern fascination about metonymy, i.e. the free flow of signification without referents, Lacan maintains the importance of metaphor as well. Metaphor is defined as the replacement of one signifier by another in a process of repression. This process interrupts the free flow of signification and creates another level of reality underneath that which commonly counts as reality. See Lacan, 'The Agency of the Letter in the Unconscious or Reason since Freud', in *Écrits: A Selection*, trans. Alan Sheridan, New York: W.W. Norton, 1977, p. 164.

78 Fredric Jameson has talked about the political unconscious: see *The Political Unconscious: Narrative as a Socially Symbolic Act*, Ithaca, NY: Cornell University Press, 1981. One of the great advantages of Lacan's approach to psychoanalysis is that it can be used in order to analyse social processes since it has been developed with this broader horizon in mind. See Rieger's use of Lacan in *Remember the Poor* and *God and the Excluded: Visions and Blindspots in Contemporary Theology*, Minneapolis, MN: Fortress Press, 2001.

79 For a postmodern perspective that prefers metonymy over metaphor see, for instance, Paul de Man, 'Semiology and Rhetoric', in Hazard Adams and Leroy Searle (eds.), *Critical Theory since 1965*, Tallahassee, FA: University Presses of Florida, Florida State University Press, 1986.

80 Albert Memmi, *The Colonizer and the Colonized*, Boston, MA: Beacon Press, 1967, p. 88.

81 See Rieger, *Remember the Poor* and *God and the Excluded*.

82 Jacques Lacan, 'Seminar 20, *Encore*', in Juliet Mitchell and Jacqueline Rose (eds.), *Feminine Sexuality: Jacques Lacan and the École Freudienne*, New York: W.W. Norton, 1982, p. 144.

83 Frantz Fanon, *The Wretched of the Earth*, trans. Constance Farrington, New York: Grove Press, 1968, p. 48, italics original.

84 Frantz Fanon, *Black Skin, White Masks*, trans. Charles Lam Markmann, New York: Grove Press, 1967, p. 14.

85 Homi Bhabha, *The Location of Culture*, London: Routledge, 1994, p. 45.

86 Quoted in Bhabha, *Location of Culture*, p. 6.

87 Terry Eagleton, *Ideology: An Introduction*, London: Verso, 1991, p. 198.

88 For the theological underpinnings see Rieger, *Remember the Poor* and Rieger (ed.), *Opting for the Margins: Postmodernity and Liberation in Christian Theology*, Oxford: Oxford University Press, 2003. There is a parallel between subaltern studies and liberation theology: Beverley sees it in terms of the 'preferential option for the poor' and the effort of 'listening to the poor' (Gutiérrez), in other words, not just looking at our speaking about the subaltern but building relationships: John Beverley, *Subalternity and Representation: Arguments in Cultural Theory*, Durham, NC: Duke University Press, 1999, p. 38.

89 Fanon, *The Wretched of the Earth*, p. 41. Fanon talks about the totalitarian character of colonialism and the need of the settler to portray the native as absolute evil.

90 See Duchrow et al., *Solidarisch Mensch werden*, for an analysis of the situation of the middle class and very helpful suggestions about steps that can be taken in the right direction. The authors surmise that the future of the globe might depend on the solidarity of the middle class with the working class: p. 413.

91 The first Subaltern Study Group was founded in India, and another one was founded later in Latin America. Note that there exists a good deal of diversity within both subaltern study groups. What ties them together might perhaps best be described as a set of 'experimental spaces' related to a common concern for the margins: see Beverley, *Subalternity and Representation*, p. 22. The term *subaltern* comes from Antonio Gramsci, *Selections from the Prison Notebooks of Antonio Gramsci*, trans. Geoffrey Nowell Smith, New York: International Publishers, 1971, p. 52ff. and captures the common concern of contemporary subaltern studies for the situation of the lower classes – particularly those groups at the margins who do not possess a unified class consciousness.

92 Beverley, *Subalternity and Representation*, p. 87, for instance has raised the question whether subaltern identity is hybrid or binary. Walter Mignolo's notion of border thinking, shaped by analysing the relations of the dominant parts of the world with Latin America – Occidentalism rather than Orientalism – is also instructive here: this thinking is not structured in terms of traditional subject–object relations, where the subject remains untouched and independent of the object, and where the object can be known as such. This binary needs to go. Border thinking and its truth grow out of 'the wounds of the colonial histories, memories, and experiences': Mignolo, *Local Histories/Global Designs: Coloniality, Subaltern Knowledges, and Border Thinking*, Princeton Studies in Culture/Power/History, Princeton: Princeton University Press, 2000, p. 37.

93 Beverley, *Subalternity and Representation*, p. 2.

94 In her 1999 book, *A Critique of Postcolonial Reason: Toward a History of the Vanishing Present*, Cambridge, MA: Harvard University Press, pp. 308–11, Spivak has rewritten her earlier statement that 'the subaltern cannot speak', saying that 'it was an inadvisable remark'. Nevertheless, she goes on to show the many ways in which the subaltern continues to be silenced.

95 Bhabha, *Location of Culture*, p. 47, reflecting on the work of Frantz Fanon. The other 'is always ambivalence, disclosing a lack' (p. 52).

3

Empire and Transcendence

The thesis of the end of transcendence with the emergence of Empire

Michael Hardt and Antonio Negri, in their book *Empire*, present as their basic hypothesis: 'sovereignty has taken a new form, composed of a series of national and supranational organisms united under a single logic or rule'.[1] For them, the concept of Empire is something completely different from imperialism, which was 'an extension of the sovereignty of the European nation-states beyond their own boundaries', while 'Empire establishes no territorial center of power and does not rely on fixed boundaries or barriers. It is a *decentered* and *deterritorializing* apparatus of rule that progressively incorporates the entire global realm within its open, expanding borders.'[2]

Beyond this fundamental difference, the authors defend the thesis that there is another fundamental difference that results from the first: what in the modern era was transcendent is now made immanent. For them, the dominant theme in modern politics and metaphysics was the elimination of the medieval form of transcendence, of religious character, which inhibited production and consumption, and the constitution of a new transcendence more appropriate for the new modes of association and production: a transcendent political apparatus. The sovereignty of the modern state became a *locus* of sovereignty that transcends and mediates the plane of immanent forces. In this sense, they affirm that 'Thomas Hobbes's proposition of an ultimate and absolute sovereign ruler, a "God on earth," plays a foundational role in the modern construction of a transcendent political apparatus.'[3]

Based on the thesis that the transition from modern imperialism to the present system of Empire emerges from the twilight of modern sovereignty, Hardt and Negri also defend the hypothesis that

What the theories of power of modernity were forced to consider transcendent, that is, external to productive and social relations, is here formed inside, immanent to the productive and social relations. Mediation is absorbed within the productive machine. The political synthesis of social space is fixed in the space of communication. This is why communications industries have assumed such a central position. They not only organize production on a new scale and impose a new structure adequate to global space, but also make its justification immanent.[4]

The end or decline of the sovereignty of the modern nation-state has led to an abandonment of the notion of transcendence in the area of productive and social relations, and even the justification of Empire and any and all actions within it are given in an immanent way. The reason for this is that, if modern sovereignty was based fundamentally on the *transcendence* of the sovereign over the social plane,

capital, on the contrary, operates on the plane of *immanence*, through relays and networks of relationships of domination, without reliance on a transcendent center of power. . . . The laws by which capital functions are not separate and fixed laws that stand above and correct capital's operations from on high, but historically variable laws that are immanent to the very functioning of capital: the laws of the rate of profit, the rate of exploitation, the realization of surplus value, and so forth.[5]

From these ideas, they affirm: 'Capital therefore demands not a transcendent power but a mechanism of control that resides on the plane of immanence.'[6]

As they call the new global form of the economy dominated by the logic of capital Empire, we can then draw the conclusion that for them Empire ignores the notion of transcendence as well as a *locus* that transcends productive and social relations. They do not ask if the passage from a specific form of domination to another did or did not create a new form of transcendence, as occurred in the passage from the medieval era to the modern, but simply identify transcendence with the modern sovereignty of the nation-state and declare the end of transcendence, together with the end or decline of the nation-state.

Can a system as large and complex as the global Empire function and be maintained, controlled, or commanded without any reference to a transcendental authority? Hardt and Negri affirm that 'Imperial control operates through three global and absolute means: the bomb, money, and ether.'[7] The conjuncture of nuclear bombs (which create a new metaphysical horizon of absolute violence), money, and the

[Handwritten margin notes at top: "nuclear bombs — absolute violence / money — means of absol control / mechanisms of Empire's control: ① media, educ. system, culture"]

market as global means of absolute control and the administration of communications, the educational system, and culture constitute the mechanisms of Empire's control. Clearly, of those three, the absolute violence of war and nuclear arms constitutes the ultimate and fundamental mechanism of control and domination.

In their next book, *Multitude*, Hardt and Negri affirm that

> what is specific to our era . . . is that war has passed from the final element of the sequences of power – lethal force as a last resort – to the first and primary element, the foundation of politics itself. Imperial sovereignty creates order *not* by putting an end to 'the war of all against all,' as Hobbes would have put it, but by proposing a regime of disciplinary administration and political control directly based on continuous war action. The constant and coordinated application of violence, in other words, becomes the necessary condition for the functioning of discipline and control.[8]

Now, if war has become the foundation of politics, the distinction between legitimate and illegitimate violence or war becomes key in the construction and maintenance of this global order. In the modern world, one of the pillars of nation-state sovereignty was the monopoly on legitimate violence within the country's borders and against other nations. Today, according to these authors,

> Violence is legitimated most effectively . . . not on any a priori framework, moral or legal, but only a posteriori, based on its results. It might seem that the violence of the strong is automatically legitimated and the violence of the weak immediately labeled terrorism, but the logic of legitimation has more to do with the effects of the violence. The reinforcement or reestablishment of the current global order is what retroactively legitimates the use of violence.[9]

The violence of the weak, or of those who are against the hierarchy of the global Empire, is labelled violence, while the violence of the strong, of the victors who maintain the present order, is considered legitimate, that is, not violence, or as a form of special violence, a purifying and restoring violence of the threatened order. In traditional pre-modern societies and in modern societies, this distinction was made in the name of transcendence: in traditional societies in the name of religious transcendence, and in modern societies in the name of the sovereignty of the nation-state. As Hardt and Negri defend the thesis that in the present global order there is no transcendence, they propose that the distinction between legitimate and illegitimate violence, between just and unjust war, is based on the strength itself of the violence of the strongest. Immanent violence is the foundation of this distinction. Therefore, they affirm that 'only one distinction does matter, and it is superimposed over all others: violence that preserves the contemporary hierarchy of global order and violence that threatens that order'.[10]

When even 'absolute violence' is justified in the name of the maintenance of the imperial order, in the name of Empire itself, there is nothing that transcends it and there is no need for any reference to a transcendent authority or transcendent values. This Empire is an empire that expands in its own name, through the expansion of submission to its absolute power.

Nevertheless, how is it possible to speak of aspects of Empire such as *absolute* violence, a new *metaphysical* horizon', the '*absolute inversion of the power of life*', '*imperial arbiter*', and at the same time say that these do not have transcendent status?[11] Does being an absolute power over life or an imperial judge – divine or demonic qualities – not signify being above everything else, being transcendent? Can such an imperial system, without any transcendent justification, be attractive to other countries and groups who remain on the margins of Empire or to those who are thinking of leaving the system?

For Joseph S. Nye, Jr, a former US Assistant Secretary of Defense, even though military power is essential for global stability, it is not sufficient. He says: 'We must not let the illusion of empire blind us to the increasing importance of soft power', the ideological and cultural attraction that the USA exercises in the world.[12] It is clear that he recognizes the limits of this soft power:

> Some tyrants and fundamentalists will always hate us because of our values of openness and opportunity, and we will have no choice but to deal with them through more effective counterterrorism policies. But those hard nuggets of hate are unlikely to catalyze broad hatred unless we abandon our values and pursue arrogant and overbearing policies that let the extremists appeal to the majority in the middle.[13]

The use of military power is not only insufficient, but must be placed at the service of the defence of values such as freedom, otherwise the arrogance of government in the name of military power will have the effect of strengthening tyrants and fundamentalists.

This sort of discourse can be interpreted as mere rhetoric to justify domination based on military power. It might be. But, as Joan Robinson says, 'any economic system requires a set of rules, an ideology to justify them, and a conscience in the individual which makes him strive to carry them out'.[14] In the end, no one likes to have a bad conscience, and pure cynicism is quite rare, for 'even the Thugs robbed and murdered for the honor of their goddess'.[15] And Nye justifies the use of military power against those whom he labels tyrants and fundamentalists in the name of freedom. Military power is not used in the name of the system itself. There is a higher value, freedom, that justifies the use of military power and does not transform the Empire into something arrogant, something that could not attract those at the margins or outside the domain of the Empire.

The concept of transcendence and the development of Empire

The question that is raised here is whether or not Empire truly destroyed and/or needs the concept of transcendence for its functioning and legitimation in the face of itself and those whom it subordinates. A second question that we can raise concerns the necessity or utility of the concept of transcendence in the comprehension and critique of Empire; that is, of the theoretical necessity or non-necessity of the critical unveiling of the new concept of transcendence in Empire. In order to discuss this, we are going to remain for now with the thinking of Hardt and Negri.

Let us take the passage in which they present 'Empire' as a concept:

> We should emphasize that we use 'Empire' here not as a metaphor ... but rather as a *concept*, which calls primarily for a theoretical approach. The concept of Empire is characterized fundamentally by a lack of boundaries: Empire's rule has no limits ... Second, the concept of Empire presents itself not as a historical regime originating in conquest, but rather as an order that effectively suspends history and thereby fixes the existing state of affairs for eternity. From the perspective of Empire, this is the way things will always be and the way they were always meant to be ... as a regime with no temporal boundaries and in this sense outside of history or at the end of history. Third, the rule of Empire operates on all registers of the social order extending down to the depths of the social world. Empire not only manages a territory and a population but also creates the very world it inhabits. It not only regulates human interactions but also seeks directly to rule over human nature. The object of its rule is social life in its entirety, and thus Empire presents

the paradigmatic form of biopower. Finally, although the practice of Empire is continually bathed in blood, the concept of Empire is always dedicated to peace – a perpetual and universal peace outside of history.[16]

Hardt and Negri present four fundamental characteristics of the concept of Empire: the power of Empire has no limits; it presents itself as an eternal reality, suspending history; the power of Empire functions in every register of the social order, to the depths of the social world and to such a point that it seeks to rule over human nature itself; Empire is dedicated to a perpetual and universal peace outside of history in spite of its continual bloodbath. It is interesting to note here that these four characteristics of Empire bring to mind the characteristics of those religious myths that sacralize a social order.

Peter Berger, for example, assuming Thomas Luckmann's concept of religion, says that it is 'the capacity of the human organism to transcend its biological nature through the construction of objective, morally binding, all-embracing universes of meaning'.[17] The efficacy of religion, whether in traditional language or in an apparently secularized language, in the legitimation of a social order rests on the fact of its relating the precarious reality of social institutions and the social order itself with the supreme reality and in this way 'bestowing upon them an ultimately valid ontological status, that is, by *locating* them within a sacred and cosmic frame of reference'.[18] In this way, religious legitimations confer on the institutions 'a semblance of inevitability, firmness, and durability that is analogous to these qualities as ascribed to the gods themselves'.[19]

The characterization of Empire made by Hardt and Negri refers to the function exercised by religion in the processes of legitimating some social order. But, it is clear for them that the present Empire does not use pre-modern religious language for its legitimation. However, if it does not make explicit use of religious language and makes no reference to another type of transcendence, how does Empire justify this pretension of unlimited, eternal power capable of ruling every aspect of social life, even human nature itself, and demand continuous sacrifices of human blood with the promise of eternal peace? Is it possible to answer this question without reference to some notion of transcendence, whatever it may be?

Before answering these questions, it is important to emphasize here that the authors make it clear that these characteristics are not attributed by them, but are productions of the Empire itself and of the productive and social relations of Empire: 'From the perspective

what is 'real' is the sacrificial
logic of Empire

of Empire, this is the way things will always be and the way they were always meant to be.' That is, the four characteristics of Empire are not 'real', but are from 'the perspective of Empire', especially the idea that Empire is an eternal reality, suspended from history. We can briefly note here, since we will be treating this theme in greater depth later, that what really is 'real' is the sacrificial logic of Empire: the demand to bathe itself continually in blood in the name of perpetual peace. The demands for blood in the name of peace and justice are understandable only by appealing to a notion of transcendence, whether to a god that demands sacrifices in exchange for salvation or to the sovereignty of the nation-state/Leviathan. But, as Hardt and Negri defend the thesis that transcendence no longer exists under Empire, they do not explore in depth the critique of this sacrificial logic or the critique of a perverse transcendence that not only legitimates sacrifices of human lives in the name of perpetual peace or development but, what is most important, turns evil – the bloodbath – into good. The critique of a perverse transcendence presupposes the idea that all forms of social organization produce from and within their productive and social relations divinizations and transcendences. And, if this is the case, the question no longer concerns the denial or defence of the transcendences of a specific social order but discernment among the transcendental images and concepts that either ground and legitimate or criticize that social order.

There is an affirmation by Hardt and Negri that reveals a theoretical problem in their approach to this question: 'What the theories of power of modernity were forced to consider transcendent, that is, external to productive and social relations, is here formed inside, immanent to the productive and social relations.'[20] Now, one thing is the place where something is formed, another is how the theories or ideologies of power of a certain era are or are not forced to consider this object. The fact that the theories of power of modernity were forced to consider transcendent the biopolitical production of order does not mean that it has really been a product of the action of a transcendent being and that it has not been generated within productive and social relations, since, as they affirm, modern theories were forced to consider transcendence for reasons of their time. The discovery that this power has no transcendent origin, but occurs in immanence, also does not mean that the theorists of the Empire and legitimating discourses do not treat it as transcendent. From one non-imperial point of view, the perspective of the victims of empires, all power is the immanent result of productive and social relations, but from the point of view of the dominators they are or can be considered transcendent.

65

To affirm that there is no longer transcendence or any reference to the transcendent in the logic and discourse of the power of Empire, only because the biopolitical production of order is 'discovered' to occur within productive and social relations, is to fall into a dualism that radically separates transcendence and immanence in social orders.

Marx, who as a young man had reduced religion and the 'transcendent world' to a simple symptom of an alienating and oppressing society, made the critique of religion a method of analysis:

> It is, in reality, much easier to discover by analysis the earthly core of the misty creations of religion, than, conversely, to develop from the actual relations of life the corresponding celestialized forms of those relations. The latter method is the only materialistic, and therefore scientific one.[21]

He proposes to analyse and discern divinizations beginning with real life, rather than simply discarding them. In this line of thought, Franz Hinkelammert – one of the contemporary authors who have explored at length the relation between transcendent concepts and social systems[22] – states: 'Societies and human beings are self-reflected in and through their divine forms.'[23] Therefore, the question is not whether divine beings exist or not, but whether we can analyse the transcendent concepts or values and divine forms produced by historically contextualized productive and social relations in order to understand the most profound dynamics that rule those societies. Only such a method can lead us to a more helpful critique of the characteristics of Empire that Hardt and Negri themselves describe.

The facts that Empire's present means of control do not possess a specific location and are articulated in relation to productive functions do not signify in themselves that Empire does not possess or claim to have a transcendent status. On the other hand, without a notion of transcendence it is difficult to explain and understand the characteristics to this point analysed in the work of Hardt and Negri.

Let us consider a text of Edward Said, from his preface to the 2003 edition of his *Orientalism*:

> Every single empire in its official discourse has said that it is not like all the others, and that its circumstances are special, that it has a mission to enlighten, civilize, bring order and democracy, and that it uses force only as a last resort. And, sadder still, there always is a chorus of willing intellectuals to say calming words about benign or altruistic empires, as if one shouldn't trust the evidence of one's eyes

watching the destruction and misery and death brought by the latest *mission civilizatrice*.

. . . What matters is how efficient and resourceful it sounds, and who might go for it, as it were. The worst aspect of this essential-izing stuff is that human suffering in all its density and pain is spir-ited away. Memory and with it the historical past are effaced as in the common, dismissively contemptuous American phrase, 'you're history.'[24]

Said's text well summarizes the characteristics of empires, whether from the time of imperialisms or that of Empire, in the conception of Hardt and Negri. All empires affirm – in an explicitly religious or more secular way – exceptionality and, therefore, their civilizing mission. What Said highlights, with more emphasis than Hardt and Negri, is that this civilizing or divine mission is realized with the use of force and, therefore, with sacrifices and oppressions. But, because it is under-stood as sacrifice – human suffering imposed in the name of progress, civilization, or a divine mission – this human suffering is eclipsed and eliminated from memory. All that remains is the efficacy of progress, the salvation brought by 'modern Western civilization'.

There is an intrinsic correlation between this notion of exceptional-ity and the deletion of human sufferings from memory. Since human sufferings necessary for the fulfilment of an exceptional or divine mission are sufferings or sacrifices necessary for 'salvation', they are therefore not-sufferings. Sacrificial logic redefines the sufferings of the victims as a necessary aspect of the path to salvation, or better yet, as 'good'. In this way, the sufferings and deaths of the victims are deleted from memory as such and recalled as necessary sacrifices.

But where does this imperial character of exceptionality come from? Said affirms that, in the present cases, it is justified through an abstract thinking that denigrates the relevance of historical and contextual con-text, which is similar to Hardt's and Negri's idea that Empire presents itself as suspended from history, as something eternal. However, the abstract or 'eternal' character of the discourse cannot itself explain the foundation of its exceptionality and, more importantly, the inversion that presents as benign the sufferings and deaths imposed in the name of the 'mission'. What type of mission, given by whom, and what is the relation between the Empire and this mission that permits this inver-sion? What type of rationality can conceive of a benign and altruistic Empire?

To answer these questions it is fundamental for us to unmask the 'spirit' that moves the present Empire. And for this we must explore in depth the question of the transcendence produced by the productive and social practices and by the discourses of imperial intellectuals.

Security, Liberty, and the Free Market

President George W. Bush, in his graduation speech at the United States Military Academy at West Point in June 2002, said, 'America has no empire to extend or utopia to establish. We wish for others only what we wish for ourselves – safety from violence, the rewards of liberty, and the hope for a better life.'[25] Without entering into the discussion here whether the United States really has or does not have imperial intentions or a utopia, we want to analyse the relation between security against violence – which is today understood fundamentally as terrorism – liberty, and a better life. Do these three objectives correspond to three distinct tasks and paths or are they the result of a fundamental task already assumed? Our hypothesis is this: in the perspective of Empire, there is a fundamental path for attaining these three objectives and this path is linked to a notion of utopia or transcendence.

To begin this discussion, we want to introduce a reference document of the Canadian International Development Agency, a country few would accuse of being imperialistic. In her presentation of the document, 'Canada's International Policy Statement (2005)–A Role of Pride and Influence in the World: Development', the International Cooperation Minister Aileen Carroll says that the world has achieved significant progress in recent years in the area of human development.[26] However, this victory is unequal, and 20 per cent of humanity still struggle to satisfy their basic needs.

> Such poverty offends our most basic values of decency and fairness. There is simply no good reason why, in the twenty-first century, half a million women a year should be dying during childbirth, or why thousands of children should be killed every day by easily preventable and treatable diseases. Such poverty is a moral affront to all of us, and this reason alone compels our response.

Ethical indignation is presented here as sufficient reason for actions and policies of international co-operation. But, soon after this foundation in morality, the minister presents another reason, this one more pragmatic and systemic: 'Increasingly however, such poverty also poses a direct risk to Canada and our allies. We understand there are links between acute poverty and state failure, and between state failure and global security.' Ethical indignation can affect people of goodwill, but does not function as sufficient argumentation in the real world of politics and economics. Therefore, she presents the reasoning of the system: the poverty of poor countries signifies risk for global security, because poverty and failed states have or might have a relation to terrorism and violence.

At first glance, this presentation of the pragmatic argument might be interpreted as a rhetorical necessity in the political game of Canada or any other country. In the political arena, pragmatic arguments are traditionally more convincing than arguments based only on moral sense. In this way, some might say that the principal reason to support human development in poor countries is moral and that the argument intrinsically linking human development and the security of the global system or Canada itself would be only a secondary argument, of the more pragmatic order.

However, in the body of the document itself, the order is reversed. First comes the reasoning of the system:

> Our future is intertwined with that of people around the globe struggling to secure democracy and human rights . . . Failure to achieve significant political, economic, social and environmental progress in the developing world will have an impact on Canada in terms of both our long-term security and our prosperity. Security and development are inextricably linked . . . Development has to be the first line of defence for a collective security system that takes prevention seriously.

Then, in second place, subordinate to Canadian interests and global security, follows the moral concern: 'While there is a moral imperative to respond to the humanitarian crises that erupt when states degenerate into conflict and chaos, Canadian interests are better served if these can be prevented.' This shows that behind a discourse apparently founded on ethical indignation operates a pragmatic rationality: what justifies the preoccupation with human development, a better life for all in the world, is, in the first place, a preoccupation with the security of the global order. The reason for co-operating with the non-wealthy countries in the struggle to overcome poverty is not that overcoming in itself but the maintenance of the security and stability of the global order. Efforts for the social and human development of the poorest countries are conditioned and limited to the demands and necessities of security. And this document is from the Canadian International Cooperation Minister, not the Ministry of Defense.

Let us now take a document specifically concerned with the question of security: the 2002 'National Security Strategy of the United States of America'.[27] President George W. Bush, in the introduction to the document, dated 17 September 2002, begins: 'The great struggles of the twentieth century between liberty and totalitarianism ended with a decisive victory for the forces of freedom – and a single sustainable model for national success: freedom, democracy, and free enterprise.' This victory, however, does not mean that there is no more danger: terrorists and tyrants who do not accept economic and political freedom continue threatening the peace. The United States will use its unparalleled military power and its large political and economic influence to preserve the peace by building good relations with the world's great powers and 'by encouraging free and open societies on every continent'. This also includes encouraging the advance of democracy and open economies in Russia and China 'because these are the best foundations for domestic stability and international order'.

In order to maintain the peace and the global order, preventive attacks against the enemies must be complemented by the 'encouragement' of political and economic freedom throughout the world, because the foundation of the stability and peace of the global order is freedom. And 'the United States will use this moment of opportunity to extend the benefits of freedom across the globe. We will actively work to bring the hope of democracy, development, free markets, and free trade to every corner of the world.' The reason for this emphasis on the free market in a document concerning national and world security can be found in section six:

A strong world economy enhances our national security by advancing prosperity and freedom in the rest of the world. Economic growth supported by free trade and free markets creates new jobs and higher incomes. It allows people to lift their lives out of poverty, spurs economic and legal reform, and the fight against corruption, and it reinforces the habits of liberty. We will promote economic growth and economic freedom beyond America's shores.

The path to security, then, passes fundamentally through the promotion of the free market, which will promote economic growth throughout the world. This is because 'the concept of "free trade" arose as a moral principle even before it became a pillar of economics' and 'this is *real freedom*, the freedom for a person – or a nation – to make a living'.[28]

If freedom of commerce, presented as true freedom, is a fundamental moral principle for economic progress and peace, then it is perfectly understandable that President George W. Bush affirms in his introduction that 'Freedom is the non-negotiable demand of human dignity' and that he assumes as the great mission the expansion of this freedom:

> Throughout history, freedom has been threatened by war and terror; it has been challenged by the clashing wills of powerful states and the evil designs of tyrants; and it has been tested by widespread poverty and disease. Today, humanity holds in its hands the opportunity to further freedom's triumph over all these foes. The United States welcomes our responsibility to lead in this *great mission*.[29]

The argument of the two documents presented here do not affirm the legitimacy of violence or the use of military power in the name of the power of the strong or the mere preservation of the global order. Military interventions as well as political and economic pressures are justified in the name of liberty and peace. From there comes the notion of a 'mission' to spread 'true freedom', free trade, or the free market throughout the world. There is something that transcends the global order and military power: freedom, the non-negotiable demand of human dignity, which is truly embodied in the freedom of the market.

Therefore, the analysis of the notion of transcendence within the discourse and practice of the free market becomes fundamental for understanding the spirit of Empire.

The World as a Perfect Market

Alan Greenspan, chair of the US Federal Reserve Board for two decades (1987–2006), was and continues to be one of the most influential people in the world economy and in international finance. In his book *The Age of Turbulence*, written after he left the Federal Reserve, Greenspan says that 'the reinstatement of open markets and free trade during the past quarter century has elevated many hundreds of millions of the world population from poverty'.[30] We saw above how the struggle against poverty, by being intimately linked to the struggle for security and, with that, to the stability of the global order, is an important theme for the present system and for its principal defenders. It is interesting to point out here the notion that the free market was reestablished in the past quarter century. For Greenspan, what marks this period is the rediscovery of market capitalism after the expansion of state interventionism from the 1930s through to the 1970s: 'After being forced into retreat by its failures of the 1930s and the subsequent expansion of state intervention through the 1960s, market capitalism slowly reemerged as a potent force, beginning in earnest in the 1970s.'[31] Beginning in the 1970s, market capitalism has re-emerged to the point that it presently prevails, with greater or lesser intensity, throughout the world.

It is important to note that for Greenspan what prevailed from the 1930s to the 1970s was not the capitalism that he defends, market capitalism. He is clearly not arguing that in this period the United States and Europe, as well as other countries under Western influence, were living under a socialist or communist regime. No one doubts that this period is part of the history of capitalism. The distinction that he makes between these two historical periods reveals the notion of capitalism with which he is working. He operates with a 'pure' concept of capitalism, or an ideal type, beginning with which he analyses empirical capitalist economies and distinguishes phases of the 're-emergence' and 're-establishment' of market capitalism.

Greenspan's description of the situation gives us an idea of what constitutes this ideal model of capitalism:

> The *spreading* of a commercial rule of law and especially the protection of the rights to property has fostered a worldwide entrepreneurial stirring. This in turn has led to the creation of institutions that now anonymously guide an *ever-increasing* share of human activity – an international version of Adam Smith's 'invisible hand'.[34]

'Pure' or perfect market capitalism would be an economic system where the rule of commercial law and the protection of property rights would be enforced in an absolute way, without any form of intervention by the state or organized civil society that limits it, and all human activities would be oriented or co-ordinated anonymously by the market mechanism that Adam Smith called the 'invisible hand'. The words 'spreading' and 'ever-increasing' reveal the positive judgment of this drawing closer to what is presupposed as 'perfect' or 'pure'.

This notion of market capitalism completely free of external interventions not only assists in discerning the historical stages of capitalism and in judging the 'quality' of the type of capitalism in operation but is the goal that orients the great strategies of political-economic action.[33] This is why President George W. Bush affirmed that 'we will promote economic growth and economic freedom beyond America's shores'. For the defenders of this model, this goal has been present in capitalism since its inception, as Thomas Friedman affirms in a clear and direct way:

From the first stirrings of capitalism, people have imagined the possibility of *the world as a perfect market* – unimpeded by protectionist pressures, disparate legal systems, cultural and linguistic differences, or ideological disagreement . . . That is why the debate about capitalism has been, from the very beginning, about which frictions, barriers, and boundaries are mere sources of waste and inefficiency, and which are the sources of identity and belonging that we should try to protect.[34]

In other words, the concept of the 'totally free capitalist market' functions as a transcendental concept in relation to which the empirical reality is interpreted. It enables the analysis and classification of empirical economies and supplies the major guidelines for socio-political action in the economic, political, and cultural arenas.

Moreover, the transcendental concept supplies the basis for concrete ethical judgments. It not only permits the interpretation of reality but also furnishes criteria for distinguishing the good and the bad. We know that philosophers and other theorists who study the foundations of ethics have not achieved a consensus concerning the possibility of knowing with certainty what is 'good' and 'bad' or concerning the ultimate foundation of ethical or moral systems valid for all social groups and persons. But societies cannot wait for the end of these discussions, and decisions are made without taking such debates into consideration. Since all humans carry within themselves a moral sense, or at least the capacity for distinguishing between the concepts of good and bad, without which it would not be possible to live in a group, economic decisions must also be justified in the name of some kind of notion of the good. And if there were a contradiction between the transcendental concept that orients the strategic action and ethical criteria of the group, then there would be a contradiction within the subjects of the action themselves (individual or collective) that would either paralyse them or function as frictions that reduce the efficiency of the system.

Therefore, Greenspan also deduces from the concept of market capitalism the criteria for his ethical judgment:

it was inevitable that I would generalize on my experiences. Doing so has led me to an even deeper appreciation of competitive free markets as *a force for good*. Indeed, short of a few ambiguous incidents, I can think of no circumstances where the expanded rule of law and enhanced property rights failed to increase material prosperity.[35]

If he admitted that the expansion of the rule of law creates situations that could be judged as ethically bad, he could not defend market capitalism totally free of intervention as the goal to be sought by all countries. Therefore, he affirms 'competitive free markets as a force for good'. However, in order to make this generalization, he identifies the concept of 'the good' with that of 'material prosperity'; or better, reduces the concept of the good to economic prosperity. We all know, as does Greenspan, that the good is much more than prosperity, that not all economic growth benefits the entire population, and that not all material prosperity, which is measured in monetary terms, necessarily signifies a better life even for those who accumulate more wealth. For Greenspan,

> the problem is that the dynamic that defines capitalism, that of unforgiving market competition, clashes with the human desire for stability and certainty. Even more important, a large segment of society feels a growing sense of injustice about the allocation of capitalism's rewards.[36]

But he does not abandon his position identifying material prosperity with the notion of a better life, with the good, and he dislocates the problem for those of us who do not know how to live with anxiety and the unjust distribution of wealth. The reason that we must learn to live with anxiety and unjust distribution is that they are provoked by the central logic of capitalism, which includes 'creative destruction': 'the scrapping of old technologies and old ways of doing things for the new . . . the only way to increase productivity and therefore the only way to raise average living standards on a sustained basis'.[37]

The cornerstone of the defence of market capitalism as the best way to organize society and totally free markets as the goal to be sought is the identification of quantitative growth in prosperity, measured in monetary terms, with the supreme good. Greenspan presents an abstract formal criterion – the monetary growth of wealth – and in this way, as Said reminds us, seeks to eliminate from memory the sufferings caused by the injustices of the system. Real human beings, with their preoccupations for social justice and anxious yearnings for a less stressful life, are disqualified and substituted by a notion of a 'cold' human being, one who makes monetary calculations the unique or principal criteria for finding meaning for one's life and actions. This position brings to mind Max Weber's famous affirmation concerning the spirit of capitalism:

In fact, the *summum bonum* of this "ethic," the earning of more and more money, combined with the strict avoidance of all spontaneous enjoyment of life, is above all completely devoid of eudemonistic, not to say hedonistic, admixture. It is thought of so purely as an end in itself, that from the point of view of the happiness of, or utility to, the single individual, it appears entirely transcendental and absolutely irrational. Man is dominated by the making of money, by acquisition as the ultimate purpose of his life. Economic acquisition is no longer subordinated to man as the means for the satisfaction of his material needs. This reversal of what we should call the natural relationship, so irrational from a naïve point of view, is evidently as definitely a leading principle of capitalism as it is foreign to all peoples not under capitalistic influence.[38]

Even if one affirms that Puritan capitalism, with its work ethic, has been substituted today by a market capitalism through the culture of consumption, we cannot deny the fact that the rich already possess wealth that they cannot possibly consume and yet they seek more wealth. Moreover, the primary orienting object of capitalism remains: the search for more money as the 'supreme good', that is, as the transcendental value. It is this criterion that allows Greenspan to label the competitive free market as *a force for good*.

This notion of 'a force for good' refers to a movement that cannot simply be reduced to what has occurred in the past but points also to the future. What leads Greenspan, and others who agree with him, to make this ethical judgment also in relation to what can occur in the future? We know that we cannot make logical deductions concerning the future beginning with what has happened in the past, for human history is not something predetermined. More than this, the generalizations he makes concerning the past are, like all historical generalizations in the area of the social sciences, incomplete and partial. It is clear that a person as intellectually astute as Greenspan cannot misunderstand these questions of logic and epistemology; which indicates to us that this ethical judgment concerning the market has another foundation. But, we must treat this theme a bit later.

Returning to the theme of the transcendental concept of perfect market capitalism, another question that emerges is this: is it an empirical concept, a description of an existing reality or one that can exist, or is it a transcendental concept in that it is beyond historical realizability? That is, beyond being a transcendental concept in the sense of enabling the interpretation of social reality, informing guidelines for strategic action, and supplying the criteria for moral judgments, is it also transcendental in the sense that it is beyond the possibility of being made concrete or empirical within human history?

Joseph Stiglitz, a Nobel laureate in economic science who is critical of the present model of globalization, says that with the end of the Cold War the importance of the market economy was recognized so that governments could set aside the ideological battles concerning capitalism versus communism and focus on resolving the problems of capitalism. For him, and he agrees here with Greenspan, with the end of the ideological dispute, the central question of economic discussion in the world is no longer political or ideological but merely technical: how best to direct capitalism. That is, there is no longer any doubt that capitalism is the best form for organizing societies. But Stiglitz, in contrast to the model that Greenspan calls market capitalism, defends the thesis that 'without government regulation and intervention, markets do not lead to economic efficiency'.[39] In terms of Greenspan's periodization of the capitalist economy in the twentieth century, Stiglitz defends a model closer to the capitalism that dominated from the 1930s to the 1970s.

The appropriate way to manage globalization – the notion of 'managing' globalization reveals a distinction in relation to pro-free market thinkers – is, for Stiglitz, that which was applied by East Asian governments, which oversaw very successful development. They recognized that 'success requires social and political stability, and that social and political stability in turn require both high levels of employment and limited inequality. Not only was conspicuous consumption discouraged, but so too were large wage disparities.'[40] Stiglitz defends intervention not only in the social and economic arenas, but also in the cultural, discouraging conspicuous consumption, an important theme in the consumer culture that today dominates a good part of the world. From this interpretation of what happened in East Asia – an interpretation disputed by many East Asians who see reality from the perspective of the victims of that development process – he describes in his book what might be the closest approximation of this 'perfect' management of the market economy and intervention that would benefit the developing countries as much as the developed.

For our question concerning the realizability (or unrealizibility) of the transcendental concept, we are interested here in the critique Stiglitz makes of the United States for having lost the opportunity to construct an international political and economic system based on the values and principles that could promote development in poor countries. Instead, unchecked by competition to 'win the hearts and minds of those in the Third World, the advanced industrial countries actually created a global trade regime that helped their special corporate and financial interests, and hurt the poorest countries of the world'.[41] For him, one of the fundamental problems of the unsatisfactory functioning of globalization is 'market fundamentalism', a belief that 'appeals to Adam Smith's "invisible hand" – the notion that markets and the pursuit of self-interest would lead, as if by an invisible hand, to economic efficiency'.[42] An important expression of this belief is the prescription of the 'Washington Consensus', which

> is based on a theory of the market economy that assumes perfect information, perfect competition, and perfect risk markets – an idealization of reality which is of little relevance to developing countries in particular. The results of any theory depend on its assumptions – and if the assumptions depart too far from reality, policies based on that model are likely to go far awry.[43]

Stiglitz criticizes the world of Adam Smith and the defenders of free trade, a world with no intervention or regulation on the part of governments, as being 'only a *mythical world* of perfectly working markets with no unemployment'.[44] Against this 'mythical world', he argues that

> whenever information is imperfect, in particular when there are information asymmetries – where some individuals know something that others do not (in other words, *always*) – the reason that the invisible hand seems invisible is that it is not there. Without government regulation and intervention, markets do not lead to economic efficiency.[45]

In fact, a perfectly free market presupposes a perfect symmetry in the access to information, which is empirically impossible. In this sense, Stiglitz has a point when he says that this notion pertains to a 'mythical world', or, in the language that we are using here, a transcendental concept in the sense of being beyond historical possibility.[46] But, he is wrong if he means that the Washington Consensus or those theorists who defend free trade, such as Greenspan, presuppose a market with perfect information and competition in their concrete analyses concerning the global market.

For economists in favour of the free market, the problem of the world economy and nations is that the market is not yet completely free of governmental and political intervention and regulation. If the market were already totally free, discussions surrounding elections, for example, would not be very important, since the 'invisible hand' of the market would be operating fully in an impersonal, spontaneous, and self-regulating way. Therefore, Greenspan says:

> I often wonder if the ticket of a Republican for president and a Democrat for vice president, or the reverse, would attract the vast untended center. Perhaps this issue wouldn't matter if the world were at peace. With the increasing prominence of the 'invisible hand' of globalization effectively overseeing the billions of daily economic decisions, who the leaders are would be less important. But that has not been the case since 9/11. Who holds the reins of government matters.[47]

We do not want to discuss here the question of North American electoral politics, or the problem of the attack on 11 September 2001, but to point out that for Greenspan the desired 'commercial rule of law' is still not complete. The 'invisible hand' of globalization increasingly predominates in the world, but it still has enemies who must be defeated. This is why those who occupy government positions in the United States and other powerful countries make a difference. If there were no war, if the market and its peace held the reins in the world, political discussion would no longer be important.

Along similar lines, Walter R. Mead, a senior fellow at the Council on Foreign Relations, says that

> it is a great misunderstanding to suppose that millennial capitalism is simply a matter of deregulation. . . . In millennial capitalism, the role of regulation is to protect the existence and efficiency of markets in order to allow wider access to their benefits.[48]

To the extent that there are enemies of the free market who want to intervene in the economy, governments have an important regulatory role, not in the sense proposed by Stiglitz, but in the sense of regulating society in order to diminish and even prevent entirely the regulation of the market.

Moreover, if the so-called 'market fundamentalists' presuppose that the market already functions in a complete way, then there would be no need for the notion of a 'mission' to lead the world to this 'true freedom', the freedom of free market. A transcendental concept understood as already existing is not useful in the task of interpreting the empirical world and of drawing guidelines for strategic actions.

The recognition that the free market does not perfectly rule in the world does not answer the question concerning the possibility of this becoming a reality one day. Greenspan provides a clear answer:

> A *'fully globalized'* world is one in which unfettered production, trade, and finance are driven by profit seeking and risk taking that are wholly indifferent to distance and national borders. That state *will never be achieved*. People's inherent aversion to risk, and the home bias that is a manifestation of that aversion, mean that globalization has limits.[49]

Greenspan here explicitly says that the 'fully globalized world' – the world of the total market – is something impossible to achieve. In other words, it is a transcendental concept in two senses: first, it is indispensable for interpreting the existing reality and furnishing both strategic guidelines as well as criteria for ethical judgments; second, it is beyond the limits of human history. Transcendental concepts – for example, a perfect market, the perfect planning of the Soviet Union, or churches as perfect communities – are indispensable for interpreting reality and deliberating action choices, but at the same time they are impossible to realize within history; that is, they are not realizable, in spite of being theoretically indispensable. Problems emerge when social groups do not recognize that they operate with a transcendental concept underlying their social theories and actions and do not recognize the non-realizability of the transcendent goal for which they yearn.

The reason for the impossibility of the 'fully globalized world', according to Greenspan, is not found in the transcendental character of the concept itself but in human nature: the aversion to risk, which the competitive free market exacerbates, and the tendency towards nativism, tribalism, populism, and 'all of the "isms" into which communities retreat when their identities are under siege and they cannot perceive better options'.[50]

A better choice would be to assume the path of the unforgiving competition of the market, which 'clashes with the human desire for stability and certainty' and feeds a 'growing sense of injustice about the allocation of capitalism's rewards'.[51] But many people prefer to take refuge in 'tribalism' and 'populism' and resist full globalization. There is also another group that resists the free market not because of a desire for stability or identity but because of compassion or solidarity in relation to the poor; groups motivated by religious prescriptions similar to socialist discourse: 'Although the roots for socialism are secular, its political thrust parallels many religious prescriptions for a civil society, seeking to assuage the anguish of the poor.'[52]

There are culprits for the non-realization of this fullness: they are persons and peoples who are not capable of overcoming their human nature or old religious precepts of compassion for the poor and, therefore, who are not capable of adapting to the dynamic of the free market, to *real freedom*, the freedom that President George W. Bush called 'the non-negotiable demand of human dignity'.[53] The enemies of liberty insist on resisting, and therefore, Greenspan says, 'The battle for capitalism is never won'.[54]

In this way, the struggle against terrorists, communists, interventionists, religious groups in solidarity with the poor, and all others who resist the expansion of market freedom and a 'post-compassion' culture becomes an unending salvific war/mission.

However, there is a problem in Greenspan's argument concerning the impossibility of concretizing what he calls a 'fully globalized world'. The reason for the impossibility of the perfect market is not primarily human nature but the impossibility of perfect knowledge or perfect access to information, which is presupposed in the perfect market concept. On this point Stiglitz is correct: there is always an information asymmetry and the information is imperfect. Therefore, the market by itself is not capable of co-ordinating in an efficient way the complex contemporary economic system. As a result of this, he defends state intervention into the economy in order to control the abuses of corporate and financial interests that place at risk sustainable growth, social equilibrium, and the good functioning of globalization.

The diagnosis of the non-realizability of the transcendental concept because there is no perfect knowledge impels us to accept our human condition and to learn to live with imperfect governments and markets. But, even if perfect access to information were hypothetically possible, the perfect market would remain impossible, since in a situation in which everyone has perfect access to information there would be no competition and, therefore, there would be no market. The non-realizability of transcendental concepts in the social arena derives not from the resistance of the 'enemies of humanity', but from the internal contradiction of the transcendental concept itself that results from radical difference between the imagined ideal world and the empirical world.

Curiously, in contrast to Stiglitz, the economist Friedrich A. von Hayek defends the free market and criticizes all forms of intervention in the market precisely on account of the impossibility of perfect knowledge of economic factors. Every intervention into the market with visions of altering or correcting its course – whether in the name of 'social justice' or 'socio-economic equilibrium' – presupposes an agent outside the market capable of understanding an enormous number of factors that are in play in the market. As such knowledge is not possible, Hayek argues that interventions can only produce economic inefficiency and, in this way, more social and economic problems.

In the lecture given on the occasion of his reception of the Nobel Prize in economic sciences in 1974, Hayek presents in a brief way the theological–philosophical nucleus that interests us here. The title is suggestive enough: 'The Pretence of Knowledge'.[55] Basically, the lecture is a rereading of the myth of Adam and Eve concerning original sin.

In his lecture, Hayek places the challenge of the economic crisis that occurred at the beginning of the 1970s – the crisis that would mark the turn from capitalism to 'market capitalism' or neoliberalism – in this way: 'economists are at this moment called upon to say how to extricate the free world from the serious threat of accelerating inflation'.[56] Is important to emphasize that he reduces the crisis to the problem of inflation, discarding unemployment as a fundamental problem. For him, the crisis was caused by interventionist economic policies recommended by the majority of economists of Keynesian inspiration, who suppose, according to Hayek, the possibility of understanding all the complex phenomena composing the market. In other words, the original evil that gave rise to the evil of galloping inflation and the consequent market disequilibrium and instability – in theological terms, original sin – was the pretension of understanding the market and, from there, the desire to consciously and intentionally promote the social good.[57]

Against this pretension, Hayek defends the idea that the market is a structure of such complexity that no one can understand it fully, and that, therefore, we must not attempt to substitute for the spontaneous processes of the market – today called self-organizing – conscious human control through interventions aimed at social and economic goals:

> To act on the belief that we possess the knowledge and the power which enable us to shape the processes of society entirely to our liking, knowledge which in fact we do *not* possess, is likely to make us do much harm.[58]

From the correct understanding of the market as a complex system and, therefore, having recognized the impossibility of it being fully understood, he deduces the impossibility of directing the market according to our desires and defends non-intervention in the economy and the abdication of social goals.

Evil as an unintended effect of an action that seeks the social good arises, according to him, from the fact that this action of coercion over other persons or groups by an authority 'is likely to impede the functioning of those spontaneous ordering forces by which, without understanding them, man is in fact so largely assisted in the pursuit of his aims'.[59] In other words, such action impedes the free functioning of the market.

When well-intentioned social action is seen as the source of socio-economic crisis, only two choices remain. One is to assume a position of radical nihilism and to defend the impossibility of having a better world. But this type of social theory is frustrating by nature and destined for political failure. Another choice is to believe and hope that the solution for social and economic problems will come from the unintended effects brought about by an intrinsically beneficent economic system: that is, the market and its providential 'invisible hand'.

But if it is true that we cannot sufficiently understand the factors and dynamics of the market so that we can intervene in it, how can we know that the market always produces beneficial effects or that it is essentially a 'force for good'? Is knowing that the market always produces beneficial effects not a pretension of knowledge of the market? Since one cannot prove this providential character of the market, we have here a 'leap of faith' in the affirmation of the essentially beneficent quality of the free market.

Hayek, in his last book, *The Fatal Conceit*, seeks to justify this 'leap of faith' by appealing to the idea that biological and cultural evolution produced an 'extended order of human cooperation, an order more commonly, if somewhat misleadingly, known as capitalism', which 'resulted not from human design or intention, but spontaneously'.[60] This characterization of the competitive market system as something spontaneous, the result of the evolutionary process, is also present in the classic text that has formed generations of economists, Paul Samuelson's *Economics*. According to Samuelson, 'the market economy is an elaborate mechanism for the unconscious coordination' of economic activity, a mechanism that emerged without any planning: 'Nobody designed it. It just evolved. Like human society, it is changing . . . it can survive.'[61]

In the evolution towards capitalism there occurred, according to Hayek, a break from certain values or the creation of norms capable of establishing extensive social groups that directly clash with the primitive instincts that maintain the unity of small groups – what Greenspan called 'tribalism'. For Hayek,

82

continued obedience to the command to treat all men as neighbors would have prevented the growth of an extended order. For those now living within the extended order gain from *not* treating one another as neighbors, and by applying, in their interactions, rules of the extended order – instead of the rules of solidarity and altruism.[62]

Solidarity and altruism are now considered primitive instincts that must be overcome and substituted by the defence of self-interest – which the ancients called the egoist instinct – and respect for property and contract. To the extent that solidarity is considered a primitive instinct, the new values must be acquired through education. Evolution consists in this passage from small communities, with their 'tribal' values of solidarity, to an extensive social order with the creation, diffusion, and dominion of new values that adapt to and reinforce free competition.

Hayek points out that 'this evolution was not linear, but resulted from continued trial and error, constant "experimentation" in arenas wherein different orders contended: Of course there was no intention to experiment – yet the changes in rules thrown forth by historical accident, analogous to genetic mutations, has something of the same effect'.[63] Moreover, 'not only does all evolution rest on competition; continuing competition is necessary even to preserve existing achievements'.[64]

Hayek recognizes that this process was not easy, since it meant breaking with moral values and social structures that favour more security and social stability and produced results

many of which men tend to dislike, whose significance they usually fail to understand, whose validity they cannot prove . . . The unwitting, reluctant, even painful adoption of these practices kept these groups together, increased their access to valuable information of all sorts, and enabled them to be 'fruitful and multiply, and replenish the earth, and subdue it' (Genesis 1:28). This process is perhaps the least appreciated facet of human evolution.[65]

Now, if human groups do not understand the value and effects of those little appreciated moral habits of human beings, how were they assumed and transmitted culturally? In the end, as Hayek himself recognizes, the positive effects of these painful habits occur only after time has passed, not for all, and not in the same proportion.

Hayek introduces the role of religion here. As cultural qualities were not transmitted automatically like genetic ones, he defends the hypothesis that 'mythical beliefs of some sort may be needed to bring this about, especially where rules of conduct conflicting with instinct are concerned'.[66] Further, 'like it or not, we owe the persistence of certain practices, and the civilization that resulted from them, in part to support from beliefs which are not true – or verifiable or testable – in the same sense as are scientific statements', but which merit being called 'symbolic truths'. Hayek states that 'even now the loss of these beliefs, whether true or false, creates great difficulties'.[67]

Mythical beliefs, deaths, and theologies of sacrificial character – gods that demand such painful things as sacrifices necessary for 'salvation' – are presented as one of the cornerstones of the evolution of human societies up to our societies of the market system. It is with this idea of evolution – which jumps from biological evolution to cultural evolution – that Hayek seeks to justify his 'leap of faith'. Milton Friedman, who received the Nobel Prize in economic sciences in 1976, speaks more directly: 'Underlying most arguments against the free market is a lack of *belief* in freedom itself.'[68]

This use of 'belief' – which, from a theological perspective, actually functions in Friedman's thought as 'faith' – as a 'scientific' argument is one of the characteristics of religious fundamentalism. The recurrence of these arguments in social and economic debates obliges us to extend the concept of fundamentalism beyond the religious arena. In this way, the expression 'market fundamentalism' must not be understood only as a metaphor but also as a hermeneutical key for the contemporary economy.[69] George Soros, the famous international market finance mega-investor and defender of capitalism, for example, says that 'market fundamentalism is today a greater threat to open society than any totalitarian ideology'.[70] And 'the revival of market fundamentalism can be explained only by faith in a magical quality ("the invisible hand") that is even more important than the scientific basis'.[71] Put simply, 'market fundamentalism plays a central role in the global capitalist system. It provides the ideology that not only motivates many of the most successful participants but also drives policy.'[72]

Here we have an answer to the question that we raised above: how can Greenspan, based on the generalization that he makes from past events, affirm that the free market is a 'force for good'? Beyond the reduction of the notion of the good to a formal abstraction of quantitative growth in monetary value, it is based on his faith in the market.

From the notion that the market unconsciously or spontaneously orders action we can say that the capitalist economic system is what scientists today call a self-organizing system. Paul Krugman uses this concept of 'self-organizing systems – of complex systems in which randomness and chaos seem spontaneously to evolve into unexpected order' – to say that

> the world is full of self-organizing systems, systems that form structures not merely in response to inputs from outside but also, indeed primarily, in response to their own internal logic. Global weather is a self-organizing system; so, surely, is the global economy.[73]

Beginning with the theory of complex systems, he presents a non-mythical vision of Adam Smith's 'invisible hand' concept: 'When Adam Smith wrote of the way that markets lead their participants, "as if by an invisible hand", to outcomes that nobody intended, what was he describing but an emergent property?'[74] If the 'invisible hand' is a term Smith hit upon in order to describe, ahead of his time, the self-organizing dynamic of complex systems, we must remove the providential, mythical, character that Smith himself attributed to it and that is much reinforced today. As Krugman states: 'self-organization is not necessarily, or even presumptively, a good thing . . . self-organization is something we observe and try to understand, not necessarily something we want'.[75]

But a non-mythical vision of the 'invisible hand' of the 'fully globalized world' does not serve the purposes of Empire, neither does it ensure the veracity and validity of the transcendental concept assumed through a 'leap of faith' nor justify the good feelings of being a member of a people chosen for a grand mission.

Empire as Mission

Robert Kagan, co-founder of the Project for the New American Century, in a text criticizing the idea that Europe and the United States share a common vision of the world, states:

> The transmission of the European miracle to the rest of the world has become Europe's new *mission civilisatrice*. Just as Americans have always believed that they had discovered the secret to human happiness and wished to export it to the rest of the world, so the Europeans have a new mission born of their own discovery of perpetual peace.[76]

The two have in common a sense of mission. The difference consists in the North American disposition to use, unilaterally if necessary, military power to exercise its mission.

This sense of a civilizing mission, which leads them each to represent themselves as a model of humanity or civilization, is not something recent. The very notion of 'discovery' for describing the arrival of Europeans to the continent they would label America reveals a paradigm of thought that, as Walter Mignolo says, 'presupposes the triumphant European and imperial perspective on world history, an achievement that was described as 'modernity'.[77] This invention of America

> was one of the nodal points that contributed to create the conditions for imperial European expansion and a lifestyle, in Europe, that served as a model for the achievement of humanity . . . It was the moment in which the demands of modernity as the final horizon of salvation began to require the imposition of a specific set of values that relied on the logic of coloniality for their implementation.[78]

What led Europe and the United States to believe that they had discovered the secret of humanity and, therefore, were the bearers of the civilizing mission in the world? Sigmund Freud gives us an answer: 'People will be only too readily inclined to include among the psychical assets of a culture its ideals – its estimates of what achievements are the highest and the most to be striven after.'[79] It can seem initially that these ideals exist first and determine the cultural realizations being sought; however,

> the ideals are based on the first achievements which have been made possible by a combination of the culture's internal gifts and external circumstances, and . . . these first achievements are then held on to by the ideal as something to be carried further.[80]

That is, the values or ideals to be pursued are transcendental projections that begin with an interpretation of empirical realities. And Freud concludes:

> The satisfaction which the ideal offers to the participants in the culture is thus of a narcissistic nature; it rests on their pride in what has already been successfully achieved. To make this satisfaction complete calls for a comparison with other cultures which have aimed at different achievements and have developed different ideals. On the strength of these differences every culture claims the right to look down on the rest.[81]

In other words, the idea that one has a mission relative to other cultures emerges from the process of the construction of one's cultural identity, from the affirmation of one's exceptionality, which transforms one's conquests and ideals into universal ideals that must be sought by or imposed on everyone else.[82] This process has the significant advantage of legitimating, for oneself and the subjected others, the project of domination. It is no longer seen as domination, but as a service, a mission to lead everyone to salvation, civilization, or economic progress and peace for 'inferior' and 'backward' peoples.

However, this ideological construct requires two other fundamental and necessary functions for the expansion and maintenance of the present Empire. The first has to do with the creation and the expansion of the world market. Economic globalization signifies, among other things, the creation of 'global products', goods produced in various parts of the world and sold throughout the world. For this it is necessary, beyond the technologies that enable the process of production on a global scale, to create a global pattern of consumption. In other words, without a common desire among all or most of the world's consumers, there is no world consumer market. Take, for example, mobile phones. They have become an object of desire and also a social necessity for consumers in almost every country in the world.[83] There are hundreds of millions of mobile phones in China and also in India, and there are even regions of the world in which there are more mobile phones than inhabitants. In a similar fashion, famous brands such as Nike, iPod, Louis Vuitton, and others are admired and desired throughout the world.

The desire to imitate the pattern of consumption of rich countries on the part of developing and poor populations is a fact that reveals how Europe and the United States won the 'cultural battle' and achieved their objective of presenting themselves as models of civilization and humanity. Human beings are beings of desire and they desire what their models desire; that is, they want to imitate the desire of those they consider to possess 'being'.[84] To the extent that Europeans and North Americans have managed to impose themselves on the world as those who possess 'being', they have imposed themselves as models of desire and have managed to impose their consumption pattern on almost every part of the world. In this way, the problem of creating and expanding the world consumer market was solved.

As the powerful within Empire are seen as models of humanity and progress, Empire does not need to use military force as its first recourse in the maintenance and expansion of the global order. Here enters the second function: ideological and cultural attraction as the 'soft power' of Empire. As Nye says, 'soft power is also more than persuasion or the ability to move people by argument. It is the ability to entice and attract. And attraction often leads to acquiescence or imitation.'[85]

To the extent that the economic and political elites of subordinated countries desire to imitate the life patterns of the elite in the rich countries, the work of Empire becomes much easier.[86] The subordination is desired by the subalterns themselves in such a way that it no longer needs to be imposed by force. The principal battleground, therefore, for the maintenance and expansion of the imperial order is no longer in the military arena but in the cultural sphere or in the sphere of 'soft power'. Francis Fukuyama makes this explicit when discussing how the United States should concern itself with what happens in other countries: 'the primary instruments by which we do this are mostly in the realm of soft power: our ability to *set an example*, to train and educate, to support with advice and often money'.[87] The ability to 'set an example' signifies the capacity to present oneself and be accepted as a model to be followed.

In turn, Charles S. Maier, who uses expressions like 'empire by invitation' or 'consensual empire' to refer to the present imperial order, says:

> Empires function by virtue of the prestige they radiate as well as by might, and indeed collapse if they rely on force alone. Artistic styles, the language of the rulers, and consumer preferences flow outward along with power and investment capital – sometimes diffused consciously by cultural diplomacy and student exchanges, sometimes just by popular taste for the intriguing products of the metropole, whether Coca-Cola or Big Macs.[88]

This capacity of Empire to provoke desires of imitation is not something only imperial defenders boast about. David Harvey, a critic of the present process of globalization, says:

> There is no question either, that emulation has played an important role in global affairs. Much of the rest of the world has been entrained politically, economically, and culturally in globalization through Americanization ... The emulation of U.S. consumerism, ways of life, cultural forms, and political and financial institutions has contributed to the process of endless capital accumulation globally.[89]

He goes on to say that cultural imperialism is today an important tool in the promotion of the desire to imitate the American way of being

88

and in presenting the United States as 'a beacon of freedom that had the exclusive power to entrain the rest of the world into an enduring civilization characterized by peace and prosperity'.[90]

One of the novelties of the present Empire in relation to those imperialisms of the past – its capacity to attract and use military power secondarily for maintenance of the order – is the result of its own economic dynamic and its capacity to produce and impose on the world its discourses and its transcendental utopian horizon of civilization and humanity.

The transcendence produced by Empire carries out three vital functions for domination: first, it supplies criteria for interpreting reality, establishing action strategies, and making moral judgments in accord with its values and interests; second, it is imposed as a horizon of desire – which reveals the objects that truly merit being desired – that entices and attracts people throughout the world, producing in this way voluntary subordination to Empire; third, by being a utopian horizon and thereby beyond historical realizability, it is never completely achieved and, therefore, is constantly stimulating the unending drive for capital accumulation and unlimited consumption; and, at the same time, places the guilt for the non-realization of what is impossible on those labelled 'enemies of humanity' and, in this way, justifies the demand for an unending war against those who resist the 'attraction' of Empire.

The Empire's transcendence, sacrifices, and the cruel mystique

One of the present Empire's secrets of success is that it manages to impose on the world a new historical metanarrative. In contrast to what many postmodern theorists think, what entered into crisis was not the metanarrative as such but the proposal of modernity to realize the 'earthly paradise' through reason and conscious political action. Hayek formulated, at the end of the 1950s, what can be considered a synthesis of the metanarrative that orients Empire:

> The aspirations of the great mass of the world's population can today be satisfied only by rapid material progress. There can be little doubt that in their present mood a serious disappointment of their expectations would lead to grave international friction – indeed, it would probably lead to war. The peace of the world and, with it, civilization itself thus depend on continued progress at a fast rate. At this juncture we are therefore not only the creatures but the captives

of progress; even if we wished to, we could not sit back and enjoy at leisure what we have achieved. Our task must be to continue to lead, to move ahead along the path which so many more are trying to tread in our wake.[91]

The economic elites of the world are presented here as 'captives' of progress, servants who cannot enjoy the wealth they have won because they have a mission both to guarantee peace in the world by expanding the free market system around the world in order to promote the economic progress that will satisfy the aspirations of the global population; and also to be models, leaders, who move ahead and call others to join them in this mission.

But what is the driving force of economic progress? For Hayek, it is mimetic desire: 'at each stage some of the things most people desire can be provided only for a few and can be made accessible to all only by further progress'.[92] Therefore, presenting the economic elite as models of humanity, models of desire, foments the mimetic desire that stimulates in everyone greater resolve in the search for progress. To the extent that desire and demand for products consumed by the elite increases, the market system providentially increases production, generating with this economic progress. Therefore, Hayek says, 'so long as it remains a progressive society, some must lead, and the rest must follow'.[93]

The world would be a marvellous place if this metanarrative functioned without any problems or contradictions. The first contradiction is found within the logic of mimetic desire itself. Objects are desired because they are scarce, that is, there are not enough for everyone who desires them. Abundant objects are not desired and do not stimulate competition and progress. Therefore, the objects of imitated consumption are, by definition, not accessible for all. The incessant drive to follow this pattern of consumption that is always moving ahead only has meaning to the extent that there are others who are left behind along the way. It is the essence of competition. If the finish line is not continuously moving ahead, if objects of desire are not produced and offered, the world's elite would not be fulfilling its mission always to lead the unending advance of economic progress. And in this metanarrative that drives Empire, 'even a small decline in our rate of advance might be fatal to us'.[94]

Those who do not manage to achieve the minimal pattern of consumption demanded by the community are seen as 'flawed consumers', those who remind us that we too can be left behind in the pursuit of unlimited consumption. They represent our own 'inner demons'. As Zygmunt Bauman says: 'those "left out of the game" (the *flawed consumers* . . .) are precisely the embodiment of the "inner demons" specific to the consumer life'.[95] He goes on to say:

> Increasingly, *being poor* is seen as a crime; *becoming poor*, as the product of criminal predispositions or intentions – abuse of alcohol, gambling, drugs, truancy, and vagabondage. The poor, far from meriting care and assistance, merit hate and condemnation as the very incarnation of sin.[96]

While Bauman criticizes this economic logic that is based on mimetic desire and that produces and condemns 'flawed consumers', Hayek says that this is inevitable and beneficial, since only this kind of competition-generating desire moves individuals and societies towards economic progress. He recognizes that disregarding the suffering of the poorest can seem cruel 'because it increases the desire of all in proportion as it increases its gifts to some. Yet so long as it remains a progressive society, some must lead, and the rest must follow'.[97]

The second contradiction rests in the fact that the pattern of consumption that is taken as a reference is not ecologically sustainable. The unending search for greater consumption presupposes a technological capacity to produce in an unlimited way the desired goods; and this presupposes that our environment has no biological, natural, or systemic limits. In other words, this presupposes a vision of the planet not as round and limited but as an expanding plane reaching into infinite space. Perhaps this is why Thomas Friedman, in his book *The World is Flat*, says:

> If India and China move in that direction [towards becoming free-market democracies], the world not only will become flatter than ever but also, I am convinced, more prosperous than ever. Three United States are better than one, and five would be better than three.[98]

And why stop at five? Why not hundreds of United States in the world, producing and consuming?

The third contradiction has to do with the cultural question. The homogenization of desires and the imposition of the consumer culture and 'the American way of life' enter into conflict with the diversity of historico-cultural contexts. Europeans and North Americans are not the only peoples who are proud of their cultural identity. There are many others who are also proud of their cultural traditions and who in the name of religious or cultural values, resist and combat this cultural 'expansion', which, at last look, always classifies them as inferior or backward. These people and social groups, those who resist the attraction of the postmodern consumer culture and the economic liberalism that Empire imposes and its missionaries preach, are those who, according to Greenspan, retreat into 'tribalism' or other 'isms'.

In the face of these contradictions, we have two choices: the first is to recognize that the imperial system cannot solve by itself these contradictions and to limit the desire for accumulation, seeking new paths within the system itself or struggling for some other type of social system; the second is to reaffirm the present system and try to overcome the contradictions by defining 'the guilty' in order to eliminate them. The present Empire, like all empires, assumes the second option. In this way, we have more clearly identified here the three types of enemies that the contradiction of market capitalism produces: first, the poor, the 'flawed consumers', and those who are led by compassion to be allied with populist causes in order to intervene in the market and create non-mercantile mechanisms to try to solve social problems; second, defenders of the environment who believe that the dynamic of the free market is incapable of solving ecological problems and enforcing measures of control and consumption limitations; third, the pre-moderns and defenders of cultures who do not fit in modern and postmodern capitalism and who oppose in the name of their traditional or religious values the good news of capitalist globalization. These are the 'enemies of humanity' because these are enemies of progress.

It is here that coercion arises in the most diverse forms and in the use of brute force. The challenge is determining how to do away with these enemies without Empire losing its attractiveness or the legitimacy of presenting itself as a benign empire. Providing arguments for this kind of defence is one of the functions of the intellectuals and ideologues at the service of Empire.

Joseph Nye is one of the many authors who present arguments for the brute force of the 'benign Empire':

> Individualism and liberties are attractive to many people but repulsive to some, particularly fundamentalists ... Some tyrants and fundamentalists will always hate us because of our values of openness and opportunity, and we will have no choice but to deal with them through more effective counterterrorism policies.[99]

For him, the use of military power is not the outcome of an option, for 'we will have no choice but to deal with them'. Empire is compelled to use its military power; guilt for Empire's violence rests with those who do not want to accept the values of Western individualism and liberalism. The objects of this political antiterrorism are not only the members of al-Qaida and other terrorist groups but also those who are not capable of understanding and accepting Western values. Here, there is a clear division in the world: us and them, the pre-modern fundamentalists, those who cannot accept our freedom and the free market.

Along these lines, but with an even more shocking frankness, Robert Cooper, a senior diplomat of the British government who assisted the former British Prime Minister Tony Blair in the formulation of new policies for humanitarian intervention, says the following:

> The challenge to the postmodern world is to get used to the idea of double standards. Among ourselves, we operate on the basis of laws and open cooperative security. But when dealing with more old-fashioned kinds of states outside the postmodern continent of Europe, we need to revert to the rougher methods of an earlier era – force, pre-emptive attack, deception, whatever is necessary to deal with those who still live in the nineteenth century world of every state for itself. Among ourselves we keep the law, but when we are operating in the jungle, we must also use the laws of the jungle.[100]

Few of those who agree with Cooper's thesis would dare to use such cruel and direct language. Francis Fukuyama is more subtle. In his well-known book *The End of History and the Last Man,* he says that liberal democracies, to defend themselves from those totalitarians who are destroying en masse civilian populations and economic resources, 'were led to adopt military strategies like the bombing of Dresden or Hiroshima that in earlier ages would have been genocidal'.[101] Without entering into the discussion concerning whether or not the bombings of Dresden and Hiroshima were militarily necessary, we want to call attention to the fact that, according to Fukuyama, these bombings were considered genocides in the past but are no longer, because they were executed or committed by liberal democracies against totalitarians.

There is something extraordinary in liberal democracy, especially in its struggle against totalitarianism, that makes suspending ethical judgments normal. In another age, those bombings were considered genocides, but not when done in the name of the defence of liberal democracy and its free market system. This is the transcendental character of the sovereign who can suspend the normal order and decree the stated exception. Exceptionally, because realized in the name of the

93

defence of market capitalism, anything is valid in the struggle against totalitarians, tyrants, and fundamentalists.

Here there is not only a suspension of moral or legal values but an inversion. What before was genocide is now presented as a salvific act. This is the logic of theological sacrifices: the conversion of an act that is normally considered evil into one that is beneficial because it is done in the name of the demands of values or entities considered transcendent. All empires, including the present one, that are presented as benign or altruistic have at their core a theological sacrifice.

In the struggle against the 'enemies of humanity', however, there is not always sufficient need or justification for the use of brute force. Especially against those who are excluded from the market game, it is necessary to use another strategy: the propagation of the culture of insensitivity. For, as we saw above, compassion for the suffering of the poor tends to lead to alliances with populists, interventionists, or even socialists. One of the ways to carry out this strategy is to eliminate from memory and remove from sight the actual sufferings of concrete persons. As Fukuyama says, 'even benevolent hegemons sometimes have to act ruthlessly'.[102] This constitutes one of the duties of Empire for the maintenance of the global order.

This culture of human insensitivity is something strategic today because, as Zygmunt Bauman says, the production of 'human waste' – those excluded from the market system, those who Latin American theologians call 'the left behind' [those left out] –

is an inevitable outcome of modernization, and an inseparable accompaniment of modernity. It is an inescapable side-effect of *order-building* (each order casts some parts of the extant population as 'out of place,' 'unfit,' or 'undesirable') and of *economic progress* (that cannot proceed without degrading and devaluing the previously effective modes of 'making a living' and therefore cannot but deprive their practitioners of their livelihood).[103]

Hayek says that human solidarity is a primitive instinct that must be eliminated in more complex societies such as ours. But many of us continue to be touched by the sufferings of others. It appears that there is a contradiction between our old human nature and the efforts of Empire to construct a world as a perfect market. Against compassion and cultural and spiritual traditions that valorize human solidarity, the ideologues of the totally free market defend the end of what they call 'paternalism' and introduce a new spirituality compatible with the spirit of Empire. Roberto de Oliveira Campos, a former economic advisor in the Brazilian government, well summarizes this challenge, saying that 'modernization presumes a *cruel mystique* of the behaviour and the cult of efficiency'.[104] A 'mystique' to overcome the temptation to compassion in order to assume a new cult. 'Cruel' because this new cult means subordinating human life to profit numbers: that is, it presumes an insensitivity or cynicism in the face of the sufferings of those less 'competent' and less efficient – the poor.

Wasted lives, those sacrificed in the name of the advance of market capitalism, are the lives whose sufferings and dignity are deleted from the memory of those who are comfortable in the present system. These lives demand not only the recovery of their memories but also theological critiques of the idolatrous theologies of the Empire. Idols, in the Biblical tradition, are gods that demand sacrifices of human lives.

All social systems produce their transcendental concepts, which come to serve as the ideal model for the interpretation of reality and supply guidelines for strategic action. More than this, a society's transcendental concept serves as the source of criteria for ethical critique and the utopian horizon that channels the desires of society's members in a direction compatible with the ruling social dynamic. This process is a necessity for all types of social order. The question is not whether a system possesses a notion of transcendence or not but how the society relates with its transcendental concept. The main focus of this critical reflection on the present global order was not whether it possesses a notion of transcendence or not. We hope that we have shown that it does. The fundamental problem is something else: is the relation society maintains with its notion of transcendence sacrificial? We hope also to have shown that this is the case. Our challenge, then, is how to construct a notion of transcendence that orients our interpretation of reality and our actions but is not sacrificial; one that is humanizing and assists us in the construction of a more human and just social order, sensitive to the sufferings of other persons and other peoples.

Notes

1 Michael Hardt and Antonio Negri, *Empire*, Cambridge, MA: Harvard University Press, 2000, p. xii.
2 Hardt and Negri, *Empire*, pp. xii–xiii.
3 Hardt and Negri, *Empire*, p. 83.
4 Hardt and Negri, *Empire*, p. 33.
5 Hardt and Negri, *Empire*, p. 326.
6 Hardt and Negri, *Empire*, p. 326.
7 Hardt and Negri, *Empire*, p. 345.

8 Michael Hardt and Antonio Negri, *Multitude: War and Democracy in the Age of Empire*, New York: Penguin Press, 2004, p. 21.

9 Hardt and Negri, *Multitude*, p. 30.

10 Hardt and Negri, *Multitude*, p. 32.

11 Hardt and Negri, *Empire*, pp. 345–6, italics added.

12 Joseph S. Nye, Jr., *The Paradox of American Power: Why the World's Only Superpower Can't Go It Alone*, New York: Oxford University Press, 2002, p. xvi.

13 Nye, *The Paradox of American Power*, p. xi.

14 Joan Robinson, *Economic Philosophy*, Chicago: Aldine, 1962, p. 13.

15 Robinson, *Economic Philosophy*, p. 21.

16 Hardt and Negri, *Empire*, pp. xiv–xv.

17 Peter Berger, *The Sacred Canopy: Elements of a Sociological Theory of Religion*, New York: Doubleday, 1967, p. 176.

18 Berger, *Sacred Canopy*, p. 33.

19 Berger, *Sacred Canopy*, p. 36.

20 Hardt and Negri, *Empire*, p. 33.

21 Karl Marx, *Capital: Critique of Political Economy*, Volume 1: The Process of Capitalist Production, trans. Samuel Moore and Edward Aveling from the 3rd German edition, Chicago: Charles H. Kerr & Co., 1906, p. 406, n. 2.

22 Among his many works on this subject, see especially Franz Hinkelammert, *Crítica a la razón utópica* ['Critique of Utopian Reason'], San José, Costa Rica: Editorial DEI, 1984.

23 Franz Hinkelammert, 'Prometeo, el discernimiento de los dioses y la ética del sujeto: Reflexiones a partir de un libro' ['Prometheus, the Discernment of the Gods, and the Ethics of the Subject'], *Pasos*, 118 (March–April 2005), p. 10.

24 Edward W. Said, *Orientalism*, 25th anniversary edition, New York: Vintage Books, 2003, p. xxi.

25 Available at http://tinyurl.com/okrgmv.

26 'Canada's International Policy Statement (2005) – A Role of Pride and Influence in the World: Development', available at http://www.acdi-cida.gc.ca/ips-development.

27 Available at http://www.informationclearinghouse.info/article2320.htm.

28 Italics added.

29 Italics added.

30 Alan Greenspan, *The Age of Turbulence: Adventures in a New World*, New York: Penguin Press, 2007, p. 14.

31 Greenspan, *Age of Turbulence*, p. 14.

32 Greenspan, *Age of Turbulence*, p. 15; italics added.

33 Concerning the notion of non-interference in the economy, Karl Polanyi writes: 'Market economy implies a self-regulating system of markets; in slightly more technical terms, it is an economy directed by market prices and nothing but market prices. Such a system capable of organizing the whole of economic life without outside help or interference would certainly deserve to be called self-regulating' (Karl Polanyi, *The Great Transformation*, Boston, MA: Beacon Press, 1957, p. 43).

34 Thomas L. Friedman, *The World is Flat: A Brief History of the Twenty-*

first Century, further updated and expanded edition, New York: Farrar, Straus, and Giroux, 2007, p. 236; italics added.

35 Greenspan, *Age of Turbulence*, p. 16, italics added.

36 Greenspan, *Age of Turbulence*, p. 268.

37 Greenspan, *Age of Turbulence*, p. 268.

38 Max Weber, *The Protestant Ethic and the Spirit of Capitalism*, trans. Talcott Parsons, New York: Charles Scribner's Sons, 1958, p. 53.

39 Joseph E. Stiglitz, *Making Globalization Work*, New York: W. W. Norton, 2006, p. xiv.

40 Stiglitz, *Making Globalization Work*, p. 49.

41 Stiglitz, *Making Globalization Work*, p. xii.

42 Stiglitz, *Making Globalization Work*, p. xiv.

43 Stiglitz, *Making Globalization Work*, pp. 28–9.

44 Stiglitz, *Making Globalization Work*, p. 68; italics added.

45 Stiglitz, *Making Globalization Work*, p. xiv.

46 For Franz Hinkelammert, transcendental concepts are concepts 'in relation to which empirical reality is interpreted. They are imaginary concepts of reality and therefore are not realizable, but in no way are they arbitrary concepts. They constitute an idealized order beginning with the general characteristics of reality' (*Crítica a la razón utópica*, p. 56).

47 Greenspan, *Age of Turbulence*, pp. 247–8.

48 Walter Russell Mead, *Power, Terror, Peace, and War: America's Grand Strategy in a World at Risk*, New York: Vintage, 2005, pp. 73–4.

49 Greenspan, *Age of Turbulence*, p. 365; italics added.

50 Greenspan, *Age of Turbulence*, p. 18.

51 Greenspan, *Age of Turbulence*, p. 268.

52 Greenspan, *Age of Turbulence*, p. 272.

53 'The National Security Strategy of the United States of America', introduction.

54 Greenspan, *Age of Turbulence*, p. 345.

55 http://www.nobelprize.org/nobel_prizes/economics/laureates/1974/hayek-lecture.html. Note that this lecture was delivered at the end of the interventionist period in the history of capitalism (from the 1930s to the 1970s) described and critiqued by Alan Greenspan.

56 Hayek, 'Pretence of Knowledge'.

57 For a more ample consideration of this question, see Jung Mo Sung, 1997, 'Evil in the Free Market Mentality', *Concilium* 1997/5 (1997), 24–32; and Jung Mo Sung, 2007, *Desire, Market, and Religion*, London: SCM Press, 2007, Chapter 1.

58 Hayek, 'Pretence of Knowledge'.

59 Hayek, 'Pretence of Knowledge'.

60 F. A. Hayek, *The Fatal Conceit: The Errors of Socialism*, Chicago: University of Chicago Press, 1988, p. 6.

61 Paul A. Samuelson, *Economics*, 11th edition, New York: McGraw Hill, 1985, p. 38. This textbook is now into its eighteenth edition (2005). The eleventh edition was the last one authored exclusively by Samuelson. The first edition was published in 1948.

62 Hayek, *Fatal Conceit*, p. 13.

63 Hayek, *Fatal Conceit*, p. 20.
64 Hayek, *Fatal Conceit*, p. 26.
65 Hayek, *Fatal Conceit*, p. 6.
66 Hayek, *Fatal Conceit*, p. 136.
67 Hayek, *Fatal Conceit*, p. 136–7.
68 Milton Friedman, *Capitalism and Freedom*, Chicago: University of Chicago Press, 1962, p. 15; italics added. [Translator's note: The Portuguese edition with which the author is working uses 'faith' here rather than 'belief', the latter being used in the English edition: see Milton Friedman, *Capitalismo e Liberdade*, 1982, São Paulo: Abril, p. 23.]
69 See Jung Mo Sung, 'Fundamentalismo econômico' ['Economic Fundamentalism'], *Estudos de Religião* 11 (December 1995), pp. 101–8.
70 George Soros, *The Crisis of Global Capitalism: Open Society Endangered*, New York: Public Affairs, 1998, p. xxii.
71 Soros, *Crisis*, p. 127.
72 Soros, *Crisis*, p. 128.
73 Paul Krugman, *The Self-Organizing Economy*, Malden, MA: Blackwell, 1996, pp. vi and 99.
74 Krugman, *Self-Organizing Economy*, p. 3. Emergent properties are one of the products of the self-organizing of complex systems.
75 Krugman, *Self-Organizing Economy*, pp. 5–6.
76 Robert Kagan, 'Power and Weakness' *Policy Review* 113 (June–July 2002), available at: http://www.hoover.org/publications/policyreview/3460246.html.
77 Walter D. Mignolo, *The Idea of Latin America*, Malden, MA: Blackwell, 2005, p. 4.
78 Mignolo, *Idea of Latin America*, p. 6.
79 Sigmund Freud, *The Future of an Illusion*, trans. and ed. James Strachey, New York: W. W. Norton, 1961, p. 16.
80 Freud, *Future of an Illusion*.
81 Freud, *Future of an Illusion*.
82 For more concerning this process of the transformation of values from a local history into a global project, see Walter D. Mignolo, *Local Histories/ Global Designs: Coloniality, Subaltern Knowledges, and Border Thinking*, Princeton: Princeton University Press, 2000.
83 For a deeper analysis of this passage from desire to social necessity, see Sung, *Desire, Market, and Religion*, Chapters 2 and 3.
84 The theme of mimetic desire is treated in this book, in Chapter 2, concerning subjectivity.
85 Nye, *Paradox of American Power*, 9.
86 In the 1960s, Celso Furtado criticized this desire to imitate the consumption patterns of rich countries as one of the reasons for the inability of poor countries to overcome social inequality, which is today characterized as 'social apartheid' in developing countries. See, for example, Celso Furtado, *The Myth of Economic Development and the Future of the Third World*, Cambridge: Cambridge University Centre of Latin American Studies, Working Paper 16, 1974.
87 Francis Fukuyama, *America at the Crossroads: Democracy, Power, and*

the Neoconservative Legacy, New Haven, CT: Yale University Press, 1974, p. 185; italics added.

88 Charles S. Maier, 'An American Empire? The Problems of Frontiers and Peace in Twenty-first Century World Politics', *Harvard Magazine* (Nov–Dec 2002), p. 28, available at http://harvardmagazine.com/2002/11/an-american-empire.html.

89 David Harvey, *The New Imperialism*, New York: Oxford University Press, 2003, p. 41.

90 Harvey, *New Imperialism*, p. 56.

91 F.A. Hayek, *The Constitution of Liberty*, Chicago: University of Chicago Press, 1960, pp. 52–3.

92 Hayek, *Constitution*, p. 45.

93 Hayek, *Constitution*, p. 45.

94 Hayek, *Constitution*, p. 53.

95 Zygmunt Bauman, *Postmodernity and its Discontents*, New York: New York University Press, 1997, pp. 41–2, italics original.

96 Bauman, *Postmodernity*, pp. 43–4, italics original.

97 Hayek, *Constitution*, p. 45.

98 Friedman, *The World is Flat*, p. 150.

99 Nye, *Paradox of American Power*, p. xi.

100 Robert Cooper, 'The New Liberal Imperialism', *The Observer* (7 April 2002), available at http://observer.guardian.co.uk/print/0,,4388912-110490,00.html.

101 Francis Fukuyama, *The End of History and the Last Man*, New York: Avon Books, 1992, p. 6.

102 Fukuyama, *America at the Crossroads*, p. 113.

103 Zygmunt Bauman, *Wasted Lives: Modernity and its Outcasts*, Cambridge: Polity Press, 2004, p. 5.

104 Roberto Campos, *Além do cotidiano* ['Beyond the Everyday'], 2nd edition, Rio de Janeiro: Record, 1985, p. 54.

4

Humanizing Transcendence: The Human Condition and the 'Other'

At the end of Chapter 3, 'Empire and Transcendence', we raised the challenge of developing a notion of transcendence that is not sacrificial in order to orient our interpretation of reality and our actions in the construction of a society more human, just, and sensitive to the sufferings of persons and the people. This means that we need to find or set out a notion of utopia, of transcendence, which is founded on the concrete struggles against the oppressions of Empire and in the spirit of solidarity of and with marginalized and oppressed persons.

In this chapter, we want to face this task by analysing several positions on the notion of utopia and transcendence found among those who are opposed to the present model of globalization and the present Empire. We want to look at contemporary discussions on utopia for traces of and ways to construct this notion of transcendence that is both critical and humanizing. For this, we will begin with an analysis of some thinkers from the Marxist tradition and then another group that no longer fits within the more narrow definition of the Marxist tradition, even though they do not deny the importance of Marx's contribution.

The utopia of a society without inequalities and conflicts

Alain Badiou, in a text concerning the election of President Nicolas Sarkozy of France and the situation of those struggling for emancipation, says that

> after the negative experiences of the 'socialist' states and the ambiguous lessons of the Cultural Revolution and May 68, our task is to bring the communist hypothesis into existence in another mode, to help it emerge within new forms of political experience.[1]

Before moving ahead with a reflection on Badiou's proposal, it is worth raising a question: must we continue discussing themes such as communism, a proposal born in the nineteenth century, in our struggle to overcome the present Empire? In other words, are not the collapse of the socialist bloc and the declared failure of Marxism (at least by intellectuals committed to the capitalist system) enough to suggest that we should not return to the 'old' discussion concerning communism, socialism, or Marxism?

We think that the new that can emerge in the world is not a repetition of the dreams or projects of the past, but also that it is not anything so new that it has no relation to the practices and theories of emancipation or liberation in the most recent or distant history of humanity. Without reconsidering the past, we cannot construct a different future, a future that is not a mere reproduction of the present. Therefore, critical reflections on the critical theories that mobilized and mobilize emancipatory social struggles in the past and in the present are important.

Returning to the 'communist hypothesis', for Badiou, the general sense of the term 'communist' means, first of all, that 'the logic of class – the fundamental subordination of labour to a dominant class, the arrangement that has persisted since Antiquity – is not inevitable; it can be overcome'.[2] From this premise, he says:

The communist hypothesis is that a different collective organiza-tion is practicable, one that will eliminate the inequality of wealth and even the division of labour. The private appropriation of mas-sive fortunes and their transmission by inheritance will disappear. The existence of a coercive state, separate from civil society, will no longer appear a necessity: a long process of reorganization based on a free association of producers will see it withering away.[3]

The communist hypothesis proposed by Badiou begins with an affir-mation, one with which few would disagree: a collective organization different from capitalism is possible. In other words, capitalism is not the only viable way to organize the human community. Even Francis Fukuyama, who once defended the idea that history had come to an end with liberal capitalism, recognizes that history is open, since 'there can be no end of history without an end of modern natural science and technology'.[4] And this without mentioning the possible social and historical changes introduced by political and social revolutions. The problem for Badiou's communist hypothesis is found in the way in which he describes communism as an alternative form of collective organization. He presents four characteristics: first, the elimination of inequality in wealth; second, the elimination of the division of labour; third, the disappearance of the private appropriation of immense fortunes and their transmission through inheritance; and, fourth, the end of the necessity of the coercive state, which is gradually substituted by the free association of producers.

The elimination of the inequality of wealth – an objective shared by many social and political groups that do not necessarily identify themselves with socialist or communist proposals – and the disappearance of the private appropriation of immense fortunes and their transmission through inheritance are perfectly realistic objectives. The elimination of the division of the labour and the gradual substitution of the coercive state with the free association of producers, however, are objectives of a character different from the two others. First, it is not possible to implement these objectives through the political actions of the state – combined or not with the actions of civil society – as is the case with the first two objectives. While coercive state policies and pressure from civil society could eliminate the inequality of wealth and the private appropriation and transmission through inheritance of large fortunes, they cannot eliminate the division of labour and, therefore, mercantile relations, or bring an end to the state itself. The concrete experiences of socialist states demonstrate that. For Badiou, however, the non-realization of these two objectives was due basically to the failures of socialist states and, therefore, he says that 'our task is to bring the communist hypothesis into existence in another mode, to help it emerge within new forms of political experience'.[5]

The question, then, is this: is it possible to create some form of social and political organization that makes possible the realization of these objectives? In other words, are the objectives of the end of the division of labour and the end of the state historically possible?

For Badiou, communism is not a defined programme or political project since '"communism" as such denotes only this very general set of intellectual representations. It is what Kant called an Idea, with a regulatory function, rather than a programme. . . . They are intellectual patterns, always actualized in a different fashion'.[6] In differentiating communism as an idea with a regulatory function from the programme that actualizes this idea in different ways in different times and situations, he does not make it very clear whether the objective of a society without a state and without the division of labour is an objective to be pursued, because it is historically possible, or a transcendental concept that serves to orient actions but is impossible to carry out.

However, his critique of those communist parties that managed to take power and to introduce socialist or communist states provides us with a good clue.

The party had been an appropriate tool for the overthrow of weakened reactionary regimes, but it proved ill-adapted for the construction of the 'dictatorship of the proletariat' in the sense that Marx had intended – that is, a temporary state, organizing the transition to the non-state: its dialectical 'withering away'. Instead, the party-state developed into a new form of authoritarianism. Some of these regimes made real strides in education, public health, the valorization of labour, and so on; and they provided an international constraint on the arrogance of the imperialist powers. However, the statist principle in itself proved corrupt and, in the long run, ineffective.[7]

Badiou says that the party was an instrument appropriate for carrying out the revolution, but not for building a temporary state that would organize the transition toward a non-state. Since he puts the task of the construction of a state that would lead to a non-state society on the same level as the initial task of taking power, he presupposes that this non-state society, the free association of producers, is historically possible. Therefore, while recognizing that some of these regimes managed to bring about significant social and political advancements, he criticizes the party-state communist model of the twentieth century for not having been an instrument capable of carrying out this transition and for having lapsed into a new form of authoritarianism. The core of the critique is that the communist regimes created new forms of state authoritarianism rather than moving in the opposite direction: toward their own self-destruction and a non-state society. This pointed criticism demonstrates his belief that such a transition is possible. The task now would therefore be to create new forms of political experience and organization that are appropriate for the realization of this objective.

The possibility or not of the construction of a society based on the free association of producers, or any other form of designing a society characterized by freedom, justice, and co-operation, is an important discussion in the struggle to overcome the present Empire and in the construction of alternative societies and an alternative globalization. In the end, politics and social struggles presuppose the distinction between what it is impossible and what is possible.

Agnes Heller, in a perspective different from Badiou, notes that Marx does not say anything about how the associated producers are going to make their economic decisions in this new society. For her, the silence of Marx on this very important question is not accidental: according to him, there would be no conflicts of interest in the future society. The category of interest itself would become irrelevant. After this observation, Heller assumes Ernst Bloch's thesis that there are fertile and infertile utopias and says:

> There are many respects in which Marx's ideas on the society of associated producers are utopian when measured against our own today and our own possibilities for action, these are nonetheless *fertile*. He established a norm against which we can measure the reality and value of our ideas.[8]

The notion of a fertile utopia used here by Heller deserves more careful reflection. First of all, she uses utopia in the impossible, non-realizable sense; and not as the 'not yet' that might become possible or as something futile or pure fantasy. In this sense, a society of a free association of producers would be impossible because interest and con-flicts of interest make up part of the human condition. Hugo Assmann, one of the principal Latin American theologians who has worked on the relation between theology and economics, states it very well: in modern utopias, whether of Marxist or Christian origin, there is an anthropological presupposition that is 'somewhat naïve and excessively generous in its appraisal of the human predispositions to justice and fraternity'.[9] This is an anthropology that supposes that, when freed from the oppression of the capitalist system and the coercion of the state, all human beings will return to their original nature of solidarity and goodness, without any personal interest that enters into conflict with the interests of other persons or the community.

For Assmann, the struggle for a freer and more just society is not compatible with this naïve and optimistic anthropology, which does not take into account the actual human condition. For him, 'it is neces-sary to be dispelled of illusions about the supposedly spontaneous and natural solidarious propensities of human beings',[10] and to recognize that human beings are beings marked by selfishness and the possibility of solidarity, interested and passionate beings, beings with needs and desires. These desires are not always compatible with the needs and the will of the community and/or with the objective conditions of the environment or the society.

Beyond this anthropological question underlying the notion of the free association of producers, there is also an important economic ques-tion. In large and complex societies such as ours, no person, group, or entire community could possibly have access to or knowledge of all the information implicated in the economic processes of production, distribution, and consumption of goods necessary for the reproduction of life of the community. This signifies the necessity of specializations fragmentations of economic knowledge, practices, and decisions. ides, no group today manages to produce all the goods necessary the reproduction of its life or makes the necessary investments for are generations. Such things demand the division of labour, whether ndividual terms within a productive group or unit (family, business, mmunity, and so on) or in terms of the economic system, which ay is global. The division of labour presupposes the unequal distriion of information and knowledge and, therefore, of the power to ke decisions concerning the economic process, which in turn geners inequalities in income or wealth.

These short reflections allow us to better understand why the utopia of the free association of producers is, as Heller says, something impossible to realize. But, as we saw in the quote above, Heller does not end with her affirmation of this impossibility. She goes on to say that, in spite of being impossible to realize, these ideas 'are nonetheless *fertile*. [Marx] established a norm against which we can measure the reality and value of our ideas.'[11] This utopia is impossible to attain, but is fertile, useful nonetheless.

The fertility of the utopia, according to Heller, is in the fact that it establishes a norm by which one can measure the present reality and also the value of the ideas that legitimate or contest the present reality and that orient actions and behaviours. In this sense, the utopia of a society envisioned as a free association of producers serves as a criterion of analysis and judgement concerning the dominant capitalist system. It has a fertile or even fundamental gnoseological function. We saw in Chapter 3 that the utopia of the totally free market has this same function of serving as the criterion of analysis, evaluation, and legitimation for defenders of the free market system.

Alec Nove, an economist critical of the economic model of old communist bloc countries, disagrees with Heller's position. For his critique, however, he introduces into the reflection another position, that of the Polish thinker Wladyslaw Bienkowski, who wrote: 'let us not reject the utopian Marxist vision: perhaps one day "commodities" and "money" will disappear'.[12] Bienkowski, though criticizing those who look for a short and more direct path towards this society without commodities and money, defends the idea that one cannot determine in advance the non-realizability of this utopia.

In response to Bienkowski's position, Nove says: 'I remain unconvinced. As argued already, while of course recognizing the role and desirability of ideals, some of these utopian notions create dangerous illusions, confuse the mind.'[13] He does not agree that the utopia of a society without conflict, commodities, or money might one day be possible to actualize, and says that certain utopias, like that of Marx, create dangerous illusions and confuse the mind. While Heller says that Marx's utopia serves to analyse reality and the value of ideas, Nove says that it confuses the mind and is dangerous.

To explain his position better, Nove presents two examples of utopia. The first one is the ideal of a society without crime, which is for him a valuable and noble objective, and he believes that we ought in fact to endeavour ourselves to eliminate crime. He recognizes that this objective is impossible to attain but that we need to try; and that insofar as crime persists, nobody would defend the idea that we can live without police officers or other persons and professions that help maintain security. The second type of utopia he presents, with reference to Heller, is the notion of society without conflict, where all the persons seek the same objectives and each individual person expresses the needs of all persons. As with the crimeless society, he says that Marx's utopia is impossible, only now he adds, 'and even undesirable'. To desire a crimeless society is good, but a society without social conflict is not desirable, because for him

> anyone holding such a belief about socialism is bound to be misled, and *dangerously* misled. A belief that crime can be eradicated can lead to action designed to eradicate crime, and such action, though unlikely to be wholly successful, can have positive effects. The belief that under socialism there would be unanimity is not just false; the only action it can give rise to is the *eradication of dissent*, the *imposition* of 'unanimity'.[14]

Why is the utopia of a crimeless society not dangerous and why does it not confuse the mind, whereas the utopia of a society without social and economical conflicts is and does? Because, according to Nove, actions aiming at a crimeless society, though impossible to attain fully, lead to a reduction in crime; whereas belief in the utopia of a society without social conflicts lead only to actions aiming at the eradication of dissent and the imposition of unanimity. At first glance the argument seems quite convincing, but there is a problem.

The utopia of a crimeless society is presented and analysed by Nove in the negative form, 'without crime', whereas Marx's utopia is presented in the positive form: 'there would be unanimity'. For a policy or plan of action to be prepared and executed, the objective or utopia must be expressed in a positive form; only on the basis of a positive statement of intent can a project or plan of action be prepared. Therefore, the utopia of a crimeless society needs to be translated into something like a society where everyone perfectly obeys the law. For this to be achieved, it is necessary to have complete vigilance and 'zero tolerance' for every infraction and perpetrator. That would lead us towards a type of totalitarian, police, and fascist state, turning persons into prisoners or victims of the 'crimes' of the state in the search for a crimeless society. Since Nove does not develop his reasoning concerning the crimeless society in the form of a positive proposition and plan, he does not perceive the perverse side of this utopia when it is believed to be possible and a plan of action aiming at it is implemented. In critiquing the utopia of the stateless society, he develops the argument in the form of positive proposition, 'there would be unanimity', and so perceives the perversion that emerges when one believes that this is possible and establishes a plan of action in view of it: the eradication of dissent and the imposition of unanimity.

Therefore, the problem is not in the type of utopia, but in the belief or not in the possibility of realizing the ideal society presented in the utopia. When it is believed that it is possible through human actions to achieve fully the utopia of the perfect society (whether the vision of the perfect market, the perfect planning of the old Soviet Union, a stateless society, or a society without crime and without any violations of the law), the result is a perversion of that utopia through dominations and the imposition of sacrifices. In this sense, Nove's criticism is very relevant. This was one of the problems of the socialist countries and of many parties of communist orientation in relation to the theme of democracy: why improve democracy and develop mechanisms of control of the state by civil society if the goal is to build a society without conflicts of interests and without the state? If that goal is seen as realizable through the actions of the party or the state, democracy – which presupposes the coexistence of divergent and conflicting opinions and interests – comes to be seen as an obstacle and authoritarianism comes to be seen as an instrument for the realization of the utopia. Badiou did not perceive that the authoritarianism of communist regimes was not only the result of the intrinsically corrupt character of the state but also of the belief that authoritarianism was the means to attain the fullness of communism.

Based on his critique, Nove proposes a reformulation of Bloch's thesis. Instead of the distinction between fertile and infertile utopias, he prefers another: 'there are harmless and harmful utopias'.[15] In truth, there are fertile and infertile utopias for analysing reality and measuring the values of our ideas and our conduct; and when it is believed that it is possible to realize linearly, with finite steps, the utopia that is always perceived in terms of fullness, that utopian vision becomes harmful. The harmful thing is not the utopia in itself but the belief that it can be realized through human actions, the belief that we can fully achieve the utopia through our actions. It is what Hegel called 'wrong or negative infinity', to try to reach infinity with finite steps, and what Franz Hinkelammert called the 'transcendental illusion'.[16]

A utopia is fertile and at the same time dangerous because it can lead to the transcendental illusion and its perversions. But is it necessary? Would it not be better, as Nove thinks, to set aside the notion of utopia in order to avoid this danger? Is it possible to criticize the pretension of inevitability and the character (almost natural) of the capitalist market system (analysed in Chapter 3) and to overcome the present Empire without an alternative utopia?

The necessity of utopia and the critique of utopian reason

Slavoj Žižek, in an article on the legacy of 1968, recalls what took place when Marco Cicala, an Italian journalist, recently used the word 'capitalism' in an article for the newspaper *La Republica*: his editor asked if the use of this word was necessary and if it might not be substituted by a synonym such as 'economy'. Žižek asks:

> What better proof of capitalism's triumph in the last three decades than the disappearance of the very term 'capitalism'? So, again, the only *true* question today is: Do we endorse this naturalization of capitalism, or does today's global capitalism contain contradictions strong enough to prevent its indefinite reproduction?[17]

At the end of the article, he affirms:

> The true legacy of '68 is best encapsulated in the formula *Soyons realistes, demandons l'impossible!* (Let's be realists, demand the impossible.)
> Today's utopia is the belief that the existing global system can reproduce itself indefinitely. The only way to be realistic is to envision what, within the coordinates of this system, cannot but appear as impossible.[18]

In saying that 'today's utopia is the belief that the existing global system can reproduce itself indefinitely', Žižek affirms that current society possesses and, we might add, is moved by a utopia; in this way he is set apart from those who, like Lasky, think that the repugnance of present conditions and the seduction of a better and different world constitute part of the essence of utopia.[19] With that, he approaches the subject of utopia in a way very different from Nove and concludes that the only way to be realistic, to go beyond the pseudo-scientific ideology that naturalizes capitalism, 'is to envision what, within the coordinates of this system, cannot but appear as impossible'.

'Let's be realists, demand the impossible' is an affirmation that can seem totally naïve and romantic. How can 'demanding the impossible' be something realistic? Does not being realistic mean precisely recognizing that the impossible is impossible and that we have to keep within the limits of the possibilities of reality?

If one of the characteristics of being a realist is to live and act in accordance with the limits of what is possible, the definition of the line that divides the impossible from the possible becomes a fundamental question. And that discussion is not at all simple. Let's take as an example the question 'Is it possible for a human being to live forever?' Clearly, an immediate response would be 'no'. Some, however, might answer that progress in medical sciences and the whole apparatus surrounding genetic engineering can or is going to bring us to a situation of the perpetual postponement of death. Cryogenics makes sense only in view of this myth (or utopia) that scientific progress will lead us to victory over, or the 'defeat' of, death: when an individual is infected with an incurable disease and has enough money, he or she can contract the service and be frozen before dying and thawed when a cure is discovered. Others might answer that for God nothing is impossible and that God can raise us to eternal life or that death is only a passage from one life to another.

It is important, therefore, to know who or what system of knowledge defines what is possible or impossible and for which subject of action this is possible or not. In the case of Žižek's affirmation, he says clearly that to be realistic is to demand what the current system with its utopia defines as being impossible. As we have already seen, utopia – whether Marxist or capitalist – serves as a norm for analysing reality; that is, it determines the parameters within which something is recognized as existent – that which is – and defines the realm of the possible – that which can be. Consequently, it also defines that which is beyond the realm of existence (that which does not exist) and beyond the realm of the possible (that which cannot be). In other words, utopia establishes that categorical boundary that constitutes the dividing line between the possible and the impossible. When the dominant social system is naturalized, that which is a social construction of reality comes to be seen as natural; and what the social system does not allow and thereby places in the realm of impossibility is seen as naturally impossible.

Therefore, Žižek affirms that to be realistic is to foresee and to demand what, inside the parameters of the dominant system, can be seen only as an impossibility. Along the same lines, Boaventura de Sousa Santos, one of the principal intellectuals connected with the World Social Forum, says that there is a production of 'non-existence' whenever an experience, a social reality, or a given entity is disqualified and rendered invisible, unintelligible, or disposable by the dominant rationality. Against this, he proposes what he calls the 'sociology of absences':

an inquiry that aims to explain that what does not exist is in fact actively produced as nonexistent, that is, as a noncredible alternative to what exists. Its empirical object is deemed impossible in the light of conventional social science, and for this reason its formulation already represents a break with it. The objective of the sociology of absences is to transform impossible into possible objects, absent into present objects.[20]

To go beyond the limits imposed by the utopia of the current system is to transcend the notion itself of the transcendence of the Empire – which we saw in Chapter 3 – in the direction of another notion of transcendence and utopia. But to deny the limits of possibility imposed by the Empire and to foresee and to build what the system finds impossible is not to affirm that there are no limits for the human condition, that nothing is impossible.

We can distinguish at least four types of limit of realizability. The first is the technical limit. A person who cannot swim will not manage to swim across a river without any assistance. But this impossibility can be overcome by learning to swim or by using some instrument, such as a boat. Another example is the discussion concerning the limits of genetic engineering. The current limits are technical limits that may be able to be surpassed through the progress of science and we cannot define beforehand the limits of this scientific technological advancement. But that does not mean that we should not also discuss the ethical limits in science. That is, we cannot consider scientific progress as simply a technical problem without any relation to ethics.

A second type of limit is the systemic limit. Each system imposes on

its participants the limits within which the system in question continues to exist and reproduce itself. For example, in a system of slavery, it
is impossible for all the persons to be free. If everyone were free, this
would necessarily be a break with the present system and require the
establishment of another system that recognizes and guarantees the
freedom of all its members. Just as in the present Empire it is impossible to overcome the contradiction between the included and the
excluded, those enjoying its benefits and those left out. The reflections
of Žižek and Boaventura presented above fit within this discussion of
systemic limits.

The third type of limit is that of the human condition and history.
Human beings are a species capable of desiring or thinking beyond
what exists and what is possible for our own human condition and
beyond the objective conditions of history as such. Aside from the
earlier example concerning the idea of immortality, which in spite of
being humanly impossible is possible of being thought, we can take the
example of the search for absolute truth or perfect knowledge through
modern science. Ernst Mayr, one of the major evolutionary biologists
of the twentieth century, says:

> During the last 50 years the shift in the philosophy of science from
> strict determinism and a belief in absolute truth to a position in
> which only an *approach* to truth (or presumed truth) is recognized
> has been interpreted by some commentators as evidence that science
> does not advance. This has led the antiscience movement to argue
> that science is a wasteful activity because it does not lead to any final
> truth about the world around us.[21]

We find here three positions regarding the possibility or not of
science reaching absolute truth. The first involves the belief that the
advancement of science will bring us to an understanding of absolute
truth, this being the view within the field of science that corresponds to
the naïve utopian belief that the perfect society is possible. The second
involves the rejection of this possibility and so embraces the search for
approximations that approach the truth but without ever finally reaching the absolute truth. The third involves a commitment to the myth
of the absolute truth and so devalues science for being incapable of
leading us to this truth.

Mayr, who accepts the second position, says that 'scientific progress'
does not indicate a movement in the direction of definitive truth, but
'the establishment of scientific theories that explain more and better
than earlier ones and are less vulnerable to refutation'.[22] Therefore, he

affirms that the future of science is to develop and to advance as it has for the last 250 years and that 'science indeed is an endless frontier'.[23] This notion of the 'endless frontier' does not mean that science is capable of attaining the infinite, since, if it did, science one day would come to an end. The frontier of science is infinite: it will continue on indefinitely – so long as the human species or some other capable of producing science exists – precisely because it is incapable of achieving the definitive truth, which would put an end to its progress. The notion of absolute truth or perfect knowledge can be imagined, and serves as the objective that guides efforts within the field of science and human knowledge, but it is an objective that is beyond the human condition.

In the same way, an engineer who tries to build increasingly efficient motors needs to imagine or to take as his or her final point of reference the 'perfect motor', which does not use up any energy, and then try to approximate that end. But the engineer knows that it is not possible to achieve this 'goal' since it is contrary to the laws of thermodynamics and the 'laws' that govern nature.

If we return to the text of Badiou on the communist hypothesis, quoted at the beginning of this chapter, we can see that the objectives of eliminating the inequality of wealth and the private appropriation of massive fortunes and their transmission through inheritance are a part of the discussion concerning technical and systemic limits. Some think it is possible to achieve these objectives without breaking completely with the capitalist system by introducing economic and social reforms (technical questions) within the capitalist system, producing a type of social democracy that really works on behalf of the whole society. Others think it is impossible to achieve these objectives within the capitalist system and that it is necessary to replace it with another socio-economic system. The other two objectives described by Badiou – the elimination of the division of labour and the replacement of the state with a free association of producers – are, however, beyond the limits of historical possibility. Even though some might believe that this final objective (or the objective of perfect knowledge of the absolute truth in the realm of science) is historically possible, the discussion of its possibility concerns the limits of the human condition and history.

A fourth type of limit is that of logical contradiction. We are not, for example, able to think about or imagine a square circle. There is, then, a gap between the limits of the human condition and history and the limit of logical contradiction. It is in this space that the imagination takes root and that transcendental concepts arise, such as the utopia of a perfect society, beyond the limits of the human condition and history.

There is no logical contradiction in the expressions 'perfect planning' (from the economic model of the old Soviet Union) or 'totally free market' or 'society of harmony and perfect unanimity'. Yet these utopias, necessary as each is in its function of serving as a criterion or standard to judge the existing reality and to establish the parameters of action to modify what exists and approximate the utopia, are impossible to achieve because they are beyond the limits of the human condition and history. They are like limit concepts, which can be approximated but never reached. For Franz Hinkelammert, limit concepts transcend empirical realities and constitute

transcendental concepts in regard to which the empirical reality is interpreted. They are imaginary conceptions of reality and so are not realizable, but in no way are they arbitrary concepts. They are idealized empirical impressions rooted in the general characteristics of reality.[24]

Žižek, in his book *The Fragile Absolute*, also treats this question, while discussing what he calls 'Marx's fundamental mistake'. Marx realized correctly, he says, that capitalism unleashes an impressive dynamic force of 'self-enhancing productivity' but also that this dynamic is driven by its own inner contradiction, the final limit of capitalism, which is capital itself.[25] To describe this contradiction in brief, the economic survival of a given enterprise in a capitalist system depends on its ability to accumulate capital. In a competitive environment this demands constant innovation, which destroys inflexible enterprises and rewards the new and improved. The quickest and most efficient way to raise capital, however, is to cut costs (production costs, that is, labour). But this can be taken only so far before the firm fails (labour can only be replaced and/or exploited so much), unless a monopoly has been established, which is supposedly illegal within the capitalist system anyway. Both paths – further innovation and greater efficiency – are essential aspects of the ever-increasing productivity of the capitalist system yet both lead unavoidably to 'socially destructive economic crises'.[26] This self-propelling spiral of capitalist productivity never ends, on account of the systemic contradiction of capitalism itself.

Marx's mistake, according to Žižek, was to conclude on the basis of these insights that a final or total release of the undoubtedly impressive inherent potential of 'the self-increasing spiral of productivity' is possible, yielding a new superior social order (communism), and that this could be maintained without the contradictions and resulting social crises endured within the capitalist system: 'What Marx overlooked is that – to put it in the standard Derridan terms – this inherent obstacle/antagonism as the 'condition of impossibility' of the full deployment of productive forces is simultaneously its "condition of possibility".'[27] In other words, Žižek sees a contradiction within the utopia of communism: one cannot retain the value or goal of the spiral of productivity in order to enable a situation of abundance that frees all human beings from the chains of scarcity and the pain of the non-satisfaction of material and symbolic needs without admitting or accepting the economic and social contradictions that make possible the constant increase of productivity. Take away the contradiction and the productive potential disappears with it. In line with Hinkelammert's emphasis, Žižek recognizes that the communist utopia 'was a fantasy inherent to capitalism itself . . . a strictly *ideological* fantasy of maintaining the thrust towards productivity . . . while getting rid of the "obstacles" and antagonisms'.[28]

Economically speaking, an ever-increasing spiral of productivity demands a system of incentives, innovation, and the accumulation of wealth for new investments. Celso Furtado, in analysing the process of accumulation and industrial innovation in capitalism and socialism, says that

> the perpetuation of inequalities is . . . the other side of the efficient functioning of the incentive system. . . . As a result of the interdependence between the incentive system, which operates at the individual level, and the flow of innovations, which stimulates accumulation, industrial civilization tends to establish a ruthlessly stratified society in which ranking is based on consumption patterns.[29]

Therefore, 'the destruction of social relations characteristic of capitalism does not necessarily entail the advent of an egalitarian society if the logic of accumulation specific to industrial civilization continues to apply'.[30]

Before returning to Žižek's thesis, we need to be clear that we are speaking here about a contradiction in terms of economic realizability. The notion of communism is contradictory if analyzed within the limits of the realm of economic and social possibility, or within the limits of the human condition and history. But if we think in terms beyond the limits of historical possibility, in the space that exists between the historical limit and the limit of logical contradiction, this communist utopia can be imagined and is not contradictory, in spite of being historically impossible.

This clarification is important for continuing our discussion of Žižek's text. After describing 'communism as the self-transparent society in which the production process is directly subordinated to the "general intellect" of collective planning',[31] he says:

> our premiss is that even if we remove the teleological notion of Communism (the society of completely unbridled productivity) as the implicit standard by which Marx, as it were, measures the alienation of existing society, the bulk of his 'critique of political economy', his insight into the self-propelling vicious cycle of capitalist (re)production, survives. The task of today's thought is thus double: on the one hand, how to *repeat* the Marxist 'critique of political economy' without the utopian-ideological notion of Communism as its inherent standard; on the other, how to imagine actually breaking out of the capitalist horizon *without* falling into the trap of returning to the eminently *premodern* notion of a balanced, (self-)restrained society (the 'pre-Cartesian' temptation to which most of today's ecology succumbs).[32]

Žižek recognizes that Marx's critique of the alienation present in capitalism depends on his notion of communism as 'the implicit standard' that allows him to measure the degree of alienation within capitalist society. The notion of communism or the realm of freedom – also used by Marx – is a transcendental concept that allows Marx to recognize, criticize, and measure the alienation within real material life. According to Hinkelammert, Marx elaborated the concept of the realm of freedom or communism 'out of the search for the Archimedean point . . . which, as an absence, can make history and commodity relationships intelligible'.[33] This concept is, in this sense, 'a transcendentality existing within real material life . . . [that] explains what human relationships are not', and 'by considering what human relationships are not . . . it is possible to arrive at what they are'.[34] In this way, Hinkelammert interprets Marx's concept of the realm of freedom or communism not as an attainable goal at the end of a journey but as a horizon with which a logical and epistemological relation is established. A vision of the full existence of human possibilities, in revealing what does not exist, reveals the character of social and human relations within capitalism and, with that, motivates the struggles for more humanizing concrete historical projects. It is therefore a transcendentality within real life.

Žižek, however, since he criticized Marx's notion of communism as a fundamental mistake (for being economically contradictory), proposes in the quotation above that we discard the 'utopian-ideological notion of Communism' as 'the inherent standard' of Marxist criticism of political economy, accepting the premise that 'the bulk of his "critique of political economy" ... survives'. He therefore proposes as a theoretical task this challenge: *'repeat* the Marxist "critique of political economy" without the utopian-ideological notion of Communism as its inherent standard'.

We are not going to discuss here whether or not the Marxist critique of political economy survives without the utopian notion of communism; or how it is possible to measure the degree of alienation in capitalist society without a transcendental notion of a non-alienated human being. What interests us at the moment is Žižek's claim to justify the withdrawal of the notion of communism in the Marxist, or Marxist-inspired, critique of political economy. We saw before that the utopia of communism is contradictory if we look at it as a social project to be built within the 'real' historical economy, within the limits of human and historical possibility. Since Žižek discards it as contradictory, for him the new utopia that will have the function of being 'the inherent standard' in the new critique of political economy must be free of the contradictions that prevented it from becoming historically realizable. In short, the utopia for Žižek must be realizable. This could mean that he proposes a search for a realizable goal/utopia, but such a goal cannot be ideal or perfect and thereby cannot function as the standard for measuring and criticizing reality. Or it could mean that he proposes a search for an ideal and perfect model of society that is realizable and does not contain the contradictions of the real world. He falls into the error of the transcendental illusion. This only returns us to the discussion concerning Nove's thought on the danger of believing that the ideal is realizable.

The only way to escape this aporia is to recognize the epistemological necessity of utopia while at the same time recognizing that it is transcendental, historically non-realizable. In this way, utopia is transcendental in the sense that it allows us to think about our intervention in history and also in the sense that it is beyond the limits of historical realizability.

This leads us to the subject of the dialectic relation between the transcendental utopia – with its function as 'the inherent standard', as the 'norm against which we can measure the reality and value of our ideas' (Heller), or as 'an Idea, with the regulatory function' (Badiou) – and historical projects that must be historically realizable: that is, within the limits of the human condition and history.

Homi Bhabha, in his book *The Location of Culture*, formulates a question that also touches on this point:

Must the project of our liberationist aesthetics be forever part of a totalizing Utopian vision of Being and History that seeks to transcend the contradictions and ambivalences that constitute the very structure of human subjectivity and its systems of cultural representation?[35]

Though he does not develop a systematic reflection on this point in his book, one can see that he is faced with the same sort of problem as that on which we have developed our reflection to this point. The formulation of the question reveals a certain discomfort on his part, arising from being aware of what cannot be avoided in the project of a liberationist aesthetics, as with any project intervening in reality: it ends up being formulated in terms of or established in relation to a utopian vision that attempts to transcend the contradictions and ambiguities of the human condition and their systems of cultural representation. He does not want to deny these contradictions and ambiguities, but when he proposes a project of liberationist aesthetics he realizes that this project makes up part of a utopian vision that transcends those contradictions and ambiguities.

Franz Hinkelammert is one of the authors, if not the principal one, who has long worked on this dialectical tension between the transcendental utopia and historically realizable projects. He says that Western thought, especially beginning with the social thought of the nineteenth century, has been marked by a kind of utopian naivety, which distorts, as with a veil, the perception of social reality. There are many different social theories that seek the empirical roots of those better human dreams in order next to 'discover' some form of realizing them. In the twentieth century there took place a certain crisis of this utopian naivety, though it did not lead to its overcoming but to the appearance of an aggressive utopia in the form of anti-utopia, neoliberalism, which proposes the utopia of a world without utopia: that is, a utopia of a world without alternative utopian visions to the utopia of the total market. Alongside this anti-utopia of the Empire, we have, as we saw above, a variety of positions concerning this subject among those seeking the overcoming of the Empire.

In his book *Crítica de la razón utópica*,[36] Hinkelammert proposes

a critique of utopian thought at the level of critique of utopian reason as such. It is the question of an analysis that, in the final instance, is methodological and that seeks to reveal the categorical boundaries of current social conceptualizations.[37]

In this critique, he intends to follow the central aspects of Kantian critique since he is convinced that 'a critique of utopian reason, in the final instance, consists in a transformation of the utopian content of modern thoughts into transcendental concepts and reflections'.[38]

From his analyses of several currents of modern social thought (including Popper's and Weber's epistemologies as well as conservative, anarchist, neoliberal, and Soviet thought), Hinkelammert shows that in modernity reason itself adopted a utopian character. But, and this is important, he does not consider the possibility that this utopian aspect of modern reason might be the result of confusion and that we ought to rescue reason from its relation with utopia. He demonstrates how the utopian character of modern social thought is

> a dimension inside of it, of which we need to be conscious. Consequently, the critique of utopian reason does not propose the task of abolishing utopia. This would be the most dangerous and destructive utopia of all. Thinking in utopias makes up a part of the human condition itself. . . . Utopias are of the imagination, which links them with something 'beyond' the human condition, but without them we cannot know anything of the human condition.[39]

The discovery of the limits of the human condition is not something done a priori, but a posteriori, after the frustration of facing insurmountable limits. The reason we can think and desire beyond our condition is that we face, in the empirical world, the limits of our human condition. This is valuable for the individual, as also for social projects and utopias. The recognition that we cannot think and live without a utopian horizon that provides meaning for our journey and measures and norms for interpreting and judging reality, and also the recognition that our utopia, however desirable it may be, is not realizable in its fullness, are fundamental conditions for our reasoning not to be lost in confusion and not to be carried along by the perversions and sacrifices imposed and demanded in the name of the full realization of utopia.

Utopia and the transcendental imagination

After reflections on utopia and transcendence alternative to the Empire and related to the Marxist tradition, we now want to discuss some aspects of utopia that are being used within the principal international movement in opposition to the current model of globalization: the World Social Forum (WSF). The choice to focus on this particular movement is made for two reasons. First, reflection on utopias alternative to that of the Empire must take as a point of departure real social and political movements and not some concept or theory disconnected from social struggles. Second, the WSF, besides being an international articulation of 'opposition' of greater visibility and social impact today, has within it intellectuals who have been producing important reflections on utopia rooted in the experiences and discussions within the Forum itself. It is clear that such a plural and diverse movement as this does not have an 'official' position on the subject, nor even unanimity of thought concerning utopia. However, in order that we can advance our reflection, we are going to discuss some questions arising from the theories of Boaventura de Sousa Santos.

Santos, accepting Hinkelammert's theory that the neoliberal utopia is a conservative form of utopia that is identified with the current reality and proposes the radicalization or complete fulfilment of the present, says that

> the WSF presupposes the reemergence of a critical utopia, that is to say, of a radical critique of present-day reality and the aspiration to a better society. When it appears, it is presented as an alternative to the predominance of the conservative neoliberal utopia – that is, of the utopian belief according to which the unregulated market is the source of socio-economic well-being and the model by which alternatives must be measured (or better: discarded).[40]

With this distinction between the conservative and the critical utopia, Santos recognizes that utopia is not something exclusive of opposition to the dominant social system, but that it pertains to theoretical and social practice.

Besides, for Santos the label 'conservative' not only applies to capitalist utopias but also to many of the utopias critical of Western modernity that reverted to conservative utopias. With this, he is referring especially to communist regimes that, in the name of a critical utopia, upon being identified with the only path to that utopia became conservative.[41] Therefore, he affirms:

> The first critical utopia of the twenty-first century, the WSF aims to break with the tradition of the critical utopias of western modernity, many of which reverted to conservative utopias. The open character of the utopian dimension of the WSF is its attempt to avoid this perversion. For the WSF, the demand for alternatives is a plural demand. The affirmation of alternatives goes hand in hand with the affirmation that there are alternatives to the alternatives.[42]

The perversion that turns a critical utopia into a conservative one has been caused by the imposition of a single path or single institutional means of moving towards the utopia. This is why the WSF and Santos insist on valuing the open character of the utopian dimension, the plurality and the possibility of always having alternatives to the alternatives. In a book devoted especially to the WSF, Santos affirms that the WSF 'is a radically democratic utopia that celebrates diversity, plurality, and horizontality. It celebrates another possible world, itself plural in its possibilities'.[43]

We have here some characteristics of the utopia of the WSF: it is radically democratic and valorizes diversity, plurality, and horizontality. But, from our perspective, the major novelty appears more explicitly in the affirmation that the utopia of the WSF 'celebrates another possible world, itself plural in its possibilities'; in other words, it is a utopia that admits of multiple possibilities of mediation.

This novelty, which is also highly valued and defended by other sectors of society that hope for a new type of critical utopia and an alternate society, brings with it several challenges and tasks. We want to approach only two here. The first is the challenge of the intercultural dialogue that enables the functioning of a society based on the valorization of cultural diversity and plurality (including here religious diversity). Intercultural dialogue signifies a dialogue between different and, to a large extent, incommensurable universes of meaning. An example of this would be the dialogue between Christians (with their belief in a Triune God and God's incarnation in the person of Jesus Christ), Muslims (with their belief that there is only one, unified God), Buddhists (who do not believe in God's existence), and members of polytheistic religions.

Within a given culture, dialogues and arguments are possible without much problem because the parties involved share the same premises of argumentation, which seem to them obvious. These rhetorical commonplaces of a given culture are called *topoi*. The problem appears when members of different cultures try to understand the culture of another from the perspective of their own *topoi*, or when they use their own *topoi* as premises of argumentation with members of other cultures, who interpret that speech and engage in the argument on the basis of different *topoi*. Proceeding from the assumption that it is possible to understand a given culture from another culture's *topoi*, Santos proposes a *diatopical hermeneutics*:

Diatopical hermeneutics is based on the idea that the *topoi* of a given culture, no matter how strong they may be, are as incomplete as the culture itself to which they belong. Such incompleteness is not visible from inside the culture itself, since aspiration to the totality induces taking the parts for the whole. The objective of diatopical hermeneutics is not, however, to achieve completeness – an unattainable objective – but, on the contrary, to raise the consciousness of mutual incompleteness to the maximum degree through a dialogue that unfolds, so to speak, with one foot in one culture and the other in another. In this resides its *dia-topical* character.[44]

It is worth emphasizing two points here. The first is the explicit recognition that the diatopical hermeneutic, one of the instruments of the creation of a radically democratic society, is not capable of bringing any culture to its completeness, because this horizon that orients intercultural dialogue is not attainable, it is a utopia. For this reason, the realizable objective of the proposal of the diatopical hermeneutic is not the search for completeness, but paradoxically to raise to the maximum degree the consciousness of incompleteness. This objective of maximizing, and not in a perfect or total way, the consciousness of incompleteness goes against the tendency of any culture aspiring to totality. Conservative utopias are exactly those that promise to realize fully this aspiration of cultures to totality. In this sense, the objective of the diatopical hermeneutic is coherent with the notion of a critical utopia.

Beyond that, another characteristic of this novelty is that the line articulating the relation between the empirical and the utopian is not an institutional model or a social relation objectified by institutional systems. This is the second point. The utopia of the total market is a projection from the standpoint of merchant relations, just as the utopia of perfect planning in the economic and social life of the old Soviet Union was a transcendental projection from the standpoint of the control and planning of the Party and of the State over the economy and society. In this new, critical utopia, the articulating line and the experience from which this utopia is projected is the dialogical relation between the different, a relation between human subjects who recognize each other as human beings beyond the social roles and identities within their own cultures.[45]

Along the same lines, Walter Mignolo sets out a beautiful utopian image: 'Love is the necessary corrective to the violence of systems of control and oppression; bilanguaging love is the final utopic horizon for the liberation of human beings involved in structures of domination and subordination beyond their control.'[46] Bilanguaging refers to 'thinking in between languages' and so also cultures.[47] It is a 'way of life between languages: a dialogical, ethic, aesthetic, and political process of social transformation'.[48]

In referring to this dialogical process, Mignolo makes explicit reference to the 'dialogical thinking' explored by Paulo Freire.[49] For Freire, a dialogue is a meeting of two human beings who recognize themselves as incomplete, mediated by the world, to understand and transform the world. The dialogue, therefore, is not exhausted in the I–you relation; it is not the mere exchange of ideas. 'The domination implicit in the dialogue is that of the world by the dialoguers; it is conquest of the world for the liberation of humankind.'[50] And for this dialogue to be possible, Freire insists, several elements are necessary: a profound love for the world and all human beings, humility, and 'an intense faith in humankind, faith in their power to make and remake, to create and re-create, faith in their vocation to be more fully human'.[51] For him, 'founding itself upon love, humility, and faith, dialogue becomes a horizontal relationship of which mutual trust between the dialoguers is the logical consequence'.[52]

Mignolo says that this dialogical thinking of Paul Freire allows for the exploration of liminal thinking – a thinking that tries to overcome the distinction between that which knows and the subject/object that is known and to describe the two sides of the frontier from an exteriority (in the sense of Levinas) – on another level:

His dialogical thinking is more than an analytical concept: it is also a means for action and liberation. Liberation from what? one may ask. From social and economic oppression, but also and mainly as intellectual decolonization: not the universal emancipation of 'them,' in the Enlightenment project, but its complement, 'liberation' from coloniality, the darker side of modernity. . . . Freire talks about thinking *with* instead of thinking *for* or thinking *about* people.[53]

This way of thinking about utopia is in line with what Hinkelammert has called the 'transcendental imagination'. He draws a distinction between transcendental concepts and the transcendental imagination. Transcendental concepts 'begin with the objective social relations between subjects and take them to the limits of concepts of institutional perfection'. Transcendental imagination, in contrast, 'begins with the effectively experienced mutual recognition between subjects, [and] transcendentalizes them in a situation of perfection. In the face of the rigidity of the perfect institutions there appears the fluidity of great joy'.[54] Transcendental concepts, therefore, always have a conservative character because of preserving and taking to perfection the existing institutions or the institutions created to try to transform the society. In this way they always subject human beings to these 'perfect' institutions. The transcendental imagination, in contrast, is critical through its placing of human subjectivity at the core of what is possible, which, in turn, relativizes institutions. This utopian imagination emerges from the vision that the world can be qualitatively different, that relations between human beings are always beyond the limits of institutions and the laws of society. This vision, which emerges from alternative concrete experiences, brings with it what the biblical tradition calls a revelation.

While speaking of the transcendental imagination or critical alternative utopia, we need to pick up an issue that has been postponed to this point: the danger or temptation of the transcendental illusion, which turns critical utopias into conservative and sacrificial utopias. When the path of dialogue, respect for the other, and radical democracy is proposed, we need a transcendental notion of 'dialogue, mutual respect, and perfect democracy' so that we can attempt to approximate it. Yet this utopia also transcends our human condition and, therefore, historical possibilities. Here we again return to, and must continue to return to, the problem of the relation between the transcendental utopian horizon and historical concrete projects.

Leonardo Boff, in an article published in the 2009 edition of *World Latin American Agenda*,[55] says that, in order for us to overcome the impasse that the current model of globalization has imposed on the system of life on our planet, we must revive the socialist project. He writes: 'Not in the sense of a socialist utopia, in the sense of something limited to an unforeseeable future. Rather it is a resurgence of a project that can already be realized now in history.'[56] And he describes this project as a society where the notion of 'we' is at the centre of social life, rather than the individual or 'me', and where the economic project serves the social and ecological project for the sustaining of all life. Therefore, 'the economy should be subject to the political and the political should be subject to the ethics of solidarity and the participation of the greatest number of persons possible'.[57]

If the economy must be subordinated to politics and politics to the ethics of solidarity, this means that the economy, even in the new society, will not automatically be linked with the politics of the state, or any other institution that could be its substitute, or with the ethics of solidarity. That supposes some form of control and directing of the economy and even of politics. That is, it presupposes institutional mechanisms of restriction, control, and direction. Therefore, Boff adds that 'understanding this, socialism represents the radical realization of democracy'. Yet, in characterizing what he means by this radical realization of democracy, he says:

It is a democracy without end, as expressed by the Portuguese thinker Boaventura de Sousa Santos: a participative democracy, not only representative or delegative; a democracy alive in the family, in the community, in social organizations and in the formation of the State.[58]

We are not going to discuss here whether or not Boff's notion of 'a democracy without end', which would involve the life of the family up to the state, is the same as that of Santos, but rather the subjects of realizability and transcendence. Is a democracy 'without end' (without limit) possible within history? Boff asserts that it is possible to realize in all aspects of human life (from the family up to global relations) this democracy through putting into practice what he says is the ancestral ideal behind democracy: 'whatever is of interest to all should be debated and decided by all. Thus, democracy is the active participation of everyone in all areas of life'.[59]

This idea of democracy presupposes that every person has an understanding of the things that are of his or her interest. However, since we live in a globalized world and, as ecological thinkers never cease to remind us, everything is interconnected, this means that every person should have an understanding of every subject and participate in the decisions concerning all that happens in the world. That is obviously impossible. This apparent mixture of what is a historical project, which can be realized now within history, and what are ideal values that are behind and orient the construction of the project creates or can create a theoretical confusion. And, more importantly, it can create a great difficulty that can cause serious mistakes in the formulation of action strategies. That leads us to the question of how to translate or operationalize this transcendental ideal into what he calls the ideal democracy and, especially, within the possibilities of real democracies.

To advance our reflection, it is important to distinguish the two types of utopian ideals that appeared in our reflection on the utopia of the WSF that we saw above and that are also present in Boff's thinking: diatopical hermeneutics, which presupposes dialogue and mutual respect, and 'perfect' democracy.

The ideals of 'perfect' dialogue and mutual respect as transcendental horizons for constructing and living in a society based on diversity and plurality are ideals that pertain to the realm of transcendental imagination. Dialogue and full respect are projections of social relations between human subjects that are recognized as such, beyond social roles or cultural identities. This type of utopia brings with it a 'defence mechanism' – which is also never completed – against the temptations of authoritarianism, the imposition of unanimity, or sacrificialism. When thinking in terms of a total market society, the path is that of the imposition, in the name of this utopia, of mercantile relations for all the aspects and spheres of social life and to deny all forms of intervention or control on the part of the state or society. That also takes place, with proper adaptations, under the utopias of total planning. But when the utopian objective is that of dialogue and respect, it is not possible to impose them in an authoritarian way, since that can be shown clearly to be in contradiction with the utopian proposal itself. Therefore, it is important to distinguish social utopias that emerge from the transcendental imagination from those that emerge from transcendental concepts.

Ivone Gebara, in her text 'Rethinking Socialism in Light of New Practices', also published in the 2009 edition of *World Latin American Agenda,* instead of discussing the new definition of socialism or a new ideal model of society, wants

> to express intuitions originating in the lives of some groups that move in Latin America. . . . The point of departure and the criteria that orient these intuitions is the life of persons, the sense of daily life with its necessities and demands more or less satisfied.[60]

She explicitly assumes the line of argument that Hinkelammert labels the transcendental imagination.

She begins with a crucial question: 'In the midst of disillusionment with revolutionary theories or the promises of their governments, in the midst of the crisis of the parties and unions, and in the midst of the alienation growing in churches' what continues to mobilize different groups to continue in the struggle?[61] She finds an answer in her contacts with these groups.

> The source of the struggle is in the unbearable pain of hunger, of the lack of land, of aggression, of invisibility, of multiple forms of violence. The source is also this kind of instinct for survival, instinct for human dignity, for mutual collaboration, for love of life simply because it is our life.[62]

Her transcendental imagination is that of a world where hunger is satisfied by good food and the human dignity of all peoples is fully recognized and experienced in life and in mutual collaboration, and where life is loved.

It is worth pointing out here that the transcendental imagination expressed by Gebara links, in line with significant sectors of liberation theology, the notion of *praxis* – whose structure is determined by inter-subjective action – and the notion of *poiesis* – whose action aims at a product. Gebara begins with the concrete lives of poor persons and therefore does not forget hunger, that of the body that asks for food, and also for dignity denied. The body, therefore, with its needs and desires, is at the centre of her transcendental imagination. Here the evil is not the hunger but the impossibility of satisfying that hunger with good food. Good food (*poiesis*) and friends (*praxis*) to eat with are two basic things for living well. It is an image that reminds of us the 'celestial banquet' or God's Kingdom announced by Jesus. As Vitor Westhelle says, '*praxis* or *poiesis* become distorted when isolated from each other. *Poiesis* without *praxis* is blind and enslaving – lacks solidarity, love; *praxis* without *poiesis* is empty activism – lacks novelty, promise, and hope'.[63]

In the discussion concerning an alternative form to capitalism for organizing society, Gebara does not accept our current pre-established definitions of socialism because they perpetuate hierarchies and most of the time are useless and bureaucratic. Therefore, she seeks a new notion of socialism – or whatever becomes the label of a new model of society – that breaks with the over-institutionalized notions that suffocate persons and groups. Using her transcendental imagination as the criterion of interpretation, she says:

> If socialism signifies the concrete possibility of autonomy, discussion, decentralization, and diminution of bureaucracies . . . then this is the socialism that is emerging slowly in our midst. If socialism is the daily struggle against the perversity of the actual economic system managed by world elites, we can say that something is brewing in us. If socialism is the affirmation of human dignity – feminine and masculine in its diversity – then something is occurring in our midst, over time and in many places.[64]

She sees in these facts signs of the realization, even though partial and provisional, of this utopia. This is why she interprets reality on the basis of this imagination and in this way sees and evaluates the facts. Those who think from a utopia centred in some institution – whether the market or the state – cannot see these relations for what they are and, therefore, cannot recognize the value of these facts and relations.

In the words of Boaventura de Sousa Santos, having to do with the sociology of absences and emergences:

> Whereas the goal of the sociology of absences is to identify and valorize social experiences available in the world, although declared nonexistent by hegemonic rationality and knowledge, the sociology of emergences aims to identify and enlarge the signs of possible future experiences, under the guise of tendencies and latencies that are actively ignored by hegemonic rationality and knowledge.[65]

Gebara's beautiful transcendental imagination does not take the illusory path of denying all institutional mediations and constructing a world without relations of power or without a state. She critiques the way in which states have privileged the elite to the detriment of the poorest and proposes the collective construction of a state that 'should be the executor of the common good, the facilitator through which different groups get that which they need to survive'.[66]

A transcendental imagination that does not lose touch with reality and the human condition leads necessarily to the discussion of the institutional mediations necessary for the construction of a more human and just world: that is, the necessity of institutions emerging from human contingency itself. Insofar as we are mortal, free beings – not fully determined by genetics and instincts – and do not have perfect knowledge of reality and the consequences of our actions, the social order cannot be spontaneous. We require the institutionalization of social relations so that our social life and also social changes are possible. We can and must discuss which types of institutions or relations of human beings with the institutions are necessary, but the institutionalization is inevitable.

Therefore, the utopia of the WSF speaks of dialogue, diversity, plurality, and also democracy. Dialogue and mutual respect refer to the realm of inter-subjective relations, but it is also necessary to think about the new institutional structures of the new society and of the transition phase, which must be radically democratic. The challenge is in conceiving ideally what is radically democratic in order, from this transcendental concept, to elaborate strategic actions in the fields of politics and culture. Santos writes that

> the newness of this utopia in left thinking in western capitalist modernity . . . cannot but be problematical as it translates itself into strategic planning and political action. These are marked by the historical trajectory of the political left throughout the twentieth

century. The translation of utopia into politics is not, in this case, merely the translation of the new into the old. The tensions and divisions brought about by this are no less real for that reason.[67]

We would add that, besides these two challenges, there is another fundamental question: the dialectical tension between the utopia and the political project and strategies. As we have seen, social utopias are conceived as perfect societies, and the transcendental imaginations envision spontaneous social relations; whereas political projects are imperfect, relative, provisional, and, more importantly here, institutional. In other words, a political project is, by its very nature, contradictory in relation to the transcendental imagination of free and spontaneous relations. Between the critical utopia and the alternative political project there is a dialectical contradiction. The two must not be confused or mixed, but nor should they be totally identified or separated. The contradiction between them is not of the type of metaphysical negation in which it is necessary to opt for one and deny the other; rather, it is a dialectical contradiction where the utopia is set against the project just as the project is counterposed with the utopia. One cannot exist without the other if we want it to be a critical thought and a truly alternative project.

We can find this characteristic of a critical thought in an affirmation of Santos concerning the alternative thought on alternatives:

The first principle is that it is not enough to think of alternatives, since modern thought on alternatives has proven extremely vulnerable to trivialization, whether because the alternatives are unrealistic and discredited for being utopian, or because they are realistic and, for that reason, easily co-opted by those whose interests would be negatively affected by them. We need, therefore, an alternative thought on alternatives.[68]

He criticizes two types of alternative, which are found on opposite sides of the dialectic tension to which we pointed above. One type of alternative is that which is limited to imagining or thinking about the utopia, without preparing projects for its realization. Santos says that this leads to two problems. The first is a lack of action. Aspiring to something impossible or believing that it is possible to achieve what is impossible does not enable strategic thought or concrete action. These groups are reduced to making radical critiques that are incapable of generating real transformative actions. The second problem is that of being discredited for being unrealistic, 'discredited for being utopian'

– Santos here uses the term utopian in the popular pejorative sense. It is a characteristic of utopia to be 'unrealistic' in the sense of unrealizable within historical reality. The problem, therefore, is not being 'utopian' or unrealistic, but that this alternative contents itself with being that only.

The second type of alternative that Santos criticizes is that which is too realistic, without any tension in relation to the alternative utopia. Since it is not possible to prepare a strategic action without a utopia as its backdrop, both to orient it and serve as a criterion of interpretation and evaluation, to have an alternative proposal without an alternative utopia is to signify that the proposal falls within the categorical boundaries of the utopia of the dominant system. From this follows his observation that realistic alternatives are easily co-opted by the dominant system.

The way out of this impasse is to maintain a dialectic tension between the alternative utopia and alternative strategic projects and actions. Only in this way will the utopia not lead to naïvety and paralysis, and the feasible projects not be co-opted. The utopia must always criticize the strategic projects and actions so that they are not converted into conservative, authoritarian, and hierarchical systems, just as the projects and actions need to criticize the utopia so that it is not turned into a naïve and unreal proposal.

The transcendental concept that emerges from this observation is that of a 'perfect dialectical tension' between the utopian pole and the project/institution pole. Therefore, what we now seek is no longer the harmony of the fullness of society, which denies at the foundation the diversity and plurality of incommensurable cultures, but the maintenance of a tension in an 'optimal' situation – the best possible within human and historical means – that favours and produces creativity and a spirit of struggle that is always striving to overcome the situations of marginalization and oppression that will appear.

From this principle it is necessary to search for a formulation and a construction of an alternative state model. Santos, for example, proposes the notion of an experimental state, which

> must not only guarantee equality of opportunities to the various projects of democratic institutionalization, but also ... basic standards of inclusion, which make possible the active citizenship necessary for observing, verifying, and assessing the performance of alternative projects. These minimum standards of inclusion are indispensable for transforming the institutional instability within the sphere of democratic deliberation.[69]

It is important to highlight here that in the dialectical tension between the utopia and the socio-political project, which will never be perfect, the dominant pole must be the utopia formulated from the transcendental imagination. Only in this way can we 'control' the tendency of institutions, in the name of their transcendental concepts and the transcendental illusion, to absolutize themselves and pursue their own perpetuation, with the reproduction of hierarchies and bureaucracies that attend only or primarily to their elites.

Transcendental imagination and the option for the poor

In the course of this chapter we have seen how utopia is transcendental in the double sense that it is a condition of possibility for our thinking and acting in the world and that its full realization is beyond human possibilities. We have also seen that, especially in the social realm, we have a tendency to succumb to the transcendental illusion of believing that it is possible with our finite actions to achieve the fullness of utopia. In other words, we have difficulty in accepting the limits of the human condition and of history that do not allow us to realize our better desires and dreams. Therefore, in order that our critical utopias do not end up being transformed into conservative and sacrificial utopias, we need to recognize theoretically and existentially the insurmountable dialectical tension between utopia and realizable projects, which emerges from our condition and our limits.

This recognition of the limits of the human condition and of history is basic to preventing our succumbing to the temptations of the spirit of Empire. As we saw in the previous chapter, the heart of the spirit of Empire is a sacrificial theology that demands and justifies human suffering in the name of the realization of impossible desires and objectives through submission to an institution falsely transcendentalized. The best form of resisting this sacrificial logic/theology that converts human suffering into beneficial sacrifices is to recognize that it is beyond the human condition and impossible within history. There is no human institution capable of fully realizing that which is humanly and historically impossible. Moreover, there also is no god or divinities – which, in the end, are all imaginary or transcendental human concepts – that can realize within history that which transcends the limits of history. And, therefore, no sacrifice is justified in the name of its realization. To recognize limits is something healthy, as much in the personal realm as the social.

When we treated above the types of limit of realizability, we spoke of the existence, at least in theory, of an intermediate space between that which is humanly possible and the limit of logical contradiction: the space in which we can think about transcendental concepts and the transcendental imagination. This space is the space of mythical thought, of the mythical dimension of reason and also of theology.

To avoid misunderstanding, however, we want to reaffirm here that this 'realm' where one 'locates' transcendental concepts and the transcendental imagination is not a geographical space that is found outside the world or after history. The transcendental imagination of a society free of oppression and alienation transcends history, but at the same time it is within history as a criterion of interpretation and judgment, like a horizon that allows us to see and to evaluate the reality that the dominant rationality cannot see and does not allow to be seen. Moreover, it is within our human and social reality as a force that motivates people to struggle for a more human society. Beyond this, it is also present as an 'anticipatory sign', as a provisional reality, or, as Gebara says, as something 'brewing in us', in the human and social struggles and relations where the persons are mutually respectful and live a dignified life.

The idea of *anticipation* goes beyond that of resistance, since resistance, in spite of being basic in oppressive situations, in itself does not manage to point to the new. In resistance, the battle issues are dictated by the Empire. To live in anticipation is a capacity to go beyond the logic of the Empire, experiencing in advance the future that can surprise us, which enables us to build and raise questions and issues in confrontation with the impositions of the Empire.

However, for the construction of a notion of utopia and transcendence that guides us in the construction of a more human society, consciousness of limits is not enough. Persons with good theoretical formations and a sense of reality recognize the limits of the human condition and the impossibility, for example, of perfect knowledge, and the intrinsically relative and contradictory character of all institutions. The mega-investor/speculator George Soros, for example, defends the theory that, in spite of its deficiencies, capitalism is better than any alternative. And in his struggle to avoid the self-destruction of capitalism, threatened by what he calls market fundamentalism, he proposes the concept of open society: 'Open society is based on the recognition that our understanding is imperfect and our actions have unintended consequences', and that 'all our institutional arrangements are liable to be flawed'; therefore, 'we should create institutions with error-correcting mechanisms built in. These mechanisms include both markets and democracy. But neither will work unless we are aware of our fallibility and willing to recognize our mistakes.'[70] These ideas do not fall into the transcendental illusion.

The recognition of the limits of the human condition and the dialectical contradiction between utopia and institutional projects is a necessary step but is not sufficient for our purpose. A critical and humanizing utopia must emerge from the transcendental imagination that is rooted in the sufferings, struggles, and life of the poor, marginalized, and/or oppressed. It is this that guarantees real transcendence in relation to the dominant system and its utopia. Soros recognizes the limits of knowledge and institutions and, in the name of fallibilism, says that 'nobody is in possession of the ultimate truth',[71] but also affirms that capitalism is better than any possible alternative, making a definitive affirmation. His inability to see the radical relativity of capitalism has to do with the fact that he looks at the world from the standpoint of capitalism, which, like every culture, aspires to totality. And as we saw before, in treating the diatopical hermeneutics proposed by Santos, the incompleteness of a culture or social system is not visible from within that culture – it is only visible from outside the system. Moreover, exteriority does not signify only a geographical place but the location of subalternity and marginalization. Or, as Mignolo says, 'to describe in "reality" both sides of the border is not the problem. The problem is to do it from its exteriority (in Levinas's sense)'.[72] In the citations of Gebara's text above, this place where the dominant system is criticized and the new imagined is clear.

Recognizing limits, not from an apparently neutral theoretical position, but from the standpoint of the suffering of the most poor and oppressed, of those excluded by the dominant system, is a central question in the preparation of the transcendental imagination and of a critical and humanizing utopia. Because, while Empire tries to silence the outcries of the poor and oppressed – those sacrificed in the name of its pretension to achieve its fullness and totality – these outcries are precisely what break with the imposed unanimity, challenge the conscience of those integrated into the system, and open spaces for the new to take root.

Solidarity, which is born of compassion for the concrete persons who suffer with poverty and/or the violation of their human dignity, leads us to assume with these persons – in dialogue with them – the struggle for their liberation. In this struggle emerges the transcendental imagination of a society where all bodies are satisfied of hunger and other rights and coexist in friendship, respecting diversity and plurality. This imagination serves for the interpretation of reality and the struggle, and provides a foundation for the faith that moves us in the struggle.

But the empirical reality demonstrates to us that there are limits of the human condition, limits of the objective conditions of history, as well as technical limits and those imposed by the system in which we live. While we walk, fight, and live, we can come to see that, in spite of these limits – some surmounted, others insurmountable – we are already, in some way, living our utopia. It is ahead of us and, like a horizon that provides meaning, also moves further ahead as we move toward it; but its values and its reality are already being lived here and now, as a transcendence inside real and concrete life.

In the language of the biblical–Christian tradition, we can say that God's Kingdom – our transcendental imagination, in religious language – is within us (see Luke 17.21), at the same time in which it faces us as the utopian horizon on which we bet our lives (faith), and as an object of hope. If God's reign occurs within us because we become more human in mutual love, solidarity, dialogue, and respect, we can say that God is within us. As it says in the first letter of John, 'No one has ever seen God; but if we love one another, God lives in us and his love is made complete in us' (1 John 4.12).

The utopian horizon of the fullness of God's Kingdom as an object of hope leads us back to the space that exists between what it is humanly possible and what can be thought. Here the scene is entered by the hope that God, who raised Jesus – according to the Christian tradition – will bring about the plenitude that we live as anticipation, that we merely glimpse within history. It is nothing more than hope and faith, since certainty would be to deny the transcendental character that we have explored. Theological reflection gains relevance here, not only to affirm the possibility of God transforming this land and this world into a land without death and setting forth a 'banquet' for all but also to reveal the presence of the processes of humanization, of God's Kingdom, in the world, a presence that the theories and imperial theologies do not manage to see or allow to be seen.

In the work of unmasking and criticizing the spirit of Empire and its sacrificialism – a task that, as we have seen, can only be realized to the extent that it is countered by a critical and humanizing utopia, one elaborated in a transcendental imagination emerging in dialogue and solidarity with the sufferings and struggles of the poor and of all the victims of Empire – the recovery of that which is essential to the Christian tradition becomes relevant. Hugo Assmann, one of the premier and principal liberation theologians, summarizes it this way:

The essential newness of the Christian message, precisely because it tries to introduce all-inclusive fraternal love into history, consists in the central affirmation: the victims are innocent and no excuse or pretext makes their victimization justifiable. No projection of culpability or blameworthiness onto the victim is acceptable as justification for his being 'sacrificed'.[73]

And 'the innocence of the victim, as the central element of the Christian faith, imposes on us a link of solidarity with all the victims around us. This is the essential meaning of the famous "preferential option for the poor".'[74]

Notes

1 Alain Badiou, 2008, 'The Communist Hypothesis', *New Left Review* 49 (January/February 2008), p. 37.

2 Badiou, 'Communist Hypothesis', pp. 34–5.

3 Badiou, 'Communist Hypothesis', p. 35.

4 Francis Fukuyama, *Our Posthuman Future: Consequences of the Biotechnology Revolution*, New York: Picador, 2003, p. 15.

5 Badiou, 'Communist Hypothesis', p. 37.

6 Badiou, 'Communist Hypothesis', p. 35.

7 Badiou, 'Communist Hypothesis', p. 36.

8 Agnes Heller, *The Theory of Need in Marx*, London: Allison & Busby, 1978, p. 130, italics added.

9 Hugo Assmann, *Crítica à lógica da exclusão: ensaios sobre economia e teologia*, São Paulo: Paulus, 1994, p. 31.

10 Assmann, *Crítica*, p. 34.

11 Heller, *Theory of Need*, p. 130.

12 Wladyslaw Bienkowski, *Theory and Reality: The Development of Social Systems*, London: Allison & Busby, 1981, p. 177.

13 Alec Nove, *The Economics of Feasible Socialism Revisited*, 2nd edition, London: Allen and Unwin, 1991, p. 239.

14 Nove, *Economics*, p. 239, italics added.

15 Nove, *Economics*, p. 239.

16 See Georg W. F. Hegel, *The Encyclopaedia Logic: Part 1 of the Encyclopaedia of Philosophical Sciences*, trans. T. F. Garaets, W. A. Suchting, and H. S. Harris, Indianapolis: Hackett, 1991, §94; and Franz J. Hinkelammert, *Crítica de la razón utópica*, revised and extended edition, Bilbao: Desclée, 2002.

17 Slavoj Žižek, 'The Ambiguous Legacy of '68', *In These Times* (20 June 2008), available at http://www.inthesetimes.com/article/3751/the_ambiguous_legacy_of_68/.

18 Žižek, 'Ambiguous Legacy'.

19 Melvin Lasky, *Utopia and Revolution: On the Origins of a Metaphor*, Chicago: University of Chicago Press, 1976.

20 Boaventura de Sousa Santos, 'The World Social Forum: A Counter-Hegemonic Globalization', available at http://www.duke.edu/~wmignolo/publications/pubboa.html.

21 Ernst Mayr, *This is Biology: The Science of the Living World*, Cambridge, MA: Belknap Press, 1979, p. 79, italics original.

22 Mayr, *This is Biology*, pp. 80–1.

23 Mayr, *This is Biology*, p. 106.

24 Hinkelammert, *Crítica de la razón utópica*, p. 135.

25 Slavoj Žižek, *The Fragile Absolute: Or, Why is the Christian Legacy Worth Fighting For?*, New York: Verso, 2000, p. 17.

26 Žižek, *Fragile Absolute*, p. 17.

27 Žižek, *Fragile Absolute*, p. 17.

28 Žižek, *Fragile Absolute*, p. 18, italics original.

29 Celso Furtado, *Accumulation and Development: The Logic of Industrial Civilization*, trans. Suzette Macedo, New York: St. Martin's Press, 1983, p. 54.

30 Furtado, *Accumulation*, p. 76.

31 Žižek, *Fragile Absolute*, p. 19.

32 Žižek, *Fragile Absolute*, pp. 19–20, italics original.

33 Franz J. Hinkelammert, *The Ideological Weapons of Death*, Maryknoll, NY: Orbis, 1986, p. 53.

34 Hinkelammert, *Weapons of Death*, p. 58.

35 Homi K. Bhabha, *The Location of Culture*, New York: Routledge, 1994, p. 19.

36 The first edition of this book was published in 1984 in Costa Rica, where he lives, as *Crítica a la razón utópica*. A revised edition was published in 2002, in Spain, as *Crítica de la razón utópica*.

37 Hinkelammert, *Crítica de la razón utópica*, p. 14.

38 Hinkelammert, *Crítica de la razón utópica*, p. 15.

39 Hinkelammert, *Crítica de la razón utópica*, p. 388.

40 Boaventura de Sousa Santos, *A gramática do tempo: para uma nova cultura política*, São Paulo: Cortez, 2006, p. 417.

41 For a more systemic critique of how Soviet thought transformed critical Marxist utopia into a conservative, or sacrificial, utopia, see Hinkelammert, *Crítica de la razón utópica*, Chapter 5.

42 Santos, *A gramática do tempo*, pp. 417–18.

43 Santos, 'The World Social Forum', p. 89.

44 Santos, *A gramática da tempo*, p. 448, italics added.

45 On this subject–subject relation beyond social roles see, for example, Jung Mo Sung, *Sujeto y sociedades complejas*, San José, Costa Rica: Editorial DEI, 2005, Chapter 3.

46 Walter Mignolo, *Local Histories/Global Designs: Coloniality, Subaltern Knowledges, and Border Thinking*, Princeton: Princeton University Press, 2000, p. 273.

47 Mignolo, *Local Histories*, p. 250.

48 Mignolo, *Local Histories*, p. 265.

49 Mignolo, *Local Histories*, pp. 265–6.

50 Paulo Freire, *Pedagogy of the Oppressed*, 30th anniversary edition, New York: Continuum, 2000, p. 89.

51 Freire, *Pedagogy*, p. 90.

52 Freire, *Pedagogy*, p. 91.

53 Mignolo, *Local Histories*, p. 265, italics original.

54 Hinkelammert, *Crítica de la razón utópica*, p. 343.

55 *World Latin American Agenda* is a publication distributed throughout Latin America. It is available in several languages, including Spanish, Portuguese, English, French, and Italian, and includes articles by theologians and social scientists who are opposed to the present model of capitalist globalization. Dom Pedro Casaldáliga and José Maria Virgil are the editors. The theme for the 2009 edition is 'Towards a New Socialism: Utopia Continues'. The English edition is available at http://latinoamericana.org/English/2009LatinAmericanAgenda.pdf.

56 Leonardo Boff, 'Ecology and Socialism', *World Latin American Agenda 2009*, 2009, p. 42.

57 Boff, 'Ecology', pp. 42–3.

58 Boff, 'Ecology', p. 43.

59 Boff, 'Ecology', p. 43.

60 Ivone Gebara, 'Rethinking Socialism in Light of New Practices', *World Latin American Agenda 2009*, 2009, p. 32.

61 Gebara, 'Rethinking Socialism'.

62 Gebara, 'Rethinking Socialism'.

63 Vítor Westhelle, *The Scandalous God: The Use and Abuse of the Scandalous God*, Minneapolis, MN: Fortress Press, 2006, p. 130.

64 Gebara, 'Rethinking Socialism', p. 33.

65 Santos, 'The World Social Forum', p. 24.

66 Gebara, 'Rethinking Socialism', p. 32.

67 Santos, 'The World Social Forum', p. 89.

68 Santos, *A gramática do tempo*, p. 338.

69 Santos, *A gramática do tempo*, p. 375.

70 George Soros, *The Crisis of Global Capitalism: Open Society Endangered*, New York: Public Affairs, 1998, p. xxix.

71 Soros, *Crisis*, p. 4.

72 Mignolo, *Local Histories*, p. 18.

73 Hugo Assmann, 'The Strange Imputation of Violence to Liberation Theology', *Terrorism and Political Violence*, 3.4 (Winter 1991), pp. 84–5.

74 Assmann, 'Strange Imputation', p. 86.

Rieger

5

Towards an Alternative Subjectivity
in the Midst of Empire

In Chapter 2 we argued that empires shape not only political and economic structures but cultural, intellectual, religions, and personal realities as well. Based on that insight, we need to deal with an often-overlooked factor in contemporary debates about producing resistance and alternatives to Empire: the role of desire and with it the place of the subject. Those who seek to resist Empire tend to develop political or ethical strategies that proceed without much awareness of the power of the unconscious, where our desires are rooted. In Christian circles in the United States in particular, resistance against Empire is often seen as a conscious rejection that requires personal commitment, resolve, and a strong will. More subtle thinkers point out that resolve is not enough and that we need to form habits, which come from inhabiting particular traditions. Forgotten, however, is Paul's insight in his letter to the Romans of the self's tensions and struggles: 'For I do not do what I want, but I do the very thing I hate' (Rom. 7.15). The notion of desire reminds us that, as Sigmund Freud pointed out, we are not master in our own house. The self is not in control, and not even a strong will can always be trusted. Even the formation of habits is not necessarily strong enough to resist the maelstrom of desire set in motion by the temptations of Empire.

Subjectivity under the conditions of Empire is, as we have seen, controlled on many levels. Economic and political conditions in the Empire leave little space for the formation of an independent subjectivity, but the pressures go much deeper, since subjectivity is being actively colonized at the level of the cultural, the emotional, and even the spiritual. In this context, those on top can happily encourage others to take things into their own hands – to become active subjects, in other words – without having to be too worried that this will ever become a reality. Just the opposite: encouraging others to become active subjects in this context reinforces the myth that the powerful have gained power by becoming active subjects themselves and results in putting blame on all others who fail.

The good news, however, is that, despite all its efforts, Empire is never able to control and co-opt subjectivity and desire totally and absolutely. A first sense that subjectivity cannot be co-opted grows entirely out of an observation of the ambivalence of the status quo. The Empire's power and influence may be substantial and all-encompassing, but are never absolute, never without ambivalence.[1] Even subjectivity that has seemingly been erased by Empire keeps erupting, at times in unexpected places. It is a significant datum of history that even slaves – people who were not supposed to have any subjectivity at all – were able to reassert their subjectivity, rise up, and challenge the Empire. The Judaeo-Christian traditions are founded on such a slave uprising in the Exodus and on many other stories of resistance by people who were considered lacking subjectivity in the ancient world.

Subjectivity and desire can thus become sites of resistance to Empire. As Hardt and Negri programmatically state: 'Revolutionary realism produces and reproduces the becoming and proliferation of desire.'[2] Desire is a complex reality: it is not merely the desire for things or people but, as Lacan pointed out, it is fundamentally the 'desire of the desire of the other'. This leads us beyond moralism or naïve activism. It also leads us beyond the impasse of traditional identity politics that is based on seemingly 'natural' features such as race, gender, or ethnicity.[3] Furthermore, there is a religious component in these insights, expressed by Jung Mo Sung: 'To speak of change in desire is to approach the field of spirituality . . . These are fundamental theological questions. It falls to theology to give its contribution to this debate that is happening on diverse levels around the world.'[4]

Clearly, Empire is worried about what from its perspective might look like residual subjectivity, that is, subjectivity that has not yet been driven out. As a result, Empire constantly increases the dose of its control over subjectivity. But what we are dealing with here is more than just residual subjectivity. We are not just talking about remainders of subjectivity that have not yet been blotted out. We are talking about the emergence of another kind of subjectivity, which presents us with real alternatives. Not even the subtlest efforts to do away with people's subjectivity – including postmodern efforts to 'flatten' the self – have been successful in erasing it, as we shall see.

Foucault agrees

Another short history of subjectivity

Whether human subjectivity and desire have been subdued by force and direct repression or by more subtle efforts, Empire has never been able to exercise complete control. The history of early Christianity exemplifies this. The Apostle Paul talks about his own struggles in terms of what we might call subject formation in Romans 7. The fact that he uses the image of a struggle is of particular relevance. Why should there even have been a struggle if there were a clear line between two worlds, and if Paul had his divine marching orders and knew what to do? For some reason, Paul's own subjectivity and thus his agency is under attack: 'For I do not do the good I want, but the evil I do not want is what I do' (Rom. 7.20). This attack is not a one-time event only but refers to an ongoing struggle with evil that 'lies close at hand' (Rom. 7.21). Nevertheless, Paul does not give in, and thus the struggle for subjectivity continues. In Paul's experience, as those who endure the strongest attacks of evil are empowered by the divine (traditionally called 'election'), something happens that destroys dominant forms of subjectivity but does not leave them without an alternative: 'God chose what is low and despised in the world, things that are not, to reduce to nothing things that are' (1 Cor. 1.28). This points to an alternative source of agency, which, in turn, points to an alternative subjectivity, formed in a struggle against the status quo.

note to quote

The life and work of Bartolomé de Las Casas during the Spanish Conquest provides another example. While Las Casas was not able to escape a colonialist mindset completely – a colonialism, to be sure, that was far less severe than that of the violence of the Spanish conquest, which he resisted – he nevertheless represented an alternative form of subjectivity. This alternative subjectivity is found in the reversal of the roles of the dominant Spanish missionaries at the point where Las Casas relates the suffering and the struggle of the Amerindians to the work of Christ. Rather than identifying Christ's subjectivity and agency with the missionaries alone and thus condoning the subjectivity of those in charge – a common move of Empire then and now – Las Casas develops a growing sense of an alternative subjectivity that, however rudimentary, resists the subjectivity of Empire.[5] For the most part, Las Casas sees this subjectivity/agency of the Amerindians in terms of suffering, but it is the subversive character of this suffering that is of interest to us.

Bartolomé de Las Casas

Even at the time of the rise of nineteenth-century colonialist mentality shades of different subjectivities remained in existence. In some ways we still lag behind some of Friedrich Schleiermacher's deepest insights developed during this time. His rejection of punishment and reward in education is only one example. While postmodern sensitivities have a sense for some of the perennial problems with coercion and punishment – even today a favourite register of Empire – there is also a problem with reward, because it is commonly used by the system to co-opt people, especially in a consumer society where shopping has become a way of 'rewarding oneself'. In this context, Schleiermacher points to the 'spirit of Christ' as an alternative motivation that cannot be co-opted as easily and that prevents people from being turned into machines.[6] The resulting alternative subjectivity deserves a closer look – not because it is necessarily pristine and untouched, as Schleiermacher would have assumed, but because it is the bearer of a resistance factor that can never be totally controlled by the status quo.

Even in a postmodern world there is some hope. While the postmodern emphases on otherness and difference are easily co-opted in late capitalism, as we have seen in Chapter 2, they nevertheless point in the right direction. In this context, the difference between a 'ludic postmodernism' and a 'postmodernism of resistance'[7] still holds. Are recognitions of difference and otherness merely for the sake of entertainment and diversion – by the diversity of different cultures, for instance, by their artistic expressions as well as their cuisines? There are other ways to deal with difference and otherness that pose real challenges to accepted norms of subjectivity. Common romantic ideals of unity in difference are shattered, for instance, when differences are no longer harmless 'both ands'. The difference between the extremely wealthy and the abjectly poor, for instance, which has become a key theological subject in the work of liberation theologians, cannot be integrated into postmodern models of unity in difference. These sorts of differences need to be deconstructed and – dare we say it? – abolished. The alternative subjectivities that need to be taken into account here clearly present challenges to the postmodern Empire's attempts to establish unity in difference in a context of extreme power differentials.

Here, subjectivity can finally be reconstructed in different ways. There is no need to push for a universal model or another totalitarian idea. Just the opposite: out of the challenge to control forms of subjectivity, new possibilities emerge. The motto is 'from each according to their abilities, to each according to their needs' – a phrase commonly attributed to Karl Marx[8] but also rooted in the early Christian traditions:

There was not a needy person among them, for as many as owned lands or houses sold them and brought the proceeds of what was sold. They laid it at the apostles' feet, and it was distributed to each as any had need. (Acts 4.34–5; see also Acts 2.44–5)

We find ourselves in a situation where the subjectivity of the powerful is distorted – they are not really masters in their own house, as they believe – and where the subjectivity of the marginalized has come under attack to the point of erasure. In this situation, however, alternatives emerge from unexpected places – 'from the underside', as classical Latin American liberation theologians would have said. Alternative subjectivities that push beyond the pipe dreams of autonomy and unregulated power emerge under pressure, forged as a by-product of the repressive powers of the status quo. In the following we will take a closer look at how this happens, but Jacques Lacan's notion of *jouissance* – enjoyment, pleasure, joy – points us in the right direction: there is some mysterious energy that is not available to those whose subjectivity is the subjectivity of the status quo. Jung Mo Sung has sensed a similar dynamic, which he expresses thus:

> The subject being is not manifest in the mundane, when we live out our social roles as citizens, spouses, professors, or consumers. The subject being is manifest in resistance to concrete forms of domination, when the individual resists being reduced to a mere social role or set of roles. This is worth as much to those who occupy a high place within the institution as those who are on a lower level. And for that resistance to be able to occur, the person must deny the legitimizing rationalizations produced by institutions.[9]

Being a subject – subjectivity and agency – somehow grows out of resistance against the powers that seek to rob us of our subjectivity.

Alternative subjectivities and Empire today: four responses

Overcoming the automatic subject and the religion of the free market

Just as conventional forms of materialism were not sufficient to explain the automatic subject (see Chapter 2), moving away from material concerns into the realm of the spiritual or a narrow understanding of the religious is not sufficient to produce alternative results; the relationships between these various realities is just too complex, particularly at a time when the forces of the market create subjectivity, which then functions to reinforce the material conditions created by the market. Are there any alternatives left under the conditions of globalization, when the market is reaching ever further into the recesses of the spatial and the political, as well as of the self?

Understanding how economic mechanisms work in the formation of subjectivity is crucial. Nevertheless, since we are dealing with macro-structures there seems to be very little that can be done in order to change things at first sight. There is no one who is not affected by these structures. One of the key insights on the way to an alternative, however, is that people are affected in different ways. Those on the margins have less of a stake in the system. To be more specific, those on the margins of the global economy who are mostly excluded from it – the vast numbers of the unemployed or even the casually employed for whom the economy has little use even as consumers – have no stake in the system, except perhaps when they gather the crumbs that fall from its table. This group of excluded people is very large in the global economy as a whole, and it is growing even in the wealthy countries. There is another vast group, however, of people who are marginalized but on whose shoulders the weight of the economy rests – the workers who produce, who service, and who are essential for the overall movement of the economy. Their subjectivity is much more affected by the system, as we have seen in Chapter 2, but, since they do not reap the majority of the benefits of the system either, there are still limits on how much the system can control them. Once they begin to realize their limited stakes in the system, these workers can begin to push beyond it.

As the mechanisms of the market produce an economic surplus, and in the process determine the subjectivity of all who function within this marketplace (and even those who are excluded, and who are defined in terms of their lack of participation: the *un*-employed, the *in*-digent, the *in*-dolent), another kind of surplus is produced that does not enter economic calculations because it operates on a different plane. Jacques Lacan's notion of surplus enjoyment – discussed in the relation of men and women – points in this direction: in a patriarchal context, Lacan notes, women exist 'only as excluded by the nature of things which is the nature of words'.[10] That is to say, unlike 'man' and other signifiers of privilege, 'woman' is not an ordinary part of the dominant order of things, which Lacan analysed in terms of the dominant language or what he called 'the symbolic order'. Women exist only as repressed from the dominant symbolic order, as displaced by more powerful signifiers. The limited advantage of this position of women is that they are involved in, but not restricted to be, functions of the dominant symbolic order like men. Women participate in what Lacan calls a certain 'surplus-enjoyment', which escapes the authority and control of the formative powers of the symbolic order to a certain degree and grants both a level of independence and a level of energy not available to the status quo.[11] Marx noticed this dynamic in his own way, although we are not aware that he talked about it in these terms. He took note of what happens in the factories of capitalism where the automatic subject is shaped to such an extent that no one can escape it but where, amidst the pressure that the workers have to endure, a new spirit arises – a new kind of subjectivity – that draws on the energy of the system, that makes use of the opportunities for organizing related to the diverse kind of community pulled together on the factory floor, and that cannot be contained by the system forever. This new kind of subjectivity has proven itself, and during the long history of working-class movements progress has been made (the eight-hour workday, health insurance, pension plans, and so on). This odd logic, according to which the 'last will be first, and the first will be last' (Matt. 20.16), is also one of the – perhaps most neglected – core insights of Christianity.

While these gains have been remarkable, the ruling classes have never stopped fighting back, to the point where workers who have gained the freedom to vote in political elections are deprived of the freedom to organize unions in countries such as the United States.[12] Similar dynamics can be observed all over the globe, with the result that factories are shut down and moved to places where workers are less organized and are paid less – a process that today even affects the low-paid factory work of organizations such as the maquiladoras in Mexico when their workers begin to gain a little more influence and status. These efforts to clamp down on workers show the continued efforts to keep people in the state of the 'automatic subject' but, when viewed from the other side, witness to the constant emergence of an alternative subjectivity and agency that cannot be subdued by the system completely. Religion is, of course, part of these processes. In the US, Christianity in particular is often seen as a force that revitalizes workers on Sunday so that they can go back to work refreshed and motivated on Monday. One of the basic pastoral paradigms in this context is to 'meet the needs' of the congregations, giving people what they need to keep functioning in the system. This normalizing function of religion is often overlooked by those who follow Marx's classical definition of religion as the 'opium of the people'. In this context, a search for what Joerg Rieger has called a 'theological surplus' might point in a different direction, as it identifies alternative images of religion and of the divine that is worshipped.[13]

In order to capture this alternative subjectivity and agency, an awareness of class structures is necessary. This is a difficult task in places such as the US, where there is little recognition of the class factor and where most people assume that they are in the middle class. As Theodore W. Allen has shown for the US, there are particular structures and institutions that prevent people from recognizing class as an important factor. Allen points out how race has been used by the ruling classes in this way. The concept of whiteness, Allen's historical studies show, has been deployed since the seventeenth century in order to cover up class identities, so that white workers are led to assume that they have more in common with upper-class whites than with working-class blacks and the workers of other racial minorities. White Supremacy was created in the antebellum South of the United States in order to cover up the vast class differences among whites and thus to prevent poor whites from challenging the system. What separated whites from blacks was simply 'the presumption of liberty',[14] as poor whites were led to consider themselves as free people, no matter how few real freedoms they enjoyed. This is one important reason why the system could not tolerate free blacks.[15] As a result of this situation, the potential of white workers to acquire alternative subjectivity is doubly challenged as their own class identity is actively covered up by the system, which seeks to entangle them in an illusionary identity with the upper classes.

In this situation, the first step towards asserting an alternative subjectivity is the development of some sense of who benefits from the system and who does not. While under the conditions of capitalism all subjectivities are subject to the rules of the market and the flow of money, as we have argued in Chapter 2, not all benefit from the system equally. As relations between people come to resemble more and more closely relations between things that are traded on the market, workers are worse and worse off because all they have is their labour power. The ruling classes, who own large shares of the means of production, on the other hand, have every reason to assume that the system is working in their favour, to the point that they completely identify themselves with the system. The first step to asserting an alternative subjectivity in this situation is an initial sense that not everyone benefits equally and that this system cannot provide a true home for everyone. Religion can support or sabotage this alternative subject formation in various ways. There is a sense of not-belonging in Christianity that finds expression in Jesus' recognition that 'he has nowhere to lay his head' (Luke 9.58) and an early Christian understanding that 'here we have no lasting city, but we are looking for the city that is to come' (Heb. 13.14). There is a call to obedience in Christianity ('follow me', Mark 2.14) that has the potential of pointing in new directions but that has often been used to keep in line those who are in positions from which alternative subjectivities develop and who would thus be able to challenge the status quo, including reminders to wives to obey their husbands, to slaves to obey their masters, or to church members to follow their leaders.[16]

The lack of class consciousness and the lack of a more general awareness of not benefitting from the status quo leads to a loss of subjectivity and agency that must not be underestimated. This lack leads working-class people, for instance, to give up the last bit of agency that consists in voting their interests in democratic elections. The US is perhaps the prime example of a country where, due to a widespread absence of class consciousness, working-class people frequently vote for the interests of the ruling class, ready to forego health insurance and social security, and to tighten their belts, believing that the demands of the system require it. Nevertheless, this agency and the related subjectivity is never lost completely, demonstrated by the fact that the system remains constantly on guard, ready to suppress class consciousness whenever and wherever it raises its head. The standard accusation against those who point out class differentials is that they are instigating class warfare – thus covering up the fact that class warfare does not have to be instigated by anyone but is an ongoing fact of life by which the ruling classes appropriate the labour of the working class. Put positively, an awareness of one's place in the system and the repression that goes along with it somehow conjures up a subjectivity and agency that becomes dangerous for the status quo: people might then vote for their interests or begin to rise up in protest. As a result, the 'automatic subject' is challenged.

Subjectivity is thus reclaimed when the political and the economic subject are brought back together again. A closer analysis of economic subjectivity – the fact that, under the conditions of capitalism, the automatic subject leaves very little room for subjectivity but that there is a place of resistance for those who do not benefit from the system – has important implications for political subjectivity and ultimately for religious subjectivity as well. A refusal to participate in the political status quo grows out of a sense that the economic status quo is not functioning in the best interests of large parts of humanity; a refusal to participate in the religious status quo – the 'religion of the market' – has similar roots. In this case the special situation in the US is once again telling: whereas, particularly in Europe, workers have long since left the churches because they supported the ruling classes and their economic and political interests, in the US workers are still by and large church members. This is all the more surprising since these churches are not necessarily addressing their interests, and since they are not helping them further an alternative subjectivity. In Texas, for instance, a substantial number of trade union members are also members of churches, yet these churches give virtually no support to union causes. If these churches address economic or political issues, they side with the employers. In churches where both employers and workers are members, the employers are the ones who make their interests heard, but it has not yet occurred to the workers that they could do the same. While the employers certainly make bigger individual financial contributions to the church, the collective financial contributions of the workers are certainly not insignificant either. Religion could be quite different if working-class people were to pursue their interests, and the same is true for politics. To be sure, such a move would not have to amount to the assimilation of religion to the self-interest of yet another group but should correspond with the solidarity of the divine with the margins that is deeply embedded in the Judaeo-Christian traditions. Note also that this would by no means be merely a partisan move in favour of workers but a move that would ultimately be liberating even for employers, since they are also caught in the traps of the automatic subject and the religion of the market. Our argument here is not about some utopian future transformation, because some of these things are happening already. Liberation theology has identified similar dynamics for several decades, and current religion and labour coalitions witness to alternative subjectivities being built from below here and now.[17]

The key is in overcoming the modern bourgeois split between economic subject and political subject, as the theologian Ulrich Duchrow has argued. The problem is that most national constitutions and their laws do not allow for democracy in matters of economics. In a neoliberal system, the subjects of the economy control the subjects of politics.[18] This is no accident, as the stability of the status quo – based on the proper functioning of the automatic subject – depends on it. At the same time, we can now affirm that an alternative might indeed exist if things are seen 'from below'. In Duchrow's words: 'A new order can grow only from below, supported by the direct participation of the whole diversity of humans and groups in solidarity.'[19] Alternative subjectivities are emerging all over the world, in diverse settings and contexts.

As new subjectivities emerge from below, the role of the middle class can be seen in a new light as well. This class, which is literally in the middle between the two conflicting subjectivities, is often so strongly tied to the system that it is unable to make any contributions to an alternative subjectivity. It is this class that is often related most closely to the religion of the market, as it is more dependent on religious hope than the ruling classes, due to its weaker economic status. Furthermore, the commodity fetishism that marks relationship under the conditions of capitalism is perhaps most firmly rooted here.[20] But there are some options. One option might be the situation in Argentina early in the new millennium, where the middle class took to the streets in protest at the economic collapse of the country's economy – unearthing the common interest of the middle class with the working class, as those who do not ultimately reap the benefits from the system. In the midst of the recession of 2008 and 2009, the middle class in the US is forced to face these issues as well, since its economic status is rapidly declining amid the housing crisis and a sense that its economic fortunes can no longer be expected to rise even at the rate of average growth and inflation while the income of the ruling class keeps growing, sometimes by leaps and bounds.

Overcoming mimetic desire and sacrificial religion

Bertolt Brecht asked, 'What is a break-in into a bank compared to the founding of a bank? What is the murder of a man compared to the hiring of a man?'[21] These questions are often read in moral fashion, as the comparison of various sorts of crimes. What is more important, however, is that these questions remind us of the power of that which is considered normal and which therefore goes unquestioned. A similar comparison might be made between individual killings and killing in war – while everyone is aware of the problematic character of the former, the latter is commonly overlooked although it has far-reaching consequences, including massive loss of life on all sides and the mimetic self-sacrifice of soldiers. The question for us is, therefore, what alternatives exist to the mimetic desires of the status quo and its sacrificial religion?

Once again, a sense of class differentials might be a start. If people were to realize who really benefits from the founding of a bank, from the hiring of a man, or from the killing in war, things would be different. First, the bonds of mimetic desire between the classes who benefit more and those who benefit less would rupture. Second, new forms of solidarity would emerge among those who are dependent on banks rather than profit from them, among those who are hired, and among the foot soldiers who are now set to kill each other. Breaking the bonds of mimetic desire in the US in particular would have a global impact, because new global unity among workers might be the result (a unity that is hardly found now even among the unionized workers in the US), and because the constant flow of soldiers would be interrupted. René Girard himself has lately begun to realize the importance of paying attention to the reality of the deep tensions of the global situation and the reality of the poor, inspired by interactions with liberation theology. In this light, we need to revisit Girard's initial sense that the need to quell violence with sacrifice existed only in ancient times.[22]

Despite the deep-seated reality of standard mimetic desire, there appears to be a possibility of 'converting away from' the kind of mimetic desire that creates (and is created by) 'mimetic rivalry'; Girard talks about this under the heading 'The Good News of Mimetic Desire' and notes the possibility of 'grace'.[23] Clearly, both the notion of conversion and the notion of grace are religious concepts, which can make significant contributions to the issues at hand, since talk about conversion and grace implies the possibility of alternatives. One example of such an alternative – not addressed by Girard – is the constant fear that alternative mimetic desires emerge to become serious rivals to standard mimetic desire. As the National Security Advisor for President Nixon, Henry Kissinger, for instance, realized this problem back in the 1960s. In a 1970 memo to Nixon he wrote:

> The example of a successful elected Marxist government in Chile would surely have an impact on – and even precedent value for – other parts of the world . . . ; the imitative spread of similar phenomena elsewhere would in turn significantly affect the world balance and our own position in it.[24]

Kissinger seems to have grasped the tremendous power of imitation, but one wonders about the deeper reasons for his concern about this particular form of mimetic desire. There appears to be a deeper reality worth exploring here because, despite all the brutal repression of alternative mimetic desire by Kissinger and by subsequent US politics and despite all the aggressive advertising campaigns of capitalism, this particular 'imitative spread' of socialist politics is once more showing success in Latin America. This observation boosts the value of the following argument based on the religious dynamics of mimetic desire.

Alternative mimetic desire can be framed in terms of its religious models. The mimetic desire of appropriation, discussed in Chapter 2, is tempered by a mimetic desire of representation, the desire to be like others.[25] In Girard's account there is an alternative way of living mimetic desire, for instance by imitating a figure such as Jesus. In this case we are not merely dealing with a rival mimetic desire but with a mimetic desire that is qualitatively different. There are two kinds of mimetic desire with very different consequences: 'It can be murderous, it is rivalrous; but it is also the basis of heroism, and devotion to others, and everything.' This second form of mimetic desire includes 'the opening out of oneself' to others.[26] Mimetic desire that promotes a positive relation to the other – the relation constituted by the solidarity of the marginalized that so worried Kissinger – differs from standard mimetic desire in that it has a dynamic of its own, and this dynamic is rightly feared by the status quo.

In this situation, the Christian religion has the potential to contribute to a switching of sides, from the support of sacrifice to resistance against it. Girard notes 'the biblical tendency to "side with the victims"'.[27] Indeed, the Bible sides with those who were falsely accused and it often portrays them as innocent scapegoats, as, for instance Joseph, Job, and the Suffering Servant in the book of Second Isaiah. Girard feels that this taking of sides has contributed to putting an end to sacrifice. Nevertheless, it is only in the New Testament, he finds, that God's rejection of sacrifice becomes altogether clear: 'The Christ of the Gospels dies against sacrifice, and through his death he reveals its nature and origin by making sacrifice unworkable, at least in the long run, and bringing sacrificial culture to an end.'[28] Unfortunately, Christianity today often obscures this important development. We might even go so far as to argue that the matter has been turned on its head and that Christianity has come to understand itself as the religion of sacrifice par excellence. Going beyond Girard's exposition, we should note that at no time was this reversal more obvious than today, when we are dealing with a market system that is willing to sacrifice the lives of millions in order to secure growth and success, and which is frequently supported by mainstream Christianity.[29] Girard is aware of the general problem: 'The sacrificial misreading common to Christians and non-Christians alike has obscured the non-sacrificial significance of the Judeo-Christian Scriptures.' Fortunately, this dynamic has not been able to suppress the non-sacrificial heritage completely:

> Thus, our society could result from a complex interaction between the Judeo-Christian and the sacrificial. Acting upon the latter as a force of disruption – as new wine in old wine-skins – the former would be responsible for our constantly increased awareness of victimage and for the decadence of mythology in our world.'[30]

Nothing less than a conversion is required here, as subjectivity moves from an age-old foundation in sacrifice to something new.

Jung Mo Sung points out the magnitude of the conversion that is at stake here, when he considers Jesus' statement that God 'desires mercy, not sacrifice' (Matt. 9.13) to be an epistemological revolution.[31] Conversion and epistemological revolution happen when a different relation of self and other – a shift from rivalry to care – is envisioned. As limited resources are negotiated with potentially infinite desires, a clearer distinction between desires and real needs emerges. And once these real needs become part of the equation the picture broadens once again to include not only the needs of the self but also the needs of the other.[32] In the Gospel of Matthew the needs of the neighbour are key to salvation, when the Son of Man invites those who

> 'are blessed by my Father, [to] inherit the kingdom prepared for you from the foundation of the world, for I was hungry and you gave me food, I was thirsty and you gave me something to drink, I was a stranger and you welcomed me. I was naked and you gave me clothing, I was sick and you took care of me, I was in prison and you visited me.'

And to the surprised response when all this was done the famous answer is given: 'Just as you did it to one of the least of these who are members of my family, you did it to me.' (Matt. 25.34–40).

This alternative subjectivity that is emerging here cannot be explained with a simple reference to general human capacity. Something else is at work – the sort of thing that we are calling transcendence in this book. The Christian religion, when it is in touch with a transcendent experience of grace, functions as that which has the potential to resist negative mimetic desire and which constantly pushes for the transformation of desire. In the words of Girard: 'Wherever you have that . . . positive desire for the other, there is some kind of divine grace present. This is what Christianity unquestionably tells us. If we deny this we move into some form of optimistic humanism.'[33] What is most important about religion in Girard's account here is that it is not a 'recipe how to live' or a form of organizing, a sociological entity.[34] Girard conceives the transformation of desire as more than just an ethical prescription or the formation of a new institution. It is the 'opening towards the reign of God', which he considers to be the ultimate goal.[35] Here, a clear alternative to sacrificial religion emerges that is rooted in an experience of transcendence and grace that comes to us from the other, and that we therefore cannot control.

But even where this new positive dynamic of mimetic desire is not yet fully established, there is a dialectic that accounts for positive effects even of negative mimetic desires. Girard notes that in the world of the ruling class – the bourgeoisie – mimetic desire is crucial, and competition and rivalry determine life. This is, of course, the rut in which so many of us are stuck today, and into which the ruling classes are trying to pull as many people as possible. Nevertheless, once upon a time this bourgeois competition was a progressive force in its own right when it destroyed an older feudal hierarchy and thus generated new political and economic possibilities for its own time.[36] Perhaps we can identify here some dialectic that points into the future beyond the rule of the bourgeoisie, as mimetic desire keeps building at the margins.

There is one more thing that needs to be taken into account in this regard. In Chapter 2, we observed that the scapegoat is the only one acting in the resolution of mimetic desire. This means that there is a sort of agency that is particular to those who are marginalized and ultimately sacrificed by the system. Las Casas saw something of that agency in the Amerindians of the sixteenth century, whom he considered to be the beaten Christs of the Indies. It seems to us, though, that this is not going far enough yet, as the emphasis on the role of the scapegoat is normally limited to notions of suffering that emphasize the passive component rather than alternative agency and subjectivity.[37] Even worse, this attitude too easily feeds back into the vicious circle of sacrifice, where the agency of the scapegoat is at work for the benefit of the system. This we cannot endorse. As the scapegoat gains agency and thus subjectivity, something else beyond passive suffering emerges; the marginalized and the sacrificed gain agency where we least expect it: in the midst of suffering, which is thus no longer a merely passive matter. Suffering here takes on an active quality of resisting and overcoming the system – which is the very heart of the suffering of Christ himself, whose violent death on one of the many crosses of the Roman Empire was not the end but the beginning of something new, which turned out to be powerful enough to transform the world. This is the sort of agency that has the potential to subvert the system and to produce alternatives. Examples can be found in present-day experiences as well: a soldier, for instance, who has barely escaped his or her own sacrificial death and returns to tell the story, thereby exposing the mechanisms of death, can be a powerful voice and pose a real challenge to the system. Poor persons who refuse to give up despite the fact that the system keeps turning them into scapegoats, and who beat the system by making use of alternative resources in order to survive, can hold up a mirror to the status quo unlike anyone else. In other words, resilience to suffering and oppression can turn into resistance even if we do not readily recognize the subjectivity and agency that emerges here. As a result, when alternative subjectivity and agency manifest themselves, our very notions of subjectivity and agency are being transformed. We will deal with this below.

Overcoming shock treatment and the religion of omnipotence

While the notion of omnipotence seems to be inextricably bound up with images of the divine, we must note that this is not necessarily the self-image of the God of Jesus Christ. In contrast to the images of classical theism, the biblical God of both the Old and the New Testaments is not a divinity that is omnipotent, impassible, immutable, and untouchable. The Judaeo-Christian God's power is expressed in ways that cannot be reconciled with the notion of omnipotence, culminating in the death and suffering that Jesus endures on the cross. When this God hears people's cries (Ex. 3.7), there is no impassibility – a prerequisite for classical notions of omnipotence, because only the one who is not affected by anyone else is truly all-powerful. When this God reconsiders things and negotiates with humans (Gen. 18.22–33), there is no immutability – another prerequisite for omnipotence. When God chooses to work from the bottom up rather than from the top down (whether in siding with an insignificant people such as Israel, working through prophets rather than kings (1 Sam. 8.10–18), or in working through a Messiah such as Jesus who rejects top-down power (Matt. 4.8–10)), nothing is left of classical notions of omnipotence. Moreover, even parts of the Christian tradition that have conventionally been read in the light of the doctrines of classical theism can be read in alternative ways, as, for instance, the Nicene Creed. The declaration of the divinity of Jesus in this creed might be interpreted as a domestication of Jesus in terms of the precepts of classical theism, but if the Nicene Creed is read the other way around – in terms of the life and ministry of Jesus reconstructing notions such as omnipotence, impassibility, and immutability – affirming the divinity of Jesus ultimately implies a deconstruction of the use of classical theist attributes for God and a radical reconstruction of the divine.[38]

As human efforts to imitate divine omnipotence show, omnipotence cannot be maintained indefinitely. These semblances of omnipotence can deconstruct, they can destroy people and their projects, but they are not able to reconstruct anything in lasting fashion. Like the top-down shocks on which they are built, they eventually wear off. Perhaps the best example of human efforts to mimic divine omnipotence are the bombing campaigns of the US wars in Afghanistan and Iraq, started by the administration of George W. Bush: throwing bombs out of airplanes is a consummate sign of top-down power, and the largest and most advanced planes, such as the B-52 bombers, have to face relatively little risk of being harmed in the process (no B-2, the latest generation of stealth bomber, has ever been shot down); here, omnipotence goes together with impassibility, immutability, and untouchability. Nevertheless, omnipotence and shock work best in the short term or within a fairly limited time-frame. This is true for military power as a whole, which, as Machiavelli knew, is hard but brittle. The best way to resist this sort of power initially is to know what is happening and why.

Ewen Cameron, the father of the shock doctrine discussed in Chapter 2, was not successful in his efforts to reprogramme people. As Naomi Klein has pointed out: 'No matter how fully he regressed his patients, they never absorbed or accepted the endlessly repeated messages on his tapes. Though he was a genius at destroying people, he could not remake them.' His program of 'psychic driving' did not work. Klein extends this observation to the followers of the Chicago School of Economics, who advocate the application of the shock doctrine to economics: 'Disaster capitalists share this same inability to distinguish between destruction and creation, between hurting and healing.'[39]

A similar strategy was followed in the first days after the US invasion in Iraq, but there the project failed as well for various reasons. Creating a clean slate by destroying the country's infrastructure, including not only its industry, its schools, and its communication networks but also its invaluable historical artefacts, was supposed to enable the birth of a new world of privatized industry, schools, and communication, and the availability of an unlimited supply of inexpensive consumer goods. A short time after the destruction was accomplished and victory declared, large numbers of entrepreneurs were flown to Iraq with the expectation that fast-food chains such as McDonald's and big-box stores such as WalMart would soon be open for business. What might be called 'economic driving' – the constant rehearsal of simple economic messages that resemble the messages taped by Ewen Cameron and played to his patients for endless hours – did not work either. Perhaps the patients just did not know what it meant to be told that 'you are a good mother and wife and people enjoy your company' (Cameron's message) or that 'privatization, free markets, and cutting taxes and government is the solution to all problems' (neoliberal capitalism's message), but the deeper question is whether complex personalities and societies can ever be run by such efforts.[40] Failed experiments as diverse as the reconstruction of Iraq and the rebuilding of hurricane-stricken New Orleans – in both cases the shock doctrine was applied, as described in Chapter 2 – bear witness to the problems.

The failed efforts at reconstructing Iraq illustrate what is at stake. Unlike the Marshall Plan that helped rebuild Germany and Japan after World War Two, the reconstruction of Iraq was not aimed at achieving the self-sufficiency of the Iraqi economy through the creation of local jobs and the development of a tax basis that would fund a social net. The reconstruction of Iraq was supposed to be accomplished by major US contractors such as Halliburton, Blackwater, Bechtel, and Parsons, who would subcontract with other foreign contractors who would then hire foreign workers instead of Iraqi workers. These companies imported even basic building materials, which could easily have been produced by the shut-down Iraqi plants. Klein notes that 'even the job of building "local democracy" was privatized', a plan that ended in failure and with the dismissal of the company, which was hired for that purpose under a contract valued at $466 million.[41] Again, Klein notes: 'Freed of all regulations, largely protected from criminal prosecution and on contracts that guaranteed their costs would be covered, plus a profit, many foreign corporations did something entirely predictable: they scammed wildly.'[42]

It stands to reason that it was precisely those projects – which for the most part were not completed satisfactorily – that contributed to the mounting resistance in Iraq against the US occupation and to the emergence of alternative subjectivity and agency. Unemployed Iraqis who lost their jobs to the cheap labourers imported by US contractors from elsewhere tended to sympathize with the resistance against the US, and some even joined it. Even Iraqi businesspeople became part of the resistance, because they resented unrestricted imports and foreign ownership of Iraqi assets and thus started funding resistance activities. In addition, privatization left state workers such as soldiers, doctors, nurses, teachers, and engineers without work – groups of people who could have helped moderate tensions, including religious ones.[43] In Iraq, the vacuum that was created by the shock doctrine's erasure of everyday life was quickly filled not by the dream world of free market capitalism but by mosques and local militias. The shock doctrine created a breeding ground for radicalism and alternative subjectivities. Klein concludes that religious fundamentalism is 'the only source of power in a hollowed-out state'.[44] But there may be more to this matter, and deferring to religious fundamentalism and extremism muddles the waters more than it clarifies things, especially in a context where Islam is already seen in a negative light.

In order to broaden our horizons, consider this situation in terms of its 'unintended consequences', which Chalmers Johnson, following the lingo of the CIA, has called 'blowback'. Years earlier, the *Kubark*

Counterintelligence Interrogation Manual had noted the problem: 'Interrogates who have withstood pain are more difficult to handle by other methods. The effect has not been to repress the subject but to restore his confidence and maturity.'[45] In other words, the destruction of subjectivity may backfire and strengthen forms of alternative subjectivity, which should not be dismissed too quickly as sheer 'radicalism'. In Nietzsche's famous words, that which does not kill us makes us stronger. Social psychology points to a similar insight: the social psychologist W. Keith Campbell notes that the experience of a deep shock can arrest the normal mechanisms by which the psyche protects itself, thus creating the possibility for transformation.[46]

It appears that something like this is precisely what happened in Iraq, because immediately after the US invasion the Iraqi people produced strong efforts to build democracy. Rather than becoming passive, various groups organized spontaneous elections in towns and provinces. The US commanders were not prepared for this reaction and L. Paul Bremer III, the US envoy to Iraq, quickly abandoned the idea of convening an assembly that represented all sectors of Iraqi society. Instead, Bremer handpicked the political leaders himself. Massive peaceful demonstrations against this practice were the result, with people chanting 'yes to elections, no to selections', manifesting alternative forms of subjectivity and agency that were not foreseen by the US forces. It was in response to this emergence of alternative subjectivity and agency that the abuse of prisoners escalated, something that is normally seen only in the midst of the pressures of war, not during times of reconstruction.[47] Yet, even as the repression of these alternative subjectivities was ratcheted up, resistance grew further. Torture began having the opposite effect. As one prisoner who was released from Abu Ghraib Prison stated, 'Abu Ghraib is a breeding ground for insurgents.'[48] Surviving systematic abuse and torture makes people ready to resist, especially those who were imprisoned by 'mistake'. Resistance to shock is further enhanced when shocks have been experienced and survived in the past.

Elsewhere, similar situations have occurred, particularly in Latin America where shock therapy was first implemented on a broad scale, beginning in the 1970s with systematic repression through military dictatorships. Latin America's turn to the left in recent years demonstrates a remarkable resilience to similar shocks, seen for instance in an ability to withstand efforts at toppling duly elected leaders of state and undermining democratic electoral processes. More and more countries are beginning to develop their own collective subjectivity and agency under new leadership, including Venezuela (Hugo Chávez), Bolivia (Evo

Morales), Ecuador (Rafael Correa), Brazil (Luiz Inácio Lula da Silva), Nicaragua (Daniel Ortega), Chile (Michelle Bachelet), Paraguay (Fernando Lugo Méndez), Argentina (Cristina Fernández de Kirchner), and El Salvador (Mauricio Funes). All these countries challenge to a certain degree the neoliberal economics as introduced by those who administered the shocks in Latin America, which have led to further repression of the masses and to further growth of the gap between rich and poor. The surprising discovery is that the repressive character of neoliberal economics and the related shocks to the poor and the middle class (as in the Argentinian economic crisis from 1999–2002) has led not just to frustration but also to new agency. Perhaps one of the clearest signs of this newly developing agency is that several of these countries are preparing to leave the International Monetary Fund (IMF), and some have left already. They are objecting particularly to the IMF's neoliberal dogmas of privatization, corporate freedom, and reduction of social spending, which were introduced on the back of the shock doctrine and its application but which have worsened the situation of the majority of the people. In 2007, Latin America made up only 1 per cent of the IMF's lending portfolio, down from 80 per cent in 2005.[49] Other countries are following, including Russia and Thailand.

These moves set the stage for broader transformations of subjectivity. The new-found subjectivity that is part of this resistance is no longer being built on the creativity of just a few charismatic individuals. Mutual support is crucial because the new forms of resistance cannot be sustained by isolated individuals – they could be too easily coerced back into the system. Struck by a natural catastrophe that was used as the launching point for the shock doctrine, community leaders from New Orleans went to Thailand in order to study how the people organized themselves and how they started to rebuild after the Tsunami, having to fend off efforts to grab their ocean-front land. After returning home, these New Orleans residents began taking things into their own hands and started their own projects of rebuilding.[50] In sum, this new kind of subjectivity is based on a different kind of intersubjectivity that emerges among those whom the system tried to shock into compliance in different ways. This intersubjectivity emerges at all levels, from the personal to the political and economic. One example at the macro level is Bolivia's proposal of an alternative free trade agreement (ALBA), based on the idea that 'each country provides what it is best placed to produce, in return for what it most needs, independent of global market prices'.[51] Once again, the motto of this emerging intersubjectivity is: 'From each according to their ability, to each according to their needs.' Alternative subjectivity and intersubjectivity emerges as

progressive networks organize power from the grassroots up, producing alternative ways of life that challenge the status quo.

In the Christian tradition, this emerging intersubjectivity might be
seen in the resurrection of Christ. Not giving in to the execution of
this alternative Messiah by the seemingly omnipotent powers that be,
the divine takes the side of those against whom the shock treatment
was directed and thus enables new hope. While the crucifixion was
real – Christ was not merely in a state of suspended animation but
killed and buried – the resurrection thwarts the Roman Empire's and
the Jewish High Priests' efforts to do away with Jesus Christ for good.
The power at work in this resurrection is not top-down omnipotence
but resistance from the bottom up, which begins when a few women
do not give in to the shock treatment of the crucifixion but assemble
at Jesus' grave, and when they spread the word about the risen Christ
and reassemble the scattered and dispirited group of his disciples in
his presence at the margins of the Empire in Galilee (see, for instance,
the account in the Gospel of Luke, chapter 24; Luke does not mention
Galilee, but the other Gospels do).

There is something else that cannot be wiped out completely by the
omnipotent shocks imposed by the status quo. Klein notes that memory, both in its individual and collective forms, 'turns out to be the
greatest shock absorber of all'.[52] The interesting question, of course, is
what kind of memory it would be in our current situation of Empire
that helps us absorb the shocks. Memory of religious images may not
necessarily help in this case, especially if these images reinforce the
Empire's notion of omnipotence. Memories of the divine as omnipotent, for instance, too easily reinforce images of the omnipotence of
the powerful: from this perspective, those who command superior
military force, the greater economic powers, and the sheer mass of the
global economy must ultimately be right. There is however another
sort of memory, what some have called 'dangerous memory'.[53] In
the Christian tradition, this is the memory that the basic symbols of
Christianity do not fit in with the symbols of the Empire. One of these
dangerous memories holds, for example, that the Christian confes-
sion of the lordship of Jesus is a challenge to the Roman Emperors,
who claimed the exclusive right to the title 'lord'.[54] Such memories,
of course, are not the memories of the mainstream but have stayed
alive, mostly under cover and on the margins, flashing up at moments
of great danger (Walter Benjamin) and contributing to the creation of
something new.[55] Klein talks about the formation of a new narrative:
'As soon as we have a new narrative that offers a perspective on the
shocking events, we become reoriented and the world begins to make

sense again.'[56] We will need to keep investigating, though, from where this new story emerges – a story that is ultimately not completely new because it is rooted in dangerous memories – and how it contributes to the organization of intersubjectivity.

At the heart of a subjectivity that is resistant to the top-down shocks of the Empire is an outlook that appreciates movements from the bottom up. The people who are broken by top-down shocks are those who are not aware of the bottom-up alternatives, those for whom there is only one way, the way of top-down omnipotence. If this one way turns against them, there is nothing left, and their memories of former times of greatness and omnipotence will be of little help. Moving away from the top-down shock strategy of Empire, religion shapes up differently, as it recaptures its memories of bottom-up movements. These bottom-up movements, it can be argued, return religion closer to its origins and founding moments, as many of the founders and founding events of the major world religions derive from below.

With this in mind, we might be able to turn around and re-appropriate an insight promoted by Milton Friedman of the Chicago School of Economics, which says that 'only a crisis – actual or perceived – produces real change'. While this insight has been at the heart of the Empire's shock doctrine, perhaps there is a lesson here for the subjectivity and agency that develops in the resistance against empire as well: most of us would benefit from paying much closer attention to the real crises of our time. Without a clear perception of the tremendous crisis in which we find ourselves – reaching from the ever greater inequality of wealth to the as yet unforeseeable snowball effects of global warming – real change may not be possible.

We will now take a closer look at what happens to subjectivity in the midst of this crisis.

Overcoming the realism and the religion of the status quo

The advantage of the position of the real (see Chapter 2) is that the marginalized are not completely determined by the powers that be – unlike those who are part of the system. Lacan talks about a kind of surplus enjoyment[57] that escapes the authority and control of the status quo. As Slavoj Žižek explains, 'it is not a surplus which simply attaches itself to some "normal," fundamental enjoyment because *enjoyment as such emerges only in this surplus*'.[58] In other words, the subjectivity of the marginalized is not merely a function of the status quo and cannot be explained in terms of the realism of the status quo: the 'realists' in power are not even able to envision that real subjectivity can really exist outside their control, although they remain nervous about the margins. Furthermore, the so-called realism of the status quo overlooks the fact that the formation of dominant subjectivity is complex and produced on the back of others. Even the common and well-meaning admonitions of mainstream religion not to be so 'selfish' and 'greedy' support this system, because they presuppose the reality of individualistic subjectivity. The subjectivity that this realism acknowledges, however – the rugged individualism of the 'self-made man' – does not exist; it is a myth that covers up the fact that the powerful and the wealthy have acquired their wealth and their power on the back of others and that their subjectivity and agency is endorsed and choreographed by the system. Even the subjectivities of super-rich eccentrics such as Donald Trump or Paris Hilton are part of the system, as such subjectivities emerge in relation to the large numbers of others whose stories are never told, such as the workers mowing the lawns on Trump's or Hilton's properties who inevitably contribute to the increase of their fortunes, which fund their subjectivity. The subjectivities of Trump and Hilton are part of the system even when they step out of line, as the rich and wealthy are supposed to be able to 'do anything they want' – as long as they do not turn against the system itself.

In this situation, a new look at the underside is required. The insights of subaltern studies can be helpful here, a field of study that is primarily concerned not with conventional studies of the subaltern that aim at representation but with discerning its subjectivity, agency, and energy.[59] John Beverley is right: 'If cultural studies adequately represented the dynamics of "the people," there would be no need for subaltern studies.'[60] What is this new subjectivity that presents itself here?

Resistance to Empire confronts us with an unexpected reversal between subject and object, according to which those who thought their subjectivity secure will lose it and those who were considered mere objects will gain it, parallel to an old insight of Jesus: 'For those who want to save their life will lose it, and those who lose their life for my sake will find it. For what will it profit them if they gain the whole world but forfeit their life?' (Matt. 16.25–6). Resistance has to do with a reversal in subjectivity, where those who were considered non-subjects or non-persons (in the language of liberation theology) become the true subjects, while dominant subjectivity is exposed as a fraud. 'Gaining the whole world' is apparently not the way to true subjectivity. Elsewhere Rieger has described the mechanisms at the root of this alternative subjectivity in this way, pointing out how alternative subjectivity exposes false dominant subjectivity:

resistance has to do w/ a reversal in subjectivity

This switch in the relation of subject and object, in which the repressed object mirrors the truth of her repression back to the repressing subject (who is now haunted by the truth of his own actions and by his inability to deal with the object that he thought was under complete control), is what lies at the basis of resistance.[61]

In other words, what was considered the 'repressed object' becomes the new subject, while the 'repressing subject' is exposed as unable to maintain control. This new subjectivity is gained only where the false subjectivity of the status quo is challenged.

Alternative subjectivity grows out of the pressures of being 'subjected' and 'objectified', gushing forth precisely at the point where these pressures are unable to exert absolute control and to shape everything in their image: omnipotence – the ability to control everything absolutely – is an illusion that Empire wants to maintain but that does not exist. Franz Hinkelammert has put things in a slightly different way:

> The subject is not a substance – something that exists and subsists by itself alone or in relations inside systems or 'webs' – but a 'lack that cries out', a potentiality or set of potentialities that make it possible for the human being to oppose and resist the attempted reduction by the dominant social system.[62]

Dominant subjectivity, seeking to project an impossible omnipotence, fails to realize this lack that is at the heart of the subject and thus falls prey to the reduction by the dominant social system. Alternative subjectivity, on the other hand, is made painfully aware of its limits at every turn but – precisely for this reason – is able (and forced) to explore alternative ways of being that are not available to those beholden to the status quo. Elsewhere, Hinkelammert has put it like this: 'To become a subject is to respond to this absence positively . . . without eliminating it as an absence.'[63] From the perspective of subaltern studies similar issues are promoted:

> To go to the subaltern in order to learn to be radically 'fragmentary' and 'episodic' is to move away from the monomania of the imagination that operates within the gesture that the knowing, judging, willing subject always already knows what is good for everybody, ahead of any investigation.[64]

The openness, fragmentation, and lack that are part of alternative subjectivity are therefore not negative markers but essential for its ability to resist the status quo and to develop real alternatives.

Of course, we are dealing with a different sort of subjectivity and agency here. We are neither talking about the top-down action of the powerful, seemingly autonomous subject that is a function of the status quo, nor are we talking about the streamlined actions of specific institutions of the status quo, whether they are religious, economic, or political. True subjectivity and agency is formed in situations of pressure, first as lack and fragmentation but then shaping up as counter-pressures that respond to the repressions of life. Perhaps this is the truth behind mysterious sayings of Jesus such as the following:

Blessed are you when people hate you, and when they exclude you, revile you and defame you on account of the Son of Man. Rejoice in that day and leap for joy, for surely your reward is great in heaven; for that is what their ancestors did to the prophets. (Luke 6.22–3)

In this situation, new energy sources are tapped that are not available to those who function within the confines of the status quo ('Woe to you when all speak well of you, for that is what their ancestors did to the false prophets.' (Luke 6.26)). This alternative subjectivity takes form in different sorts of agency that are often not seen in their constructive potential; alternative agency includes not only the active construction of alternatives but also manifests itself in protest, insubordination, withdrawal, migration, revolt, and the kinds of cultural practices that are related to these moves.[65] There are other parallels in the Christian tradition. As suggested in Chapter 2, the subjectivity and agency that are emerging here can be rethought in terms of how some strands of the Christian tradition envision Jesus' subjectivity and agency, which can do without Satan's offer to rule the world (Matt. 4.8–10), which Jesus rejects. But had Jesus rejected Satan's offer because he assumed that this particular kind of rule over the world (or any other sort of 'power over' the world) would be given to him a little later by God anyway, this offer would not have presented much of a temptation. As Jesus' life and ministry show, he ends up assuming a different sort of subjectivity and agency that is defined not by top-down rule but by solidarity with the outcasts. This is what ultimately leads to his execution at one of the thousands of crosses of the Empire that were reserved for political rebels – that is, for those who assumed any kind of subjectivity and agency that was in tension with the subjectivity promoted by the Empire. The Apostle Paul, author of the oldest writings in the New Testament, gives expression to this alternative subjectivity in the following way:

God chose what is foolish in the world to shame the wise; God chose what is weak in the world to shame the strong; God chose what is low and despised in the world, things that are not, to reduce to nothing things that are. (1 Cor. 1.27–8)

Clearly, there is a tension between two subjectivities here that cannot be reconciled; what Paul's statement describes as God's choice ('election' is the traditional theological term) is ultimately a judgment of which subjectivity will endure in the long run. Alternative subjectivity is thus not just a harmless alternative that stands next to dominant subjectivity and complements it: rather, alternative subjectivity challenges dominant subjectivity and ultimately overturns it.

This alternative subjectivity, however, must not be romanticized, as should become clear from the tradition of the oppressed. The oppressed know that their subjectivity is produced by all kinds of forces, including the forces of the status quo; and while this alternative subjectivity pushes against and beyond the 'automatic subject', it is not autonomous either. But neither can the oppressed afford to give up whatever is left of their subjectivity, because their survival depends on it. In this context, neither individualism nor communitarianism are attractive options. Individualism is the false sense of subjectivity of the powerful, who are never individual subjects, even though they may think so. But communitarianism, often pronounced as the solution to individualism, is a problem too, since it mirrors individualism's false sense of subjectivity. Communitarianism shows little awareness of the fact that group identity and collective subjectivity are not autonomous either, and that they are also produced in the tensions of life and on the back of others. The result is what might be called a 'collective individualism', where the group emerges as a fairly homogeneous collective individual, manifest for instance in the communities of the privileged and their homogeneous gated communities. The ethos of postmodernity in which these battles of individualism versus communitarianism are often waged does not help much in resolving this dilemma, for it questions subjectivity precisely at a time when marginalized people are gaining some subjectivity.

Not talking about subjectivity in general, but about the subjectivity that emerges at the margins, puts us on a different path. Laura Donaldson, a Cherokee thinker, helpfully reminds us that we need to pay attention to what is actually happening at the grassroots,[66] because this gives us a clearer understanding of the fact that the oppressed retain some sort of subjectivity and agency even under the conditions of the postmodern or postcolonial Empire.[67] Gayatri Spivak, who initially wondered whether the subaltern could speak, revised her earlier argument in this direction as well (see above, Chapter 2). This is the reality, which we experience in the margins of our own contexts, not only in Brazil and Argentina, but also in the United States, and this is what keeps reminding us of a sort of transcendence that is not seen from the perspectives of the status quo.

In this context we can talk about another kind of surplus. What is produced by imperial capitalism is not simply the surplus of the powerful but another kind of surplus that finds expression in the traditions of the oppressed. Jacques Lacan's notion of 'surplus enjoyment' refers to a resource available only to the repressed, at the underside, and not to those who are part of the status quo ('rejoice and leap for joy', Luke 6.23). Hardt and Negri put it like this:

> The production of the common always involves a surplus that cannot be expropriated by capital or captured in the regimentation of the global political body. This surplus, at the most abstract philosophical level, is the basis on which antagonism is transformed into revolt. Deprivation, in other words, may breed anger, indignation, and antagonism, but revolt arises only on the basis of wealth, that is, a surplus of intelligence, experience, knowledges, and desire.[68]

In other words, the oppressed and marginalized are not just the ones excluded, fragmented, and confronted with a lack; they have their own sort of wealth ('blessed are you', Luke 6.20–3). There are levels of insight and energy here that are unknown to the status quo. Since this wealth is not recognized by the system, there are certain niches or safe spaces that open up. Based on this alternative production of subjectivity related to another surplus, some of our preconceived notions of resistance change: what if the work of resistance were done not primarily in people's spare time (through large numbers of additional meetings at night, for instance) but in the networks in which we live our daily lives.[69]

At this point, the religious surplus comes into view more clearly. God is not limited to being the supreme warrant of the status quo – the product of the surplus of the system and the automatic subject – although that is indeed the god of Empire and thus the most prevalent image of God in every age. God can also be conceived in terms of the opposite of the status quo, and this is the story told in many of the Judaeo-Christian traditions, especially the ones on which Jesus draws and which inspire him to step up against the politico-religious status quo (see, for example, Mark 3.1–6, where Jesus heals a man with a crippled hand, which is against the official Jewish Sabbath law, with the result that the religious leaders and the political power-brokers conspire to kill him early on in his ministry). There are aspects of the divine that cannot be controlled by Empire and that keep bubbling up despite the system's best efforts to subdue them (in *Christ and Empire*, Rieger talks about a 'theological surplus' or a 'Christological surplus'). If people's subjectivity cannot ultimately be controlled, why should we assume that there is a divine reality that can be controlled altogether? This is one of the key insights of this book that is developed in each chapter.

The difference, of course, is that this alternative kind of surplus is produced on the underside. It is linked to particular acts of repression in a repressive system. Union organizers have a saying that 'the boss is our best organizer'. Top-down repression generates not just pressure but also counter-pressure and a surplus from which resistance grows. Empire itself, without being aware of it, thus creates the conditions for a new thing. New subjectivity, however, emerges precisely in the places where Empire least expects it. Once these places are recognized as genuine places for the creation of alternative subjectivities (we are using the plural deliberately, since the acts of repression are diverse, although the systems of repression are linked), new energies and resources are discovered. Hardt and Negri put it this way: 'Some resources remain scarce today, but many, in fact, particularly the newest elements of the economy, do not operate on a logic of scarcity.'[70] As Thomas Jefferson realized, ideas are enhanced when they are communicated – a key insight, which is especially relevant in the information age. Here a whole new understanding of the wealth of the underside and its alternative subjectivities emerges. While dominant ideas may benefit from these dynamics as well, traditional top-down models of domination and influence are challenged at least implicitly, since the world can flourish without them. Even the findings of contemporary science, such as neuroscience and its models of the brain, provide helpful images of situations where rulers are more and more parasitical and sovereign power less and less necessary.[71]

In this context, we can take a new look at the formation of relationships between the various emerging subjectivities. While the particular acts of repression differ to a certain degree, there is a larger system of repression in place, which fuels these acts of repression. This larger system produces certain family resemblances that account for the potential solidarity among the various repressed groups. What is created here, as a result, is a collective subject that is not 'additive', in the sense that each experience of repression would be presented as unrelated to any other. This sort of addition is the problem of a sort of essentialized identity politics, where struggles of different identities (such as black people, women, ethnic minorities) are being added up and compared but not really identified in terms of the common roots of repression. As we move beyond addition and discover relationships between various forms of repression, a new collective subjectivity emerges, which is characterized by an open-ended solidarity where no one group and no one leader calls the shots. Beverley sums it up: while the people remain heterogeneous – there is no need to homogenize them – they are unified in antagonistic relations with the powers that be.[72] Such approaches can be seen in the world of religion, for instance where different religions are working together in interfaith groups not in order to produce religious homogeneity but in order to apply their various religious traditions in struggles against top-down domination and for the common good, so that all can live.

One of the key differences between dominant subjectivity and subaltern subjectivity is the way in which unity is understood. The unity of those in power demands homogeneity, even though it may allow for some differences. The realism of the status quo demands that certain key issues are not questioned, such as the commitment to the 'free market' that guarantees the freedom of the most powerful members of society, or an understanding of democracy that excludes the world of economics. The unity of the people, on the other hand, is not homogeneous but involves different social agents with differing identities and histories.[73] This points to the real, which is not homogeneous either. The real is never the "thing in itself" but that which is produced by the repressions of the system, and therefore is able to expose it and resist it. Participating in the real unites because it resists co-optation and maintains an awareness of the common repression that is endured. Unlike reality, which is the way the world is perceived from the perspective of the status quo, the real is the common pain of repression that creates new forms of solidarity and alternative subjectivities and agencies.[74] But there is also a positive aspect that must not be overlooked, since the real produces something new that is not of the system ('in the world yet not of the world', paraphrasing John 17.6–19) and thus makes a difference.[75] Alternative subjectivity and agency produce positive alternatives that create what realism and the religion of the status quo never thought possible. Nevertheless, we must not forget that those alternatives maintain an openness that cannot be found in the dominant system, and thus can never ultimately be pinned down.

Finally, new forms of intersubjectivity emerge here that lay the foundations for a new humanity. In the words of Jung Mo Sung:

When one is manifest and experienced as a subject in resistance to oppressive relations, one can recognize oneself as a subject and, at the same time, recognize the subjectity of other people beyond any and all social roles. It is what we were speaking of earlier as the experience of gratuity in the face-to-face relation.[76]

The new relationship that is built by those who embody alternative subjectivity allows for a face-to-face encounter that is not possible in a system where subjectivity depends on power differentials, that is, where the subject can only be understood as that which is subjecting others and bringing them under control – an understanding that is often perpetuated today in notions of 'leadership' promoted not only in the world of business but also in politics and the Church. There is a transcendent moment here because these new forms of intersubjectivity cannot be 'made' or controlled, and they push beyond any system. This is a 'truly spiritual experience of grace and justification by faith', which 'justifies the existence not only of the oppressed person, but also of the person who feels the indignation'.[77] This sort of justification – an embodiment of God's justice that opposes the Empire's notion of justice, as Christianity discovered early on in the Roman Empire[78] – may be the best antidote yet to the automatic subject of capitalism.

Conclusion: subjectivity and resistance

Perhaps one of the most important processes in the development of alternative subjectivity is the development of what might be called 'antibodies'. Empire seeks to erase independent subjectivity as much as possible, and alternative subjectivities are under attack to the point of the attempted erasure of their bearers in torture, disappearances, and executions. The Latin America of the various military regimes in the 1970s and 1980s is an example, although not even the most brutal repression could ever root out alternative subjectivities completely. In the aftermath of this destruction we need to make sure that it will be ever more difficult in the future for the structures of Empire to root out alternative subjectivities.

Alternative desire is at the heart of alternative subjectivity. Yet desire cannot be changed easily, and moralizing or sermonizing – the common responses of those whose world is confined to the system – will not work. In this context, it is important to dig deeper and to realize that desire, like subjectivity, is shaped in relationships and through repressions. Once this is clear we will be able to see the tide of alternative desires that is already rising in a system that is becoming more and more repressive of more and more people. This alternative desire is thus truly a collective phenomenon, and it has the potential to create a new human nature.[79] Yet this alternative desire also needs to be organized. Without organization it disappears. This may be the wisdom embodied in alternative religious and other movements when they form on the underside of history.[80]

No middle road exists in this polarized situation of Empire: 'No one can serve two masters, for a slave will either hate the one and love the other, or be devoted to the one and despise the other. You cannot serve God and wealth', the Matthean Jesus declares (Matt. 6.24). Those in the middle are usually pulled into the defence of the powers that be, in order to create a (mostly illusionary) sense of stability. But those in the middle might also opt to step back from a system that does not allow them to form alternative subjectivities and join in the emerging relations of intersubjectivity from below.

Notes

1 This notion of ambivalence is developed by Homi Bhabha in *The Location of Culture*, London: Routledge, 1994, p. 86. It is developed further in the context of theological discourse in Joerg Rieger, *Christ and Empire: From Paul to Postcolonial Times*, Minneapolis, MN: Fortress Press, 2007, p. 11.

2 Michael Hardt and Antonio Negri, *Multitude: War and Democracy in the Age of Empire,* New York: The Penguin Press, 2004, p. 356.

3 See Joerg Rieger, 'Theology and the Power of the Margins in a Postmodern World' in Joerg Rieger (ed.), *Opting for the Margins: Postmodernity and Liberation in Christian Theology*, 2003, Oxford: Oxford University Press, pp. 179–99.

4 Jung Mo Sung, *The Subject and Complex Societies*, unpublished translation by Peter L. Jones, p. 39.

5 Rieger, *Christ and Empire*, pp. 180–7.

6 Rieger, *Christ and Empire*, p. 223.

7 Cf. Teresa L. Ebert, 'The "Difference" of Postmodern Feminism', *College English* 53.8 (December 1991), p. 887, defines ludic postmodernism as 'a theatre for the free-floating play . . . of images, disembodied signifiers and difference'. The term 'postmodernism of resistance' is coined by Hal Foster in *The Anti-Aesthetic: Essays on Postmodern Culture*, Port Townsend, WA: Bay Press, 1983, pp. xi–xii. Foster differentiates between a postmodernism that critiques modernism merely in order to return to 'the verities of tradition (in art, family, religion . . .)' and a postmodernism that counters not only modernism but a self-congratulatory postmodernism as well.

8 Karl Marx, *Critique of the Gotha Program*, 1875, part 1, available at http://www.marxists.org/archive/marx/works/1875/gotha/ch01.htm.

9 Sung, *The Subject*, p. 62.

10 Jacques Lacan, 'Seminar 20, *Encore*', in Juliet Mitchell and Jacqueline

Rose (eds.), *Feminine Sexuality: Jacques Lacan and the* école freudienne, New York: W.W. Norton, 1985, p. 144.

11 Lacan, 'Seminar 20', 143–4. Slavoj Žižek, *The Sublime Object of Ideology*, London: Verso, 1989, p. 52, follows up on the notion of 'surplus-enjoyment'.

12 The bill on the Employee Free Choice Act of 2007 (H.R. 800, S. 1041) before the 110th US Congress was designed to rectify this. For the text, see http://www.govtrack.us/congress/billtext.xpd?bill=h110-800. As of this writing, the bill has not yet become law.

13 See Rieger, *Christ and Empire*.

14 Theodore W. Allen, *The Invention of the White Race*, London: Verso, 1994, p. 248.

15 Allen shows the long history of this approach, starting in the seventeenth century: *Invention of the White Race*, pp. 239–53.

16 For the latter, see Hebrews 13.17, almost immediately following the previous passage.

17 In the US, we would like to highlight the work of Jobs with Justice (JwJ) and Interfaith Worker Justice (IWJ). Other examples include the tradition of the Worker Priests in France, which goes back to the middle of the twentieth century and initially inspired several Latin American liberation theologians.

18 Ulrich Duchrow, Reinhold Bianchi, René Krüger and Vincenzo Petracca, *Solidarisch Mensch werden: Psychische und soziale Destruktion im Neoliberalismus – Wege zu ihrer Überwindung*, Hamburg, Oberursel: VSA Verlag, Publik Forum, 2006, p. 394: 'Under the current capitalist conditions those who depend on their salaries have little opportunity, to form sufficiently strong powers of negotiation with globally mobile capital. They can be played off against each other.' Still, those people can make a difference collectively, as producers and consumers: 'Nothing more and nothing less is at stake here than to end the bourgeois split between the subject of the economy (free property owner, bourgeois) and political citizens (citoyen/citoyenne):' p. 395.

19 Duchrow et al., *Solidarisch Mensch werden*, p. 397. The strategy that Duchrow proposes is first to starve the capitalist system through demythologization of its ideology and clear refusal (strikes, boycotts of banks and cheap consumer goods) and resistance. The second step includes developing local–regional alternatives to capitalism (exchange-based rather than money-based; co-operative banking, alternative energies, local food production), reclaiming resources in all areas (dignified work, agriculture, public goods such as water, just taxes – capital pays less and less, social networks, fair trade, renewable energies), and developing an alternative macronarrative of hope: pp. 398–417.

20 As observed in Chapter 2: value, is thus 'relation between persons expressed as a relation between things'.

21 Bertolt Brecht, 'Die Dreigroschenoper', in Bertolt Brecht, *Gesammelte Werke in 20 Bänden*, vol. 2, Frankfurt-am-Main: Suhrkamp, 1967: 'Was ist ein Einbruch in eine Bank gegen die Gründung einer Bank? Was ist die Ermordung eines Mannes gegen die Anstellung eines Mannes?'

22 René Girard, *Violence and the Sacred*, trans. Patrick Gregory, Baltimore: The Johns Hopkins Press, 1979, p. 14: 'Violence undoubtedly exists within our society, but not to such an extent that the society itself is threatened with extinction.' The later interaction of Girard with liberation theology is important in

this regard because it emphasizes the deep tensions of the global situation. Hugo Assmann, 'Das Opferwesen in der Wirtschaft', in Hugo Assmann (ed.), *Götzenbilder und Opfer: René Girard im Gespräch mit der Befreiungstheologie*, trans. Horst Goldstein, Thaur: Verlagshaus Thaur and Münster: LIT Verlag, 1996, p. 277, affirms that, from the Latin American perspective, the real-life consequences of the logic of sacrifice are pretty obvious. For Girard's own recognition of the importance of a connection to the reality of the poor, see Girard in Assmann, *Götzenbilder und Opfer*, pp. 285–6.

23 René Girard, 'The Good News of Mimetic Desire', *The Girard Reader*, ed. James G. Williams, New York: The Crossroad Publishing Company, 1996, p. 63. Girard, in Assmann, *Götzenbilder und Opfer*, p. 290, says explicitly that the analysis of mimetic desire is in the service of conversion, '*Umkehr*'.

24 Quoted in Naomi Klein, *The Shock Doctrine: The Rise of Disaster Capitalism*, New York: Metropolitan Books, 2007, p. 451.

25 Jung Mo Sung, *Desire, Market and Religion*, London: SCM Press, 2007, p. 49.

26 Girard, 'Good News', p. 64.

27 René Girard, 'Mimesis and Violence', in *The Girard Reader*, p. 17.

28 Girard, 'Mimesis and Violence', p. 18.

29 See, for instance, the work of Jung Mo Sung and Franz Hinkelammert.

30 Girard, 'Mimesis and Violence', pp. 18–19.

31 Sung, *Desire, Market and Religion*, p. 50.

32 See Jung, *Desire, Market and Religion*, p. 33.

33 Girard, 'Good News', p. 65; Girard also uses the Christian notion of grace in Assmann, *Götzenbilder und Opfer*, p. 291.

34 Girard in Assmann, *Götzenbilder und Opfer*, p. 271.

35 Girard in Assmann, *Götzenbilder und Opfer*, p. 306.

36 Girard in Assmann, *Götzenbilder und Opfer*, p. 283.

37 See the discussion of Las Casas in Rieger, *Christ and Empire*, Chapter 4.

38 See Rieger, *Christ and Empire*, Chapter 2.

39 Klein, *Shock Doctrine*, p. 47.

40 This question also applies to the three basic economic tenets of the Chicago School: privatization, deregulation, and cuts to government services: see Klein, *Shock Doctrine*, p. 444. For Klein's account of Cameron's messages see *Shock Doctrine*, p. 32; Cameron would play such messages for up to twenty hours a day for weeks.

41 Klein, *Shock Doctrine*, p. 348 and more generally pp. 347–50.

42 Klein, *Shock Doctrine*, p. 356.

43 Klein, *Shock Doctrine*, pp. 351–4.

44 Klein, *Shock Doctrine*, p. 359.

45 Reference in Klein, *Shock Doctrine*, p. 323.

46 Reference in Kathleen McGowan, 'Wenn das Leben auseinanderfällt', *Psychologie Heute* (October 2007), pp. 20–7. See also Hermine Mandl's comments, available at http://herminemandl.wordpress.com/2007/09/20/was-uns-nicht-umbringt-macht-uns-starker/.

47 Klein, *Shock Doctrine*, pp. 361–8.

48 Klein, *Shock Doctrine*, p. 370.

49 Klein, *Shock Doctrine*, p. 457.

50 Klein, *Shock Doctrine*, p. 465–6.

51 Emir Sader, a Brazilian sociologist, quoted in Klein, *Shock Doctrine*, p. 456.

52 Klein, *Shock Doctrine*, p. 463.

53 See Johann Baptist Metz, *Glaube in Geschichte und Gesellschaft*, Mainz: Grünewald, 1977, pp. 176–80, following Walter Benjamin. Part of the notion of dangerous memories is that it points to unrealized hopes: Metz, *Glaube*, p. 176.

54 Rieger, *Christ and Empire*, Chapter 2.

55 'To articulate the past historically does not mean to recognize it "the way it really was" (Ranke). It means to seize hold of a memory as it flashes up at a moment of danger': Walter Benjamin, 'Theses on the Philosophy of History', in Hannah Arendt (ed.), *Illuminations: Essays and Reflections*, trans. Harry Zohn, New York: Schocken Books, 1969, p. 255.

56 Klein, *Shock Doctrine*, p. 458.

57 Lacan, 'Seminar 20, *Encore*', p. 144; the exact term used in the English translation is 'supplementary *jouissance*'.

58 Žižek, *Sublime Object*, p. 52, emphasis in original.

59 Vinayak Chaturvedi, *Mapping Subaltern Studies and the Postcolonial*, London, Verso, 2000, p. xiii, summarizes these concerns in terms of the questions of agency, subject position, hegemony, and resistance to determinism.

60 John Beverley, *Subalternity and Representation: Arguments in Cultural Theory*, Durham, NC: Duke University Press, 1999, p. 113.

61 Joerg Rieger, 'Liberating God-Talk', in Catherine Keller, Mayra Rivera, and Michael Nausner (eds.), *Postcolonial Theologies: Divinity and Empire*, St Louis, MO: Chalice Press, 2004, p. 217.

62 Hinkelammert, as paraphrased by Jung Mo Sung, *The Subject*, p. 81.

63 Franz J. Hinkelammert, *El grito del sujeto: Del teatro-mundo del evangelio de Juan al perro mundo de la evangelización*, San José, Costa Rica: Editorial DEI, 1998, p. 6.

64 Dipesh Chakrabarty, 'Radical Histories and Question of Enlightenment Rationalism', in Chaturvedi, *Mapping Subaltern Studies*, p. 275.

65 Rieger, 'Liberating God-Talk', pp. 217–18.

66 Laura Donaldson, 'The Breasts of Columbus: A Political Anatomy of Postcolonialism and Feminist Religious Discourse', in Laura Donaldson and Kwok Pui-lan (eds.), *Postcolonialism, Feminism, and Religious Discourse*, New York: Routledge, 2002.

67 Rieger, *Christ and Empire*, Chapter 7, introduces the term 'postcolonial Empire', which at first sight appears to be a paradox.

68 Hardt and Negri, *Multitude*, p. 212.

69 See also the argument in Hardt and Negri, *Multitude*, p. 350; Hardt and Negri, however, seem to discount the value of additional organizational meetings too easily.

70 Hardt and Negri, *Multitude*, p. 311.

71 Hardt and Negri, *Multitude*, p. 338f.

72 Beverley, *Subalternity*, p. 105.

73 See also Beverley, *Subalternity*, p. 90.

74 This argument is further developed in Rieger, 'Developing a Common

Interest Theology from the Underside', in Joerg Rieger (ed.), *Liberating the Future: God, Mammon, and Theology*, Minneapolis, MN: Fortress Press, 1998.

75 Beverley, *Subalternity*, p. 103; subaltern studies is both deconstructive and constructive.

76 Jung, *The Subject*, p. 63. For a note on the English term 'subjectivity' see above, p. 52, n. 11.

77 Jung, *The Subject*, p. 49.

78 See Rieger, *Christ and Empire*, Chapter 1.

79 Hardt and Negri, *Multitude*, pp. 348, 356, point out that the 'multitude' can be seen as a new human nature. Note also their rephrasing of Lacan's insight about the unconscious being structured like a language: 'The multitude is organized something like a language' (p. 339).

80 Many examples could be given for this. One example is the short statement by John Wesley that 'Religion must not go from the greatest to the least, or the power would appear to be of men': John Wesley, *Works*, ed. Thomas Jackson, 3rd edition, London: Wesleyan Methodist Book Room, 1872, vol. III, p. 178.

6

The People and the Empire: Towards a
Political Overcoming

Having studied the vices and consequences of Empire, the question arises of the possibility of a political overcoming of the tendencies and consequences of imperial concentration. Moreover, it becomes necessary to investigate the possibility of a non-imperial political practice that begins to develop even within the environment of Empire to produce its alternatives, to generate the conditions of its modification, and to form the anthropological *ethos* that allows the overcoming of the subjectivity generated in the imperial space. We do not postulate the possibility of a closed model, a noble vanguard that indicates the just way, nor even of a 'utopia' that would function as a full alternative; neither do we believe in a spontaneous mobilization of the masses, or that a direct irruption of the multitude could give form to new systems that completely modify the ways of social management. The people can emerge in a moment indicating a presence that shakes the system, revealing its obvious contradictions and limitations, but it has to be put on the right track through alternatives that, while changing schemes of power, will have to be reformulated beginning with new dialogues, new equilibria, and the social and ecological realities themselves that must be taken into account. What emerges as a possibility here is the creation of options that, from new cultural forms – but also from economic reformulations, from a combination of macro- and micropolitics – could generate hope for human relations that allow the life of human beings in their condition as such; that is to say, to overcome the biological state of life in order to be able to develop equitable forms of life itself. In the words of the World Social Forum (WSF): 'a different world is possible', or, indicating its vocation to recognize alternatives to the alternatives, using the expression of the Zapatista motto, 'a world where all worlds fit'.

This is a challenge for all, but especially for Christian theologians, if we consider ourselves heirs and claim, as we do, that the communities formed from Jesus of Nazareth arose (among other dimensions that we do not ignore) as antihegemonic proposals opposed to the constitution of the Roman Empire. The constitution of primitive Christianity itself is, as its traces show, plural in its social insertions, theological orientations, ways of conceiving the world, and in the relations of the communities of faith among themselves and with the imperial world.[1] This diversity had its limits, no doubt, in some central affirmations that were, little by little, generating an orthodoxy, which were reformulated in other social sectors different from those in which they originally grew and ended up being appropriated by the Empire itself. But in this process over three centuries there was a wealth of experiences (later overseen by 'official Christianity', although in some lasting cases cryptically), which ranged from communities where the people generated alternative myths and histories to the impositions of the elites who were taking possession of the symbolic legacy of Jesus' movement.

Affirming the 'laocratic' option

The idea of a plural world therefore implies overcoming the pretension of the concentrated and univocal power that we call Empire. In this sense we are playing with the tension and antagonism between the imperial vision and what we have come to call 'laocracy' (as much in Christian theology, which we will not explore here, as in the political practice projected from a vision inspired by the perspective of the messianism of Jesus, which is the focus of this chapter). This concept, which we introduced without much explanation in the first chapter, will help us establish an opposing vision to the imperial, based on the validity of the *res publica*, but will simultaneously recognize the possibilities and limits of the democratic and republican as an alternative to the imperial ethic.

Effectively, in every historically based society today, even in those considered the most consistent in their politics of equality and social justice, there is always an 'untouched remainder' who, whether through the conditions of the social system or through their own situations, do not participate (or do, but to a very unequal extent, from a subaltern position or from an oppressive captivity) in the benefits of collective life and the resources necessary to sustain it, at least in a proportion that dignifies them. The existence of this 'remainder', of this subsistence of exclusion, marks the limits of any human attempt to 'construct the Kingdom of God on earth'. It is true that some systems manage to mitigate these consequences significantly, up to limiting them to minority expressions in their societies. But in the imperial system this exclusion affects the majority – although in an unequal way and differently for different persons and sectors of society – in some of the facets of life: economic activity, political participation, the validity of the collective or personal rights, the experience of cultural identity and creativity. These diverse oppressions force those who endure them to look for ways of expressing their claims, sometimes from sectorial claims, sometimes unifying their demands. When all these exclusions coincide with the same social sector or with the same population, and where possibilities of reaction or expression are limited to the minimum, we are on the threshold of the human: they are the 'wasted lives' that globalization generates, the inhabitants of concentration or extermination camps, reduced to a peripheral existence in the cities of poverty, the undocumented persons subject to ignorance and expatriation, the inhabitants of jails, and so on.[2]

Meanwhile, the Empire concentrates wealth and power, controls distribution and uses the legal apparatus and the function of hegemony, to the point that those sectors that benefit and participate in the imposed system, that employ imperial politics and imperial biopolitics, accumulate in their own hands vital and symbolic resources, and to the same extent this space of marginality increases, along with the forms and consequences of this exclusion. There are more of those who cannot possibly gain access to vital resources, and there are simultaneously fewer resources that remain available to them. The dynamic of the Empire is to possess everything and, because of this, any thing or resource that must be saved for others marks a limit. For it must advance over all it created, while the exclusion that it produces is ever-increasing because every time it must exclude more who request the same good. If the market must control everything, any endeavour to produce or employ goods outside its norms must be fought. Consequently, it brings together the claims of those who are losing access to the goods that the market controls, at the same time as it tries to expand. Then, as it concentrates these claims, it shrinks the place from where they can be made, closing them into an ever-diminishing but increasingly overpopulated space. Because the Empire as an empire must leave no corner untouched; the pretension of Empire is to occupy everything, as much in an extensive sense (the geographical and demographic space) as in the subsystems (education, health, services) that still wholly or partially escape its logic. Those who complain about co-opted state systems nevertheless create something worse: the appropriation of the totality by private interests, a 'seizure' where the treasury is replaced by the private interests of imperial oligopolies.

Nevertheless, the Empire does not manage to retain this totality, because the increase of its power and accumulation necessarily produces an increase in marginality, of oppression and exclusion. The walls built on the Mexican–American border, the stockade around Melilla, and the shameful barrier imprisoning the Palestinians are illustrative. This generates a tension that the imperial system, as such, tries to hide, because somehow it marks its own limit, its space of powerlessness, which, although weak and marginal, resists, cannot be convinced or included, and transcends it. The transcendence, then, is not marked as 'metaphysical' but as the scarcely physical, not as 'suprasystemic' but as 'infrasystemic', as that which the system excludes, shuts up, condemns. Nevertheless, somehow, although useless and unknown, although hidden and repudiated, the limit generates anxiety in the system. It is, on the one hand, what remains to be conquered or destroyed, but at the same time it is what the system refuses to see or to consider, and must not understand because it would denote a 'lower limit', a zone that is impossible to conquer since to include it the system would have to be opened, to be modified, to deny its construction and immutability, and to admit the need to control its own ambition and put limits on its excess. It would have to recognize that there are spaces that cannot be resolved by its logic – by its market. This is why, for the imperial mentality, only the 'final solution' – to deny what it cannot assimilate, exclude it from its consideration, objectify it, or finally even murder it or bring about its death – appears as a requisite for the imperial pretension to omnipotence. The prison of indefinite confinement that the United States supported through the colonial possession of Guantánamo during the George W. Bush administration is a public example of this politics of destruction, as are also the policies that Israel maintains in relation to the Palestinian people. When these practices are exhibited publicly and go so far as to touch an ethical core that reveals the total inhumanity of the system, those who inhabit the Empire but are not completely lulled by it cannot consent. Nevertheless, these extremes are only the hyperbole of what the Empire does. Hence the truth of what Giorgio Agamben would say: 'we all live in a concentration camp'.[3]

Nevertheless, the excluded, as excluded, is necessary for the imperial utopia. It is necessary, in a certain ideological sense, since the imperial system, to be supported, must demonstrate its capacity for exclusion and needs to make visible its power, the validity of its threat. Since the Empire denies the precariousness that supports it, it must exhibit its destructive force, and for this it must kill what it cannot contain: it is a necessity of death, which not only comes from its denial of the other but from its will to deny the other within itself, and therefore it excludes and kills that other to keep from revealing its own interiority, the fragility of the potentiality that feeds it, and the emptiness of the symbolic and the agreements that support it. Killing the excluded intimidates the dominated. For if the foundation of democracy rests on a fragile, floating, indefinable concept of people (as we saw in Lefort's analysis), equally vacuous is the foundation of the imperial, which rests on a hegemony on which initially dissimilar interests agree but are then brought together in a circle of mutual dependence that only can exist through the imposition of those who formulate it, an imposition that is supported by violence, physical and symbolic. This power of violence must in some way be made visible, perceivable within the system, if it is to be exercised outwards: that is to say, to mark a border. The excluded, the *laos*, is, for the imperial system, both what it does not count and what is necessary for the demonstration of power. It is the limit that the Empire does not want to have recognized but that it contains.

But this limit, to which we will return, exercises a tension, a force that is exterior to the system but that, as we said, also exists hidden within it: it is its dialectic of the immanent and the transcendent. When this force (*kratos*) appears with such magnitude that the system cannot disavow it and is upset by it, we can say that we are in a 'laocratic moment'. It is necessary to clarify that 'laocratic' cannot imply a system of government or a way of structuring power. This would be a conceptual incompatibility since, if the excluded – the exterior thing – has power or structure, it ceases to be excluded. The laocratic is this moment of force in which the useless and excluded are included as a question, critique, challenge and opposition to the current ruling system. To put it in terms of Jesus' parable, it is the unexpected presence of the beggars at the banquet (Luke 14.15–24).

If Empire is the way of control, the cohesion of power (of the powerful), then the laocratic is the moment of the crisis of power and, in its most extreme forms, the uncontrollable: chaos. Here it is necessary to distinguish laocratic movements from the imperial 'putsch'. The latter provoke a moment of suspense caused by the empire itself, when through military, financial, or political coups it produces a 'shock' to dismantle the forces that might control it and in this way impose its own dynamics.[4] The former is the moment of convulsion that is generated when a sector of the people make their claim heard beyond the articulated forms of regulated politics. Nevertheless, the laocratic does not always irrupt in such a visible, explosive way, although there are historical occasions in which this has happened, in what we call revolutionary moments. But the laocratic also occurs in manifestations that are not necessarily violent or completely detectable within its historical moment but that somehow begin to corrode the ideological foundation and alliances that support the Empire. It is exactly these breaches that allow the appearance of micropolitics as a space of resistance to Empire and of anticipation of other balances of power. The laocratic also happens in the necessary complementarity of the 'microphysics of power', to use Michel Foucault's expression, with movements of major importance that affect the large structures of domination.

Moreover, precisely as an expression of the weak, it is especially characteristic of this irruption of the unexpected to be manifest in marginal ways. A critical marginality, which can eventually transform itself into a convener of other marginalities and constitute a moment of strength, is possible. When conformed as a force, however, it faces its biggest risk: that of assuming for itself the very modes of power that it questions. The biblical texts, in many cases arising from experiences of oppression and hope, usually exemplify this reality: that of power manifest in the marginal, but that simultaneously becomes distorted in the ways of a new accumulative normality. For example, David is the youngest of Jesse's sons, who is not even summoned before the visit of the prophet Samuel (1 Sam. 16), who is the most unthinkable of the warriors who will face Goliath (1 Sam. 17), and who is later the outsider in the palace and condemned to death (1 Sam. 19), the 'rural bandit' (1 Sam. 23.14–25.25), the one exiled in hostile territory (1 Sam. 27), until he becomes the most popular king of Israel. Nevertheless, his actual character becomes, in turn, an agent of injustice: his laocratic moment occurred, after which it normalized in power. Just as it seems that David conquered the throne, the inverse takes place: the environment of the dynamic of the throne conquers him.

The marginal can also turn into a sign of the transcendent, as occurs in some cultures with popular canonizations, to which we will return later. Facts of daily life, minor irruptions, later turn out to be acts that give meaning to human life and praxis. As a biblical example, this occurs with the birth of Jesus, and is demonstrated in the marginal birth of a child for whom 'there was no place in the inn', who is recognized only by a few poor shepherds of the region and a few foreigners. Nevertheless, when Herod finds out about the birth of Jesus, the possible messiah of Israel, he deploys the power of death that he wields as an agent of the Empire. He addresses the threat of a new power that may rise against him from a dark and remote place by mandating the murder of all the children of the village of Bethlehem born around the same time as Jesus. This slaughter of the innocent is a sample of the imperial dynamic in the face of the most humble laocratic event. Beyond the generated myth and its later over-mythification,[5] what history reveals is precisely the inability of the system to assimilate the laocratic event, the possible emergence of a limit to its power, the presence of what transcends it. Moreover, it reveals the possibility that this transcendence expresses itself in a fact that in its moment is only a minor occurrence, a significant marginality.

The laocratic as political hope

It is certain that the laocratic, when it appears in a more open and visible form, tends to garner its own strength, a strength that allows it, somehow, to question the imperial and subvert it. It is articulated on a claim of presence, and this claim takes – beyond the moment in which it gains momentum – explicit forms that place in evidence the limits and flaws of the ostensible totality. In it there also occurs an ideology (or diverse ideological forms).[6] In constructing its ideological configuration, it takes previously existing elements, whether in the hegemonic forces or in the resistances that have already been generated in the system, as well as popular memories and other laocratic moments. It is also constructed on hopes and wishes, on projects and visions, on the utopian. This generates different types of political parties, ideologies and experiences that try to contain 'the popular': syncretic constructions from where are inserted into the political space those who suffer through the unequal distribution of resources, by the impositions of confiscatory powers for privatization that harvest the common good, until then excluded or ignored.

No doubt the expression 'populism' resounds in an ambiguous way, with a certain negative connotation for many sectors, including the left or fashionable progressives, especially those who stick to conceptual purities or who focus on 'institutional quality', the formal regime, and confuse it with the content of democracy. The sense that we here assign to 'the popular' does not necessarily refer directly to certain experiences of populism, though we do not disavow them, but to symbolic formations – politics – of representation, which emerge precisely not from a constructed proposal but from certain unexpected irruptions of popular culture within the political environment. Of course, this is a necessarily ambiguous phenomenon, since any popular construction is certainly also a bearer of elements of the hegemony in the midst of which it formed. The popular is not the product of a pure laboratory of alternative subjectivities but a complex mixture of elements interlaced with what those with few resources from their society refill the spaces of life. With this in mind, Míguez and Semán define popular culture as a

> system of representation and practices constructed in situated inter-actions by those who have lower levels of participation in the distri-bution of resources of instrumental value, social power and prestige, and who provide mechanisms of adaptation and response to these circumstances, both on the collective and individual levels.[7]

An added value of this definition is that it allows us to differentiate and focus on several levels of meaning of 'the popular'. This mistreated term has often been used, in a pejorative sense, to indicate the masses, an undifferentiated set of people who act almost by reflex, spontane-ously responding to stimuli. The popular may contain elements of that, but this is not what defines it. The popular, as this definition sets it out, may be a majority or may not be. *Massiveness* is not what character-izes it; rather, it is characterized by its place in the social structure. A government is not 'popular' because it finds more-or-less large-scale support, because it secures the adherence of a significant number of voters, or because its representative figures use a language related to the dialect of the suburbs or the sayings of the folkloric tradition. It is popular when it assumes the interests and representations of the most neglected sectors of society, even, sometimes, against certain potential majorities influenced by hegemonic currents.

Another way of discrediting this term has been to take it as a syno-nym of the rude, the coarse, as opposed to 'the cultured', that which is elaborated from more sophisticated sources. The definition itself allows us to recognize that the popular is constructed from sectors with minimal access to material and symbolic resources. This does not mean, however, that the products of popular culture do not contain a collective elaboration that is nourished by a plurality of memories and traditions retold throughout history, and that underlie the creations and resources of the popular.

Another way in which it has been used, and especially in regard to the dependence of its use in English, has been to understand 'the popular' as that which attains a certain diffusion across the mass media. Popular then becomes synonymous with being recognizable, with having spread through wide sections of the population. Even some thesauruses list 'popular' as synonymous with famous, well-known, or multitudinous. But this conception does not take into account that the origin of this form of 'popularity' does not rest on what the people create, but on what is given to them to consume, in elements generated from outside 'the popular', with the use, many times, of enormous resources to capture popular subjectivities.

We have pointed in another direction with our concept of 'the popular'. In this sense, we do not tie it to one particular social class, although undoubtedly the access to the resources mentioned in the definition used prefentially locates it in a social sector characterized by subalternity. This enables us to characterize within the popular a variety of constructions, without any one necessarily exhausting it or preventing the same concept from being applied to others. The proposals of young subcultures, the readings of reality of general theories, the preoccupations expressed by those who suffer abandonment in old age, movements that confront the consequences of child abandonment as much as working and rural struggles, or the efforts of native peoples to keep their memories, tongues, and lifestyles: all these can be everyone's, according to their moment and expression, their mode of construction and their dynamic; expressions of 'the popular' as forms of representations, as a set of practices, although they are not majorities nor spread by the mass media, in the power of the dominant classes. Precisely as a system of representations 'the popular' generates, following van Dijk's definition, a certain ideological perception, that which is going to be given expression in ideologies of a populist slant.

In this sense, this representation of the popular marks both possibilities: of adaptation and response, of partial acceptance and a rejection of the impositions of the system, which generally happen simultaneously. Both of these shape 'populism', and from there it is exposed to critique from the more pure left. Nevertheless, these social actors, exactly as the result of their position at the 'lower levels of participation in the distribution of resources', include the claim for major resources, especially and in the first instance material, within their political agency. It is in this claim that the laocratic moment can be generated – the excess that the Empire generated and cannot control.

In this way, one can also understand this uncertain limit, this flexible border at the low end of the system. The mark of exclusion is neither definitive nor permanent in all cases, and the 'culture of the excluded', by expressing it somehow, also takes on the fetishistic marks of the included and the burden of its own exclusion. For example, 'urban recyclers' who live off the selection and resale of waste are, on the one hand, the ones excluded from the labour world who seek a form of survival. On the other hand, to the extent in which they develop this activity, they set up in urban and suburban spaces, intervene in the market, affect other activities, and summon political actions, whether of repression or protection. This is to say nothing of the underworld of commerce in addictive drugs. The excluded do not disappear, and, as human beings, they generate their own representations and forms of life, which finally confront the imperial reality because they cannot but occupy the same space, especially to the extent that Empire tends to occupy the entire space. Yet precisely because they can manifest at this flexible border, because they can infiltrate in spite of the walls and guards, the consequences of exclusion take place within the system itself and affect it. To give another example, the subculture of marginal crime in the favelas of São Paulo or Rio de Janeiro, in the Central American 'gangs', or in the uprisings of youth in the marginal districts of Paris take place in the centres of big cities, demonstrating the fact of their exclusion in the very places where Empire establishes its nodes of power. This means that the popular can also emerge in its negativity, since it does not always manifest in a constructive or purposeful way (and this is part of the limitation in which exclusion immerses them): it is often the pure expression of the same violence that the system generates, the claim as a cry of despair, the simple denial that they themselves experience.

'Populist' constructions are a result of this plurality and contradiction, of this conjunction of claims not necessarily linked but that at some moment become coincidental, at least in the symbolic in which they express themselves. As Laclau postulates:

> the *sine qua non* requirements of the political are the constitution of antagonistic frontiers within the social and the appeal to new subjects of social change – which involves, as we know, the production of empty signifiers in order to unify a multiplicity of heterogeneous demands in equivalent chains.[8]

They contain the popular in its ambiguity but its strength precisely resides in this possibility of containing it, of expressing it. In this manner, populism is nourished with the same contradictions as the system, but it re-defines them from another place of perception, from its lower border. Somehow, even contradictorily, it expresses the laocratic moment.

The fall of the Soviet Union can also be understood as beginning with these laocratic moments. Of course, it would be a frank simplification to say that it was the *laos* of the states under the power of the Kremlin that produced the implosion of the Soviet state. The concentrated interests of the imperial alliances clearly seized the opportunity, expanded and deepened it, to settle there. But it would be equally awkward to think that the popular dissatisfaction with the bureaucratic 'nomenclature' had nothing to do with it. Although there is no denying the imperial nature of the capitalism we have today, the Stalinist experience and its derivatives also show that the same tendency can exist in other regimes. It was precisely 'democratic centralism' as a political organization that made possible the October Revolution, but also, in bureaucratic continuity of the Russian communist party, placed the party in check from the beginning. This concentration of power, which is assumed to be representative of the popular, but which forces it into previously known ideological moulds, returns to generate an 'untouched remainder', whether in population terms, in distribution of resources, or in participation in decisions concerning the public, that is to say, political power. The tension of having to resist the Empire often makes the oppositional impulses assume modes that resemble, at least in their dynamics of strength – although not in their social configuration – the Empire itself. Antonio Gramsci has warned that the worst thing that can happen to a force of opposition is for it to be structured in a way similar to its enemy.[9]

In this sense, the 'populism' that is generated from the laocratic moment places into evidence the limits of democratic formality, that which pure institutionality cannot resolve. Populisms, the expression of the 'populus' in all its complexity, prolong in time certain laocratic claims, but precisely by prolonging them in time and representing them in the political space they exceed and submerge them, and simultaneously formalize them. In this way, populism opens up space for a new exclusion, having included forms of power that necessarily become linked with its own original moment.

As we have seen, imperial dominion can also be sustained in a formal democracy. It is no wonder that certain cultures of progressivism and democratic institutional quality that do not dare to question the neoconservative parameters of Empire stigmatize as 'populisms' precisely those movements that in Latin America have managed to break the neoliberal mould and erect alternatives of power.[10] They even go so far as to label them 'terrorists', parts of the 'axis of evil', in this way not recognizing the democratic mechanisms of those who exercise the government. Something similar happens with Hamas in Palestine, which contains and expresses the popular claim but also settles on a conception of Islam that places it in tension with a wider political project. Nevertheless, in spite of the democratic moment in which it gains representation, it is not recognized because the Empire cannot accept the idea of a democracy that does not satisfy or adapt itself to its logic.

This tension between formal democratic progressivism and populism becomes more acute precisely when 'serious' intellectual classes have lost their critical capacity, or the 'elite' continue their out-of-touch discourses. In addition, there are those populisms that are

> taking into account and confronting the loss of legitimacy precisely from the narrow socially excluding republican democracies, with their appropriated institutional forms marginalized for that reason. The popular, in reopening an agglutinative politics, appears checking falsely reconciled societies across different forms of democratic depoliticization, where any real opposition is judged to be pernicious.[11]

It is true that this 'populism' deformalizes the articulated forms of power. This is precisely why it is anti-imperial. As in Genesis, creation proceeds from chaos. When everything is so formalized, when the system is unified in its responses, it is because it has managed to exclude the contradiction, and, having done so, it ignores the symptoms of oppression. It presents itself as the earthly paradise, the reconciled society, the full life, the Kingdom of Heaven. However, as one cannot historically be any of those things, it can be better portrayed as an anaesthetized cancer, the symptoms of which hide but are equally fatal for humanity and the environment.[12]

Although it sometimes finds a partial channel in some partisan expression, the populist fabric is not tied to an organic function of the political apparatus (nor that of social class, in the Marxist sense) because it would not then be able to express the unarticulated, the unresolved of the imperial logic. The popular will always be moving, quick to avoid any attempt to constrain it – even the democratic formality that sometimes tries to express it, even the attempts of 'populism' to contain it. 'Democratic immanence' – the rise of instrumental reason, in the legal sense, as the ultimate end – avoids the critique of the institutional deviations of the democratic; that is why the popular must envision itself as something that transcends the democratic, which always leaves a remainder of exteriority that is manifest in the laocratic moment. This does not mean that the democratic is not the normality that must precede and be recovered in a modified way following the expression of the *laos*. This, although it seems quite distant, is one of the facets of the Pauline critique of the law and his affirmation of the eschatological sense of the messianic irruption, to which we will return later.

This is why the laocratic appears politically as an expression that cannot be exhausted in a democratic order, although it cannot do without that order. It is the necessary exteriority that antagonizes the democratic 'from below'. In theological terms, it is the irruption of the messianic *kairos* that suspends the law, not because it annuls it, but because it overcomes it by means of grace. It does not suspend it from the sovereignty of power, but nor does recognize it as the law of death.

Here appears the necessary distinction between 'imperial' and laocratic sovereignty or, as we will see, messianic sovereignty. If the Schmittean conception emphasizes that sovereignty is the ability to suspend the law, then we can point out that Empire suspends it while it itself becomes the law.[13] Nevertheless, there is another misapprehension of the law, another 'suspension' of the recognition of the law, which is not born of the power to abrogate it with impunity, but of not recognizing it as being a law of death. It is a sovereignty that is not born of the power to suspend the law, of the capacity to produce the exception through one's superiority over the law. It is just the opposite, that which seeks to circumvent the law because it experiences it as a threat to its life. It is the disobedience that emerges precisely from its challenge to the power that generates the law and its consequence. Precisely as an intended ignorance of the law from a non-power position it cannot create a stable sovereignty, but the transitory expression of the uncontemplated, that which the same law does not know. Nevertheless, it does not cease to be a form of popular sovereignty, a force that although it irrupts only in a sporadic way, shows exactly (not from the law but from its ignorance), the limit of the imperial sovereignty that has appropriated the law, which it has moulded to its advantage, which it has transformed into a 'law of the market', which it imposes and possibly suspends according to its form of power.

Nevertheless, in 'normal' times, 'the people' (in its plurality of meanings and constitution) must be able to accept the democratic game. Far from destroying the democratic, its function is, somehow, to re-establish the balances of the power that makes democracy possible, that guarantees the republican, that returns to the public its meaning when it has been emptied by the imperial conjunction. Just as grace, in Pauline theology, recognizes and returns to the law its real status and function, the laocratic moment revitalizes the democratic, returns the meaning of *res publica* to the action and presence of the people – the sense of community that finds a place in state formality.

While modern democracies offer a formal frame of government, the claim of the moment of the expression of the *laos* (beyond the legal conditions of citizenship) is the search for the balances and mutual controls that democratic formality in itself has not managed to exercise. This is not necessarily explicit in the claims expressed, although popular declarations usually, at least in the countries of the developing world, make explicit their opposition to Empire, as occurs in many anti-globalization organizations. Popular participations, in their multiple forms, are the expression of a need to introduce, in democratic management, new forms of control that avoid the accumulation, as much material as symbolic, that generates Empire. Indeed, in the distributive bidding and the struggle for the recovery of resources appropriated by the *res privata*, the search for a limit to the ambitions of the material elite is expressed. When the popular claim raises the need for redistribution (for work, social plans, public services, health, and free public education), it demands a materiality; it places a material principle to the formal principle of the institution. Some critics point out that this 'materiality of the political' is precisely the Achilles' heel of populism, its opening to the clientelism that disfigures the democratic. But it is necessary to admit that, if there is no effective response to the material claims of the people, the democracy cannot be sustained as such: it becomes an imperial politics. The danger for democracy is not that it is populist but that it is not populist enough. In this sense Jesus was a 'populist', in terms of responding to the immediate need for food or health of the multitude, revealing the gratuity of the messianic times, overcoming the law of the Sabbath and the constraints of the purity laws.

This does not mean that we should identify the laocratic moment with populism, or with any other political expression. These movements can provide a channel for the claims and expression of popular sectors, or of other human groupings or parties, but somehow, in having included them in the space of the political, they also contain it, in the two meanings of the word: they incorporate it, but simultaneously put limits on it. Somehow they normalize the moment of the impetus that made the conflict clear, and thereby can be agents of new democratic experiences. In fact, in Latin America and other places these moments of strength have generated anti-imperial options that then managed to form political forces that have used the methods of democratic institutions to generate new conditions of governance, to bring about constitutional changes favourable to popular interests and to native peoples, and to limit the power of imperial capitalism. However, as has also been the case, in some experiences of the past, 'critical utopias' have transformed into 'conservative utopias', generating authoritarian mechanisms and new exclusions.

We should point out that laocratic claims do not always express themselves in the political, given that they also have to do with cultural dynamics that cannot be modified through the exercise of state power but that require continuous action in small or large everyday struggles. Minority expressions, which they cannot cease to be, aspire to a recognition of their dignity. If, as we affirm, transcendence is expressed in the weak, one will have to see in this weakness itself a manifestation of what humanity is and what Empire, blinded by power, does not recognize.

In praise of ambiguity

By the end of the first chapter we were saying that 'ambiguity', in contrast to the ambivalence proposed by Beck, is not an excuse to ignore the sense of the conflict but a recognition of its necessity, of a certain state of indefinition, of a struggle for meaning, of a distributive dispute that dynamizes democracy, and that its occlusion yields the end of the political and, therefore, the end of freedom.[14] Christianity, when it came to power, became an enemy of ambiguity, like all authoritarian logic, and thereby has constituted orthodoxies and heresies. Even the so-called 'liberation Christianity', with multiple manifestations throughout history, has often also fallen into this trap.

Ambiguity – this possibility that a thing could also be something else, that an expression could be understood in different ways, that an action could be interpreted diversely and produce effects beyond the intended, the expected and unexpected – is an unavoidable reality of the human condition, and not the worst. It is a condition of our language, of our thought itself, of our action, and, which is hard for us to accept, of our ethics. This is shown to be the case, partially at least, by the existence of the already famous 'empty signifiers' of political convocation and action,[15] as much as of the necessity to overcome the schemes themselves that we have considered (following Boaventura de Souza Santos) – the diatopic condition of our perception of the world. But this possibility of providing a force to evoke more than one interpretive dimension and more than one motivation and action, while recognizing that behind it there is even more, is something that cannot be resolved with only 'pluralism' or polisemy. Ambiguity also resides in our own logic and its different logics and illogics; not only because our senses could be filled with different meanings from linguistic vagueness or a diversity of experiences, cosmologies, and situations in life, but because our life turns out to be permeated by more than one sense and more than one nonsense. Thus, what we perceive in the expressions and actions of others always bears a certain degree of ambiguity, or ambiguities, which we can sometimes recognize and at other times overlook, whose meanings remain hidden because our own comprehension tends to be univocal. But also, and this is more difficult for us to recognize, our expressions and actions are ambiguous to others, to the eyes of others, who can see these ambiguities negatively or who can interpret them in ways different from our intention, showing that others see in us what we ourselves had not seen (and it is morally good to recognize and correct our actions from this discovery). It can also be the case that this ambiguity is a strategy of ours, an opening to wait for the response of others to help us to locate our own situation and mode of action. And that would be one of the most positive senses of this ambiguity, not only for others but also for ourselves, an aspect on which we now focus. The idea of pure expression and action, action free of ambiguity, of mixed intentions or consequences, is the heart of the Pharisaic attitude and is, therefore, exclusivistic. It is worth remembering that the main enemy of Jesus was not impurity but injustice. Jesus placed himself in the midst of the impure, of the Galilean semi-gentiles, of the impure prostitutes, of the ambiguous publicans, opposite the univocal intolerance of the Pharisees. What he seeks in their midst is the 'Kingdom of God and His Justice', and not the kingdom of abstract purities.

One can construct a political ethic overcoming the imperial from this recognition of the ambiguous condition of everything generated from the human situation. The sense of largeness that admits the ambiguity of interests, the partial concurrence that is then later denoted conflictive, must be at the foundation of politics: that is, a republican, democratic politics. This is what makes politics possible, that which returns its meaning in the face of the annulment that the Empire proposes, in the face of the claim of its dissolution in the subpolitics of the experts and its purity. The fact that the society is a fractured and ambiguous conjunction is what generates politics, just as politics generates society, and every force that unites it under a single interest does not build it up but destroys, subjugates, and oppresses it, even more if this force pushes back all control, any possibility of admitting a border or internal breakdown. The strength of democracy is its need to admit that nothing will ever be able to cover it entirely, and that it must recognize the laocratic moment by precisely the existence of this constitutive breach that is established between the actual exercise of power and its justification, and concerning which Lefort correctly notes:

Modern democracy is, we have said, the only regime to indicate the gap between the symbolic and the real by using the notion of a power that no one – no prince and no minority – can seize. It has the virtue of relating society to the experience of its institution. When an empty place emerges, there can be no possible conjunction between power, law, and knowledge, and their foundations cannot possibly be enunciated. The being of the social vanishes or, more accurately, presents itself in the shape of an endless series of questions (witness the incessant, shifting debates between ideologies). The ultimate markers of certainty are destroyed, and at the same time there is born a new awareness of the unknown elements of history, of the gestation of humanity in all the variety of its figures.[16]

It is this gap that Empire tries to conceal with its claim of totality, and therefore of absolute power in a non-threatened immanent space. In this way, it becomes transcendent in its immanence. But the breach subsists, indicating an ambiguity, a gap. It is this gap that makes manifest the 'laocratic moment', which in Lefort's language would be 'a new awareness of the unknown elements of history': the crisis, the chaotic, the uncontained, where there appears the real transcendence that dismantles the imperial claim. Our own condition as authors of this book, being theologians and simultaneously distrusting the belief that theology could newly install itself as a foundation for a unique and encompassing political ethic, is a reflection of this ambiguity. Effectively, democracy and the republican are constructed from a primary ambiguity, which is the (theological) emptiness of the place where authority resides. 'To stand on our own as if God did not exist', we would say, to paraphrase Dietrich Bonhoeffer, is a condition of modern democracy. God exists, but is not at the foundation of the democratic task, rather he is in its permanent question 'from below', from the location of the laocratic, from the excluded that transcends it, from the messianic irruption that is not based on power but calls it into question. The power that is rooted in a transcendence that legitimizes it must be questioned from the democratic, from the place of the necessary indefinition, from the 'people-*demos*'. But democratic power must be activated from another transcendence, the transcendence that is manifest among the excluded, in the 'people-*laos*'. To be a good political theologian it is necessary to renounce the idea that theology could be the unique foundation of the construction of the political and accept it as an understanding in dialogue with other perceptions of the political. This necessary lack of definition provides room for discretion, is not filled by reason but by the fact of its being unreasonable, and gives to the whole political apparatus a constitutive ambiguity. It does not mean, as Lefort expresses it well, that there should be a power gap, but 'a power that no one . . . can seize'.

Index of Names and Subjects

totality, 4, 6, 10–11, 15, 17, 22,
121, 132, 174–75, 178, 188,
190, 197, 199
transcendence, ix–x, xii, 9,
19–22, 32, 39, 59–66, 71, 100,
110, 124, 133, 150, 163, 166,
175–78, 186, 188–89, 191, 193,
196–98, 200, 203
transcendental concept(s), 73,
75–80, 86, 89, 93–95, 97, 102,
112–18, 122, 125, 127, 129–31
transcendental illusion, 108, 123,
130, 132
transcendental imagination,
122–33

unanimity, 106–7, 113, 119, 125,
132
unconscious, the, 32–34, 47, 49,
57, 84, 137, 171
unemployment, x, 37, 48, 54, 77,
81, 142, 154
unions, 42, 125, 143, 146, 148,
164, 189
United States of America (US), x,
8, 12–13, 24, 26–31, 33–34,
38, 40–46, 52–53, 68, 70–72,
76, 78, 85–89, 91, 137, 143–55,
163, 168, 175
utopia, 68, 89, 95, 100, 104–33,

135, 146, 172, 175, 178, 185,
191, 193–94

Vasapollo, Luciano, 52
Veltmeyer, Henry, 28, 52
Venezuela, 27, 155, 202
Vietnam War, 27, 34
violence, xi, 16, 20, 27, 31, 39,
43, 52, 60–62, 68–69, 71, 93,
121, 125, 139, 148, 168, 176,
181

war, 8, 13, 27–29, 31, 33–34, 40,
42–45, 61–62, 71, 78, 80, 89,
147, 152, 155
Weber, Max, 74, 97, 118
Wesley, John, 171
Westhelle, Vítor, 126, 136
World Alliance of Reformed
Churches (WARC), 5, 23
World Latin American Agenda,
123, 125, 136
World Social Forum (WSF), 110,
118–20, 124, 127, 172

Yates, Michael D., 37, 54

Žižek, Slavoj, 24, 108–11, 113–
16, 134–5, 158, 168, 170, 197,
203